The Archaeology of Southeastern Native American Landscapes of the Colonial Era

The American Experience in Archaeological Perspective

UNIVERSITY PRESS OF FLORIDA

Florida A&M University, Tallahassee
Florida Atlantic University, Boca Raton
Florida Gulf Coast University, Ft. Myers
Florida International University, Miami
Florida State University, Tallahassee
New College of Florida, Sarasota
University of Central Florida, Orlando
University of Florida, Gainesville
University of North Florida, Jacksonville
University of South Florida, Tampa
University of West Florida, Pensacola

The Archaeology of Southeastern Native American Landscapes of the Colonial Era

CHARLES R. COBB

Foreword by Michael S. Nassaney

University Press of Florida
Gainesville · Tallahassee · Tampa · Boca Raton
Pensacola · Orlando · Miami · Jacksonville · Ft. Myers · Sarasota

24 23 22 21 20 19   6 5 4 3 2 1

The Library of Congress has cataloged the printed edition as follows:
Names: Cobb, Charles R. (Charles Richard), 1956– author. | Nassaney, Michael
    S., author of foreword.
Title: The archaeology of southeastern Native American landscapes of the
    colonial era / Charles R. Cobb ; foreword by Michael S. Nassaney.
Description: Gainesville : University Press of Florida, 2019. | Series:
    American experience in archaeological perspective | Includes
    bibliographical references and index. |
Identifiers: LCCN 2019014403 (print) | LCCN 2019018272 (ebook) | ISBN
    9780813057293 (epDF) | ISBN 9780813066196 (cloth : alk. paper)
Subjects: LCSH: Indians of North America—Southern States—History. |
    Southern States—History—Colonial period, ca. 1600–1775.
Classification: LCC E78.S65 (ebook) | LCC E78.S65 C63 2019 (print) | DDC
    975/.02—dc23
LC record available at https://lccn.loc.gov/2019014403

The University Press of Florida is the scholarly publishing agency for the State University System
of Florida, comprising Florida A&M University, Florida Atlantic University, Florida Gulf Coast
University, Florida International University, Florida State University, New College of Florida,
University of Central Florida, University of Florida, University of North Florida, University of
South Florida, and University of West Florida.

University Press of Florida
2046 NE Waldo Road
Suite 2100
Gainesville, FL 32609
http://upress.ufl.edu

For Terri

Contents

Figures

▲▲▲▲▲▲▲▲▲▲▲▲▲▲▲▲▲▲▲▲▲▲▲

Tables

Foreword

▲▲▲▲▲▲▲▲▲▲▲▲▲▲▲▲▲▲▲▲▲▲▲

Early New England settlers and explorers often noted the ephemeral settlement patterns of Native Americans who aggregated and dispersed in
accordance with the seasonal availability of subsistence resources within
a defined homeland. While southeastern Natives were less seasonally mobile, a result of their greater commitment to agriculture, Europeans often
ignored Native connections to place to discredit Native claims to the land.
These politically motivated perceptions stood in marked contrast to permanent European settlements that began with the domestication of plants
and animals in the Neolithic Age. Native American migrations, as it turns
out, could span hundreds of kilometers precipitated by social, ecological, and political factors as expressed in the shifting locations of mounds,
plazas, towns, and a host of other emplacements from pre-Columbian
times to the present. These places and spaces are the outcomes of long and
complex community histories that can be revealed by combining documentary sources, oral accounts, linguistic evidence, and archaeological
inference. Moreover, this geographic palimpsest is the product of Native
fluidity and creativity as they confronted changing conditions engendered
by climate, disease, warfare, colonialism, capitalism(s), and various other
internal and external factors.

Migration and diaspora are familiar leitmotifs in the American experience manifest in European exploration, African enslavement, westward
expansion, the Gold Rush, the movement of blacks from the South to
northern cities after Reconstruction, the abandonment of areas impacted
by the Dust Bowl, and waves of European and Asian immigrants who
landed on American shores including the Chinese, Vietnamese, Irish,
Germans, Scots, central and southern Europeans, and other lesser-
known groups. My Christian grandparents left Aleppo, Syria, in the 1920s
to escape religious persecution, avoid conscription, and seek economic

opportunity. Sailing from Beirut, my maternal grandfather boarded a steamer in Marseille that took him to Ellis Island, where he was welcomed among the tired, the hungry, and the poor. Luckily, he was literate in Arabic and French, had a working knowledge of English, and could join relatives and neighbors who preceded him from the homeland. Still, I often marvel at the courage and determination it must have taken him to leave his familiar surroundings to pursue life in a very foreign land. First settling in Paterson, New Jersey, he returned to Syria to find a wife before crossing the Atlantic again on the *SS Byron*, eventually finding his way to the textile mills of Central Falls, Rhode Island, where jobs abounded before the Great Depression. This little vignette is probably different only in minor details from the family histories of many other Americans because all but the Indigenous inhabitants of this continent are immigrants. Movement was and is foundational to the American experience, and even the Indigenous peoples who we displaced have a long legacy of migration.

This book series, *The American Experience in Archaeological Perspective,* aims to illuminate the plurality of individuals and groups who contributed to American history and culture by juxtaposing the dominant narratives constructed by white elite men with the lived experience of ordinary people who varied by class, gender, race, and ethnicity. Most studies have examined the ways in which an event, process, setting, or institution was significant in the formative experience of contemporary America. This study is a slight departure from that mold as it focuses on Native Americans in the Southeast and takes a longitudinal perspective to examine how landscape is a product of and precedent for historical change and continuity.

In *The Archaeology of Southeastern Native American Landscapes of the Colonial Era,* Charles Cobb takes as his point of departure the overwhelming evidence for the regular and frequent, if not predictable, movement of people throughout the Southeast and along its margins. By using a large spatial frame of reference and a time span that bridges the Columbian divide, Cobb argues for the practical, symbolic, and metaphorical importance of the built environment in the concrete daily lives of Native Americans during the colonial era. He draws on the landscape histories of various Native groups from particular places and regions to demonstrate how their cultural configurations were a result of the intersection of local processes and wider connections linked throughout the continent to the Caribbean and the wider Atlantic world. Indeed, this historical approach does not see Native Americans as passive victims in an inevitable process orchestrated by colonial masters; rather, they were active agents who contributed to the transformation of the southeastern landscape in a process that continues to this day.

The widespread movement of Native Americans was central to this process, and they complicate the view of American migration patterns as a triumphalist westward push by Euro-Americans. Cobb uses the *longue durée* of Mississippian cultural development, its collapse/reorganization, and subsequent cultural outcomes to argue that the roots of population movements have long antecedents in the Southeast. While migration (as practiced by Natives) may be anathema to civilization with its fenced fields and orderly rows of crops, it is an enduring strategy among Native peoples to maintain their identities even as they were simultaneously being transformed. For example, the Southeast is rife with cases of coalescence in which disparate groups merged to create new communities in a process of ethnogenesis. The early growth of Cahokia in the eleventh century CE involved the immigration of peoples from a wide surrounding region as expressed in architectural, mortuary, and stylistic diversity. Elsewhere and in subsequent periods, multilingual groups and ceramic heterogeneity within towns are testimony to the coming together of different language speakers and technological traditions. By the late eighteenth century, the Catawbas, Chickasaws, Cherokees, Choctaws, Creeks, Seminoles, and others were all multidimensional coalescent groups.

Cobb's analysis identifying and interpreting the connections and patterns that emerge in the colonial era benefits from a sophisticated theoretical framework, attention to large spatial frames of reference, and the extensive work he has conducted in multiple regions throughout the Eastern Woodlands. He characterizes his theoretical approach as neo-historical anthropology that melds an interest in the material and ideological conditions of daily life tempered by a recognition of the contributions of post-colonial research. Both the real world and how Natives perceived it constrained and facilitated action. Cobb selects those case studies that best support arguments about the ways in which Native Americans were active partners in the formation of American landscapes. By tracing the histories of the Creeks, Chickasaws, and Cherokees, to name just a few groups, Cobb provides an eloquent synthesis of the outcomes of Native American landscape histories following the first arrival of Europeans. He explicates the various causes and directions of population movement and

the larger cultural, political, economic, demographic, and ecological consequences of the massive waves of migrations propelled by (sometimes
contradictory) colonial and Indigenous ambitions.

It is surely an understatement to note that the history of the Southeast
was in large part a constant struggle over people, their lands, and their
resources. Yet Cobb is able to draw together multiple lines of evidence
through time over broad spatial arenas to link the histories of droughts,
volcanic eruptions, disease vectors, warfare, slave raids, the deerskin
trade, and other episodic and time-transgressive events to identify four
seminal points that had significant consequences for Native movements
and resettlement. The first triggers were the early colonial landscape clearances and polity contractions linked to epidemic disease and the decline
of traditional chiefly power. A major result was the large-scale abandonment of a core area in the central Mississippi Valley and the resettlement
of the uplands and interior tributaries. Second, landscapes were altered
by the accelerated warring and coalescence associated with the deerskin
and Indian slave trades from about 1675 to 1750. For example, Haudenosaunee raids across eastern North America had an inestimable impact on
patterns of displacement in the Southeast and were felt all the way to the
western Great Lakes region and the Plains. Third, land sales and other dislocations came about in the early federal period with the onset of private
property and the social inequality that ensued. The federal government
and large trading companies worked together to deprive Native Americans of vast amounts of acreage, steadily reducing the land needed for
hunting, gathering, and fishing. Finally, displacement was almost complete with the passing of the Indian Removal Act of 1830 that pleased
hungry landowners who sought to expand their holdings in the quest to
accumulate capital.

Despite these efforts at dispossession, Natives employed various land-
based strategies honed over millennia to counter manifest destiny and
the efforts of the United States to further its imperialist goals. The production of place and living in and through the landscape are foundational to building a sense of human belonging and identity. The act of
constructing a mound, siting a plaza and keeping it clean, digging posts
for a communal winter house, and building a wall-trench structure all
served to define social groups at varying scales of inclusion. Similarly,
topography has both experiential and sensual dimensions as expressed in
the repeated use of prominent landscape features like Millstone Bluff in

southern Illinois and other strategic places such as the Fall Line between the Piedmont and Coastal Plain. The emplacement of recognizable features of the built environment like mounds and council houses may have become foregrounded over the "natural" environment with the demise of permanent homelands. In short, the turbulence and opportunities engendered by colonialism led to people uprooting constantly for reasons related to demography, conflict, religion, ecology, and a variety of other push and pull factors. Yet these movements and their motivations differed more in degree than in kind from earlier times.

Evidence of movement along with anthropogenic impacts to the environment are manifest archaeologically in the quarries where chert was extracted for the hoes used to till the fields to produce the surpluses that supported social hierarchies. Similarly, shifts in wood species testify to the need to exploit more distant upland vegetation due to deforestation in the American Bottom during a period of population growth at Cahokia. In other areas, intentional burning ensured the growth of understory and edge areas to attract game. These and other patterns such as site-unit intrusion of Mississippian culture in Wisconsin point to movement and accompanying landscape change. Cobb describes a dizzying array of movements over the southeastern landscape and emphasizes continuities in practice. Moreover, the dispersals he documents likely pre-adapted southeastern populations for coping with displacement when faced with the subsequent turmoil introduced by Europeans.

In using the landscape as a lens through which to view the American experience, Cobb is able to examine simultaneously the local and the distant, along with their interplay. As many Native groups in the Southeast placed more emphasis on slaves and then hides in their exchange systems, they made decisions that had unintended consequences for their political economies in the colonial era. Native groups routinely fragmented and aggregated to take advantage of the deerskin trade until a decline in the trade compelled many Native Americans who were in debt to become private farmers as they gradually made large cessions of traditional territories to the United States. The combined loss of lands and movement to family farms represented one of the most profound changes in their landscape histories and set the stage for a landscape that many seldom associate with Native Americans. The Indigenous landscape after the Revolutionary War was decreasingly communal, and privacy extended to individual possessions as indicated by a dramatic increase in the use of padlocks by the late eighteenth century. At the same time that Creeks, Cherokees, Chickasaws, and others radiated out to surrounding farms, there remained important villages with their council houses and related political and ceremonial functions that distinguished these new landscapes and the cultural practices of their inhabitants from their Euro-American neighbors. Suffice it to say that immediately beneath our feet lies the legacy of Native settlement choices and their contributions to the American experience, despite efforts to erase its traces from living memory through the dominant narrative of colonial conquest.

Finally, knowledge of these population movements has a direct bearing on some of the challenges that we currently face. If populations evacuated some of the richest arable lands in the Southeast during the Little Ice Age (ca. 700 BP), then Cobb suggests we must entertain the idea that Mississippian communities were reacting to widespread climate change and the immediate social consequences—like warfare—of ecological unpredictability. These conditions should resonate with anyone living in the world today as we witness unprecedented numbers of environmental refugees and displaced persons from Bangladesh, Central America, North Africa, Rwanda, Syria, Venezuela, and elsewhere. Perhaps lessons learned from the archaeology of the American experience can help us avoid a future dystopia.

Michael S. Nassaney
Series Editor

Preface and Acknowledgments

▲▲▲▲▲▲▲▲▲▲▲▲▲▲▲▲▲▲▲▲▲▲▲

The origins of this book are both personal and academic. Although landscapes are the foreground of the study, population relocation and migration constitute much of the background. If I were to adopt the stance of positionality to situate my own vested interest in the relationship between landscape and migration, it is probably because I am a military "brat." I was one of a cohort consisting of, I guess, tens of thousands of children with one or both parents in the US military whose lives were constantly rearranged by a litany of packings and unpackings, painful goodbyes, and anxious hellos. In no way does that experience equate to those who are addressed in this book. But I have always been fascinated by the ways in which people logistically and culturally adapt to serial migration, because that was my life. Readers will find a nod to this background in the introduction to chapter four.

Sticking with the military theme for a moment, in "The Things They Carried," Tim O'Brien's (1990) thinly fictionalized essay about his experiences during the Vietnam War (in the book of the same name), he describes the tactical decisions soldiers made about what to carry and what to leave behind under the strain of repeated patrols. For a platoon constantly on the move, the weight of objects was always a key concern. Among all the utilitarian stuff so necessary to survival, however, historical memory was also carefully packed into one's gear. Photos of loved ones, jewelry, and other things were essential traveling keepsakes for maintaining ties to a life left behind. As O'Brien's narrative reveals, even when traveling light and under duress, people think beyond the practical when they have to consider what will stay and what will go. And of course, the mind itself is a portable trunk packed with tradition and learning. Constant and/or stressful travel also shapes who we are. Although this book is not only about people on the move, it acknowledges and emphasizes the complex plaiting of landscape, place, memory, identity, and movement.

My interest in larger issues of colonialism follows a perhaps predictable path for many southeastern archaeologists. My graduate studies focused on the Mississippian-period mound-building cultures that immediately preceded and overlapped the earliest European explorers and expeditions—Native American communities that will receive considerable attention in the pages that follow. Those who study the Mississippian period (ca 1000–1500 CE) tend to rely heavily on early colonial European descriptive chronicles of Indigenous societies to animate our conceptions of what their predecessors may have been like. Oftentimes, as was my case, that route often leads to (or begins with) research on Native American sites of the colonial era. If there were a specific moment when I made that transition, it can be attributed to a gracious offer from David Hally at the University of Georgia in the mid-1990s to examine the flintknapping kits found in burial contexts related to his seminal research at the King site in Georgia (Hally 2008), a sixteenth-century Indigenous community that managed to accumulate a number of objects of likely Spanish origin. And the rest, as they say, really was history.

Since that time, I have had the benefit of the insights and expertise of a number of individuals at various institutions who have greatly expanded my horizons on the archaeology of the colonial Southeast. Soon after I began looking at the King site materials, several graduate students at Binghamton University—my academic home at that time—began an informal seminar on the archaeology of colonialism. This lasted for several years, and I have to thank Diana Loren, Lon Bulgrin, Brian Vivian, Emily Stovel, Rob Mann, Lynda Carroll, and others in that group for what turned out to be one of the more gratifying learning experiences in my career.

In 2007, I landed at the South Carolina Institute of Archaeology and Anthropology. There I was able to take advantage of Chester DePratter's generous sharing of his extensive store of knowledge over many cups of coffee. He, Jim Legg, and Steve Smith, also at the Institute, have been great partners in our sojourns across the Southeast. Since arriving at the Florida Museum of Natural History in 2014, Gifford Waters has been a patient tutor in bringing me up to speed on colonial Florida. Brad Lieb with the Chickasaw Nation and Tony Boudreaux at the University of Mississippi in many respects have been mentors as well as colleagues in our ongoing work in Mississippi, opening up yet another direction for me in colonial studies. I have collaborated with all of these individuals on a number of presentations and publications, and a lot of that work has provided much of the fodder for the ideas and research that appear in this volume. I further appreciate the efforts of legions of undergraduate and graduate students who have worked alongside me. A special thanks goes to Michael Nassaney for urging me to produce this work. We have known one another for almost 30 years now, and our paths have merged at numerous points along the way, including his own transition from a focus on the pre-Columbian cultures of the Southeast to an emphasis on the complicated, plural worlds of Native American and European encounters.

A number of individuals have assisted in the preparation of this manuscript. Neill Wallis, Rob Cook, and Brian Butler read individual chapters relevant to their own expertise. Michael Nassaney, Chuck Orser, and Tom Pluckhahn read the entire manuscript, and each provided cogent and insightful suggestions on both substance and style. I hope that I have used their insights well. Meredith Babb at the University Press of Florida was a regular source of encouragement and suggestions for framing this study to fit my worldview.

As will become apparent in this study, individuals and communities all have various ways of tethering themselves to their cultural landscape to develop a sense of stability and place. My wife, Terri Price, has provided that anchor for my own life, patiently enduring evenings and weekends listening to my grumblings over illustrations, citations, and looming deadlines. I promise to wait a year or two before embarking on another project of this scope.

Introduction

The Path Not Taken

There are two convenient paths toward a study of the transformation of American landscapes as an outgrowth of the Native American engagement with European colonialism. One can either emphasize what happened to Indigenous peoples, or one can emphasize what happened with Indigenous peoples.

There is a voluminous literature in the first regard for what is now the southeastern United States (hereafter "Southeast"). Much of this can have a somewhat gloomy pall through its descriptions of the impacts of disease, warfare, dispossession, and enslavement on Native American communities. It might be argued that this body of research, important though it is, necessarily takes Europeans-as-setting-things-in-motion as a starting part. This in turn lends itself to framing history from the viewpoint of broad trends in global history: In the Southeast, competition among European powers—notably Spain, France, and England—and advances in navigation and sailing technology led to a massive wave of colonialism in the 1500s and 1600s and numerous instances of "first contact"; with the establishment of colonies and the growing might of European powers, Indigenous peoples were drawn into the growing mercantile system as hunters of both deer and their fellow humans; as mercantilism evolved into capitalism, notions of private property and property enclosure infiltrated Native American landscapes and worldview; and finally, the formation of the United States, along with its westward ambitions, spurred a chronically adversarial relationship with Native Americans that culminated in the infamous policy of Removal in the 1830s, when tens of thousands were forced to relocate to what is now Oklahoma.

There is nothing inherently flawed with this global perspective. In fact, I use the final chapter of the book to step back from the many case studies and events described herein to reconstruct this paradigm of periodization. It is impossible to comprehend the practices of actors and communities in the colonial Southeast from the sixteenth century onward without due regard to the ongoing transformations in the world economy, the evolution of Renaissance and Enlightenment philosophies, and increasingly globalized wars being carried out by European regimes.

Yet actors on the ground—be they Native American, Euro-American, or African American—were more often making their practical decisions about where to live and how to live with respect to much more tangible opportunities and threats encountered in daily life. English traders of Indian slaves were far more interested in their own personal wealth and fortunes than they were in upholding the plantation system or the English trade balance. Young male Indians accompanying Englishmen on slaving expeditions were more likely to view their newfound wealth as a means of circumventing traditional social structures that limited prestige and power to elder males, rather than as part of a strategic effort to expand the might of their people at the demographic expense of their foes.

The following pages reflect the latter kind of history, a perspective that emphasizes the concrete daily lives of Native Americans during the colonial era as conveyed through the landscape. The structural unfolding of colonialism, mercantilism, and capitalism will necessarily serve as a backdrop to small-scale histories ranging from the Mississippi River to the Atlantic Ocean, but this was not a tidily linear history. It was one where the larger ambitions of colonial powers were leveraged, countered, and thwarted not only by Native Americans, but by the very colonial representatives who were meant to carry them out.

The trend in anthropology toward privileging a plural perspective of the past is connected to a rich scholarship devoted to historical "multiples." Many researchers have turned away from the notion that in the last five hundred years, we have witnessed movements like the Enlightenment, modernity, or capitalism as monolithic flows out of Europe and Euro-American North America that were passively accepted by, or simply forced upon, Indigenous peoples around the world. Instead, they have attempted to conceive of these phenomena as mutually constituted among numerous peoples, as multiple Enlightenments (Himmelfarb 2004; Porter 2000; Porter and Teich 1981), modernities (Cooper 2005:114–115; Knauft

2002; Trouillot 2002), or capitalisms (Blim 2000; Sahlins 1993). This is not to deny that there are central defining attributes to each of these concepts. The Enlightenment represented a turn toward humanism and the scientific method; modernity is characterized by the ascendancy of the individual and privacy alongside the rise of governmentalism; and capitalism would hardly be capitalism without commodities and alienation.

Nevertheless, the multiples movement conceives of these notions as polythetic developments rather than normative abstractions. They were shaped in distinctive ways at countless localities throughout the world by the convergence of the actions of Europeans, Africans, Asians, Native Americans, and other peoples—even if that convergence was instigated to a considerable degree by European peoples and institutions. These multivariate processes continue today. The strong anti-religious fervor of the French Enlightenment was not shared in Great Britain or in the American colonies; the current market economies of Western Europe contribute a much larger portion of their profits to social services than does the market economy of the United States; and, as we shall see in the following chapter, various European powers pursued quite different colonial strategies in the Southeast under the banner of mercantilism, all of which were countered and accommodated in scores of different ways by Native American groups. From this perspective, the landscape of the American experience from the colonial period until the present is the outgrowth of a complex, reticulated history involving the participation of a variety of peoples, not the least of whom were the southeastern Native Americans whose histories constitute the point of departure for my study.

Landscape studies are currently a thriving theoretical industry in anthropological research. Phenomenology, historical ecology, eco-functionalism, post-colonialism, and a host of other approaches have been used to address how human actions, beliefs, and experiences were entangled with the surrounding terrain and biota (cf. Ashmore and Knapp 1999; Bruno and Thomas 2008; Johnson 2012; Thompson and Waggoner 2013; Wright and Henry 2013). That said, there is not an altogether unanimous consensus on what constitutes landscape. The term does imply spatial relations across the terrain. At a material level, landscape thus is a field of resources, geographic features, and other peoples upon which a given community may align itself. To anthropologists, however, landscape also is a spatial medium of agency and meaning. Humans shape their surroundings and their surroundings, in turn, shape humans biologically as well as socially and culturally in a recursive relationship. Landscapes are lived and relational environments that are always in an emergent stage of production and reproduction. They are not static stages for human action or merely a constellation of features built up across time (Appadurai 1995; Bender 1993:3; Berleant 1997:12; Ingold 1993).

At one time, a distinction was made by anthropologists between space (landscape and the natural environment broadly conceived) and place (location and/or the built environment) (see Hirsch 1995; Lovell 1998:8–9). This distinction has dissolved, however, with the recognition that landscape itself is a collective field of spaces, and in itself may be conceived of as a space (Casey 2008; Low and Lawrence-Zúñiga 2003). In this vein, archaeologists have made the argument that the divide between built environments (villages, towns, and so on) and their surroundings is a false divide; the so-called natural setting is as much constructed as a house. In addition to these two putative ontological extremes (constructed places versus the natural world), there exists a complex network of shrines, rock art, and ritual localities constituting a polysemous landscape that is defined as much by connections and relations as physical location (Bender 1993; Fowles 2009; Steadman 2005).

Archaeological landscape methodologies vary by theoretical approach. Many phenomenological approaches focus on how the landscape was experienced and dwelled in and attempt to understand the convergence between bodily practices and space. What might it have been like to walk through a landscape structured to make actors follow a specific itinerary in order to view monuments, mortuary shrines, and other features that elicited the memories of specific events, places, or individuals? (Hamilakis 2013:154–159; Ingold 2000; Johnson 2012; Thomas 2008a; Tilley 2004; Wallis 2008). Landscapes may also be studied for their symbolic import, where monuments may be viewed as signifiers of hierarchy, or the arrangement of the built environment may reference social, celestial, or cosmological frameworks (Dalan et al. 2003:167–188; Knight 1998; Pauketat et al. 2017). The so-called southwestern school of landscape research relies heavily on a collaborative approach where ethnographic research and oral histories are used to incorporate the voices and perspectives of Native Americans today on the ways in which space and place were important to their ancestors (Fowles 2010). More ecologically minded research may rely on tools like Geographic Information Systems (GIS) to examine site distributions to elicit information about demography, resource use, political boundaries, and the articulation of communities with one another (Hare 2004; Jones 2017; Maschner 1996). Practically speaking, this book synthesizes archaeological approaches toward the landscape as conducted by others working in the colonial Southeast. That work has been strongly contoured toward the perspective of political economy and has emphasized the power relations shaping the flows of people and goods across the landscape more than human experience. In the following chapter, I draw out the implications of that slant for framing the evolution of Native American landscapes following the arrival of Europeans.

There is one way, though, in which I do impose my own methodological structure to this overview of Indigenous landscapes during the colonial era: I conceive of the Atlantic World as a meta-landscape for the Southeast, whereupon one can elucidate differential engagements with colonial powers by a variety of southeastern Native American peoples through time. The Atlantic World refers to the emergent global economy beginning with the onset of European colonization of western Africa and the Americas in the fifteenth century CE, and which involved a flowing matrix of peoples, ideas, raw materials, and finished goods around the Atlantic Ocean (Armitrage 2009; Benjamin 2009; Orser 2018). This was a world dominated by western European colonial powers until the age of revolutions in the late 1700s and early 1800s, when the United States, Haiti, and most Latin American states gained their independence. Although the Atlantic World was not a cohesive system built on a predetermined plan—and historians debate its spatial and temporal parameters and influences (see Orser 2018:10–18)—it nonetheless emerged as a complex web structured to enrich the coffers of the royal houses and merchant enterprises of Europe. At the same time, enormous wealth and suffering were seeded around its entire circumference.

Armitrage (2009) proposes three productive ways by which to enter into an understanding of the Atlantic World and its political, economic, and cultural consequences: 1) a circum-Atlantic history that adopts a transnational perspective on exchange and circulation as shaped by empires and monarchies; 2) a trans-Atlantic history that undertakes a comparative study of the political entities occupying the shores surrounding the Atlantic Ocean; and 3) a cis-Atlantic history that focuses on particular places or regions and on how their specific character was a result of the intersection of local processes and wider connections (the prefix "cis" refers to a term coined by Thomas Jefferson to refer to the particularities of the North American side of the Atlantic). It is the third perspective that is adopted in this book. Following a version of this approach advocated by Laura Putnam (2006), I will introduce a number of microhistories of various Native American peoples in the Southeast in an attempt to identify how their lives were increasingly impacted by a larger matrix of connections constituting the Atlantic World.

As we shall see, Native Americans were active partners in the history of the transformation of the southeastern landscape into a terrain eventually dominated by plantations and farms in the late 1700s and a resource that provided valuable commodities for the growing appetite of the Atlantic World. Peoples who were quick to enhance their military prowess through the acquisition of European firearms—notably the Westos and Ocaneechis—became the primary slave-raiding groups in the Southeast in the late 1600s (Ethridge 2006; Gallay 2002). They were soon replaced by even more powerful "militaristic-slaving" groups such as the Chickasaws and the Creeks. Both the demography and the economy of what would become the southern United States were shaped to a great degree from a period of intense Indian slaving that lasted only about 40 years, ca. 1685–1715. This interval witnessed the flight of large numbers of people across the landscape, population loss, and the enrichment of certain Indigenous polities.

Likewise, the deerskin trade that helped fuel the economy of the colonial South was completely dependent on Native Americans who, besides controlling much of the forested interior, had the skills and logistical capabilities to kill and skin millions of deer over the span of a century or so. Considerable fortunes were amassed from the deerskin trade by powerful European trading firms in the Southeast, such as the Scottish firm Panton, Leslie and Company, established in St. Augustine in 1783—a company whose leverage was greatly enhanced by their collaboration with Alexander McGillivray, an influential Métis born to a Scottish father and mother from a prominent Creek clan (Saunt 1999:76–79).

As exemplified by the case of McGillivray, Native American representation in the cultural bricolage of the colonial American landscape was biological as well as cultural. "Known as the Great Beloved Man by the Creeks, educated by whites, and well apprised of the workings of the larger world around him, McGillivray was well positioned to defend Creek land" through his ability to serve as a cultural broker between Indigenous and colonial worlds (Hahn 2004:275). Elsewhere, Native American women were the wives of soldiers and other Spanish citizens in St. Augustine, and they could become citizens themselves; Maria de la Cruz, a Guale woman, was listed as a property owner in the city after her husband died in 1759 (Deagan 1983:99–105). French fur traders frequently had Native American wives or partners (Nassaney 2015:107–108). By the 1700s, individuals of mixed heritage rose to prominence in territories adjoining the English colonies in the Southeast, especially among the Cherokees, Creeks, Choctaws, and Chickasaws. Mary Musgrove, the daughter of an English man and a Creek woman, served as a pivotal liaison between the new colony of Georgia and the Creek Indians starting in the 1730s (Hahn 2012). The trading post she established near Savannah with her first husband, English trader John Musgrove, was a key facility in the deerskin trade for a number of years. James Vann, the son of a Cherokee woman and English man, like Musgrove and McGillivray, grew up in a bilingual and bicultural world. His business acumen and ability to navigate the world of English and American commerce eventually made him the richest man in the Cherokee Nation, with holdings that included a store, a tavern, and a substantial plantation estate with scores of African American slaves (Ehle 1988:50; Smithers 2015:124).

These individuals and Native American peoples were not pawns whose moves were dictated by the encroachment of colonial grand masters. They were active players themselves, whose actions contributed to the transformation of the Southeastern landscape in a history that continues to evolve today. From the point of view of the long term, the modern reservations, with their hotels, casinos, and other businesses that have blossomed on Eastern Cherokee, Seminole, Creek, and other federally recognized Native American lands throughout the eastern United States, are not an historical aberration. Instead, they are an embodiment of the ongoing Native American contribution to the transformation of the American landscape and their struggle for autonomy. Moreover, there are numerous Native peoples throughout the Southeast who have not received federal recognition (though some have been formally recognized by states) who live in distinctive communities and must fight to draw attention to their identities. Their struggles, too, are an outgrowth of deep landscape histories when blending in with Euro-American communities was often necessary for survival (e.g., Greene 2010; Steen 2012).

Although this book is somewhat of a wide-ranging study topically, population movement is a leitmotif in my consideration of Native American landscapes during the colonial era. What prompted people to move, what happened while they were moving, and what were the results of those moves? Now that migration has been welcomed back into the halls of archaeology, this focus is much more acceptable than it once was. As the reader will find, a pattern of somewhat regular population relocations during the pre-European contact era in the Southeast exploded into a cascade of migrations of varying scope as European and American powers steadily ground away at the spatial and cultural autonomy of Native peoples.

There are certainly many cases of dramatic migrations throughout the course of history, ranging from the massive population movements into the Lombardy region of northern Italy in Late Antiquity to the upheavals in the aftermath of World War II. However, one is hard pressed to identify other situations like southeastern North America beginning in the sixteenth century, where Indigenous peoples began a three-century journey of constantly realigning their cultural and spatial maps in response to the incursions of European nations and the United States. I would venture that there are few parallel experiences on such a wide geographic and deep spatial scale—excepting the Americas—in modern history. As a result, it is difficult to find familiar touchstones that allow us to build a sense of connectedness to the magnitude of ongoing cultural adjustments—proactive and reactive, massive and minute—made by southeastern Native Americans.

Modern America has come to define itself as a nation of migration and frontiers. Although there is a wide streak of romanticism in this notion, empirically speaking, the colonization and federalization of what is today the United States did involve a significant westward drive by people of various origins. A widespread movement of Native Americans was part of this process, not just an analogy to it. Yet by including Native Americans in this story, we find that American migration patterns are best characterized as swirling rather than as the triumphalist westward push by Euro-Americans epitomized by Frederick Jackson Turner's (1920 [1893]) frontier thesis. The Seminoles who are a significant presence in Florida today coalesced from Creek groups who moved southward into the region in the 1700s and who integrated with local Native peoples; the territories of the Eastern Band of Cherokees in North Carolina and the Catawbas in South Carolina are the result of demographic aggregations and accommodations made with states for whom they have become important economic partners in the twenty-first century; and even lands in the South vacated by Native Americans retain their historical associations with place names. Most Mississippi citizens of a certain age would not be hard put to pinpoint the location of the bridge where the semimythical Billie Joe MacAllister leapt to his death into the river known as the Tallahatchie—Choctaw for "rock of waters."

Because my study is about landscapes, I will dwell more on movement and spatial relations than on objects. Those anticipating detailed discussions of Clarksdale bells, tinkler cones, and chevron beads will be disappointed. But it should be emphasized that there is abundant evidence in the colonial Southeast of the widespread movement of objects from their home locations as a result of the waves of people moving back and forth across the region.

A few caveats and signposts regarding my foray into landscapes are in order, beginning with what I mean by "colonial." While the term implies a contestation of power and domination between two or more peoples, it also has temporal connotations. Practically speaking, the story in the Southeast begins not with Christopher Columbus in 1492, but with Ponce de León at the head of the first officially sanctioned Spanish expedition in 1513. The book ends with Removal, the forced evacuation of most southeastern Native Americans under the administration of United States president Andrew Jackson in the 1830s. This period includes the first decades of the republic of the United States, and this inclusion reflects my unoriginal contention that American policies toward Native Americans were, for all intents and purposes, colonial in nature.

Within this span of about 300 years, southeastern Indians were not "colonized" under the traditional meaning of the term. Except for those on Franciscan missions in La Florida, who themselves had considerable latitude in their political and economic lives, by and large, southeastern Indians were not impressed into European colonial systems. Although France, Spain, and England continually attempted to impose their will on Indigenous peoples through their ambitions to incorporate the Southeast into their empires, this book will show that many Native American groups consistently and fairly successfully pursued a course of autonomy.

I have opted to maintain the anachronism of modern state and place names when discussing the location of pre-European contact and colonial-era places. In a work in which geography has such a central role, I wanted to facilitate the reader's grasp of links between places past and present. This has also allowed for the grammatical ease of saying that an Indian town was "near Tupelo, Mississippi" rather than "near what is now the modern town of Tupelo, Mississippi." To further orient the reader, several maps in chapters 3 and 4 contain most of the places and regions discussed throughout the book.

Scholars will find this work has some obvious empirical gaps. My emphasis has been on illustrating major trends and patterns in landscape histories rather than on being encyclopedic. Why do the Choctaws (and some other peoples) receive so little mention? My ambition has been to develop a study that is steeped in both archaeology and ethnohistory. There has been remarkably little archaeology on the Choctaws relative to the size and importance of their confederacy. Why is there hardly a reference to major sites like San Luis de Talimali when I discuss Spanish Florida? This was one of the largest and most important missions in Spanish Florida, and there has been considerable archaeology undertaken at the site. But the issues I wanted to raise about the Franciscan mission system were just as well served by invoking other sites. An overriding question for me in the preparation of this book was not who was included or omitted, but rather what case study or studies best supported a specific argument about the ways in which Native Americans were active partners in the formation of American landscapes.

It will become evident as one is well into the book that I have also made arbitrary decisions about which groups serve as the best examples of a given process. In chapters 4 and 5 in particular, where I discuss displacement and emplacement, many of the case studies could have occurred in either or both chapters. I ask that these choices be viewed as illustrative of the historical complexities of the colonial era rather than as part of a classificatory exercise.

The ensuing overview of these landscape histories, despite the title of the book, is a mixture of archaeology, ethnohistory, and history. As an archaeologist, I tend to use the material world as my point of departure into the past. But the rich documentary record of the Southeast, both primary sources and the abundant trove of studies by ethnohistorians and historians, that will be liberally cited in subsequent chapters represents an important analytical partner to the archaeological record. And, it should be pointed out, ethnohistorians and historians of the colonial Southeast regularly draw from archaeological studies in what has been a healthy cross-disciplinary pollination for decades. I submit this as another example of that collaboration.

I will take the first steps along the alternative path of a historical archaeology of immediacy and lived experience in the following chapter with a summary of southeastern Native American history and landscapes, complemented by a discussion of a political-economic framing of landscape archaeology. For many Native American groups, identity was predicated to a considerable degree on origin stories and cosmological beliefs intimately connected to the landscape. The importance of this worldview makes it a logical point of departure in the third chapter. Chapter 3 will also serve to demonstrate how landscape practices regarding politics, economics, rituals, and symbols were deeply integrated with Native American subjectivities. That and the following chapters will not be historically comprehensive, however. Instead, I will rely on a number of archaeological and ethnohistorical case studies to illustrate some of the key patterns in the landscape histories of the colonial Southeast prior to the wholesale removal of southern Indians by the Andrew Jackson administration in the 1830s. Foremost among these are exodus and dispersion, as the movement of Native groups accelerated throughout the sixteenth and seventeenth centuries in response to the direct and indirect pressures of colonial expansion from multiple directions (chapter 4). One of the major social responses to the unprecedented movement of groups across the Southeast was a phenomenon popularly referred to as "coalescence": the coming together of often very disparate groups to create new types of communities. As we shall see in chapter 5, coalescence was a primary means by which peoples engaged in emplacement, or the social production of new types of places, but other forms of emplacement existed as well. Next, I will consider how the introduction of novel types of plants and animals from the Eastern Hemisphere fostered dramatic changes in Native American political ecology, but even these changes were overshadowed by the political and economic consequences of the deerskin trade and the eventual proliferation of private farmsteads (chapter 6). Finally, while I wish to privilege the histories of various Native American groups in this study, there are also larger lessons to be drawn concerning the anthropology of colonialism. In my closing discussion, I will take the opportunity to contextualize Southeastern Native American landscape practices within the history of the Atlantic World (chapter 7).

A Hint of Things to Come . . .

In the year 1540, the Spanish conquistador Hernando de Soto, having navigated a significant portion of southeastern North America, entered a Native American polity of impressive scope and power (figure 2.1). Centered in what is today northwestern Georgia, the paramount chiefdom of Coosa appears to have been a somewhat linear constellation of villages and towns stretching between 150 to 250 kilometers in extent (cf. Galloway 1995; Hudson et al. 1985). As Soto's group of roughly 600 soldiers approached the eponymous capital of Coosa, they were colorfully greeted by the *cacique* (leader)

> who came out to welcome him [Soto] two cross-bow flights from the town, borne in a carrying chair borne on the shoulders of the principal men, seated on a cushion, and covered with a robe of marten skins of the form and size of a woman's shawl. He wore a crown of feathers on his head; and around him were many Indians playing and singing. (Elvas in Robertson 1993:92)

The power of the chief exemplified by this performance rested to no small degree on a fertile and demographically rich landscape. Chroniclers of the Hernando de Soto expedition observed that "the land was very populous and had many large towns and planted fields which reached from one town to the other" (Elvas in Robertson 1993:93) and that it was "one of the best lands that we came upon in Florida [the Southeast]" (Biedma in Worth 1993b:232). Indeed, the memory of Coosa's wealth and might presented a beacon for later Spanish explorers. A detachment from Tristán de Luna y Arellano's major colonization effort on the Gulf Coast visited

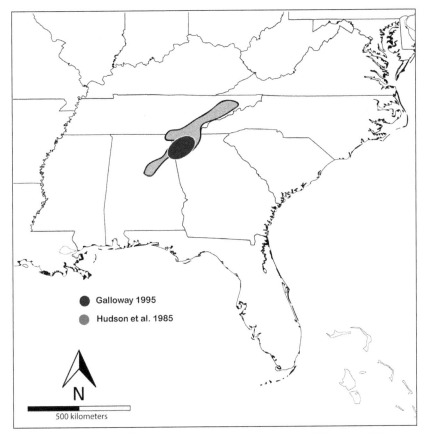

Figure 2.1. Extent of chiefdom of Coosa from two perspectives (cf. Galloway 1995; Hudson et al. 1985).

Coosa in 1560, as did members of Juan Pardo's exploratory force in the interior in 1568 (Smith 2000).

The chiefdom of Coosa may have experienced mixed fortunes following the departure of Hernando de Soto and his followers. One account from the Luna expedition 20 years later observed that "the greater part of it is unpopulated, and the populated part contains so few people that they are not enough to support any town of Spaniards which might be established" (Priestley 2010:207), whereas another noted that "truly the land was fertile, but it lacked cultivation. There was much forest, but little fruit, because as it was not cultivated the land was all unimproved and full of thistles and weeds" (Swanton 1922:231). Oddly, in less than another decade, a soldier with the Pardo expedition described Coosa in somewhat more favorable terms, noting that the capital was the largest town in the region and that the area was relatively rich (Hudson 1990:303).

How does one square these apparent contradictory views of the landscape? Is it possible that Coosa experienced a decline precipitated by the visit of the Hernando de Soto army, to be followed by a later recovery? Confounding the matter, we are dealing with the perspectives of a number of individuals over a period of many years, each of whom may have had distinctive experiences or may have recalled the same localities in different ways. A number of scholars believe that there was a genuine deterioration in the fortunes of Coosa prior to the arrival of Luna's people (Hally 1994; Hudson et al. 1989; Smith 2000:42–43). The historian Paul Hoffman (1997), however, has rejected this perspective. His close reading of the chronicles led him to argue that the seeming paradox reflects a common practice whereby early explorers embellished the virtues of places—typically to attract colonists—and later explorers focused on their drawbacks, which may seem magnified in comparison to earlier, optimistic exaggerations. Despite these inconsistencies, the capital of Coosa still appears to have retained its central status and the polity maintained its regional prominence as late as the 1560s. However, the lack of references to Coosa in this location in seventeenth-century documents suggests that the core of the chiefdom had moved elsewhere (Smith 2000:96).

A description of Coosa by Davila Padilla in 1560 contains one phrase that may help to describe its ultimate fate, and which further underscores the tensions that would be visited upon the southeastern Native American landscape for the next several centuries: "The arrival of the Spaniards in former years had driven the Indians up into the forests, where they preferred to live among the wild beasts who did no harm to them" (Swanton 1922:231). This observation would seem to rule out the disappearance of Coosa from demographic collapse brought about by epidemic disease. Or, at the least, it suggests that causes in addition to pathogens altered the demographic landscape. Instead, it is more probable that the residents of the villages and towns that comprised Coosa had decamped elsewhere by the early 1600s. Rather than being scattered into the woods, though, the polity seems to have moved en masse and reestablished itself further to the west.

Marvin Smith (1989, 2002) has conducted exhaustive research on the fortunes of the likely bearers of the Coosa tradition. Its capital at the time of Spanish contact appears to have been the archaeological site known as

Little Egypt, located on the Coosa River in northwestern Georgia (Hally 1979). It and a number of surrounding sites have yielded European artifacts that seemingly date to the sixteenth century (Smith 1992). By spatially tracking the archaeological record of sites yielding early European objects along with diagnostic Indigenous artifacts, Smith believes that a cluster of settlements comprising the original core of Coosa migrated southwesterly down the Coosa River in the late 1500s. This was followed by several more moves up and down the drainage over the next half century or so. The mobile descendants of Coosa, presumably manifested in this translocation of towns, likely became part of the Creek Confederacy by the eighteenth century.

The fate of the Coosa chiefdom is a microcosm of the objective of this study: to provide a synthesis of the outcomes of Native American landscape histories in southeastern North America following the first arrival of Europeans. What were the various causes of population movement, where did settlements come from and where did they go, and what were the larger cultural, political, economic, demographic, and ecological consequences of the massive waves of migrations propelled by colonial projects and Indigenous ambitions? As with Coosa, these other Native societies were not merely reacting to the colonial incursions of Spain, France, and England. Instead, they practiced a dynamic mixture of accommodation, resistance, flight, migration, and, in some cases, even zealous expansion. There is a very robust scholarship addressing the materiality of contact and colonial situations in southeastern North America, encompassing foodways, clothing, pottery, architecture, and other aspects of Native lifeways (e.g., Cobb and DePratter 2012; Dawdy 2000; Deagan 1983; Loren 2008; Silliman 2015). Yet we lack a synthesis of changing Indigenous approaches to culturally and physically inhabiting the southeastern terrain during the colonial era, even though this region witnessed some of the more intensive early expeditions and settlement efforts by European powers anywhere in North America in the sixteenth century.

Europeans also found their lives profoundly altered by their entrance in North America. They encountered radically new peoples, worldviews, and ecologies. As strangers in a strange land, they underwent marked changes in the ways in which they had understood the physical and social terrain from their own home lands in England, France, Spain, the Netherlands, the Holy Roman Empire, and elsewhere. Although I will touch on this aspect of southeastern landscape history when it informs on Native lifeways, it will not be a focus of this study. Yet there is no question that Native and European (and later Euro-American) landscapes were intertwined with one another to varying degrees. Further, in the same way that southern Native Americans and Europeans cannot be considered apart from one another, Native Americans from the Plains, Midwest, and Northeast also played a role in southeastern landscape histories. While I will not provide a sweeping panorama of all North American landscapes, the Southeast was, so to speak, an open system. So it will be important to consider, for instance, the peregrinations of the Shawnees from the Ohio Valley throughout eastern North America, as well as the dramatic impact of Haudenosaunee (Iroquois) war parties from the Northeast on Native American settlement patterns in the Southeast.

Further complicating the mix is the history of Africans in the Southeast. In the early years of the African slave trade—the 1600s to early 1700s—Africans and Native Americans alike were captured in large numbers on their respective continents and put to work on North American and Caribbean plantations and in other industries (Ethridge and Shuck-Hall 2009; Gallay 2002). As the estates and slave populations of South Carolina and Georgia increased in size and importance, numerous enslaved Africans escaped to Native American communities or to Spanish Florida. Many of those individuals were able to become members of their refuge settlements. As attitudes toward race continued to evolve, by the late 1700s, a number of Native American entrepreneurs had amassed their own sizable mercantile or agricultural properties and owned African American slaves. Although I will touch on some of these events and trends, they will not be a focus of this study, important though they are.

Who Met the Europeans in the American Southeast?

The year 1492 represents a seismic shift in the history of the Americas. But it was not a complete death knell for one set of cultures on the western side of the Atlantic Ocean who were displaced by invaders from the east. While the arrival of Europeans may have radically altered the cultural and geographic landscape of the Americas, Indigenous peoples still played a significant role in shaping those changes. Certainly, there were many instances where local cultures were overwhelmed. Yet there were also numerous cases where Native Americans controlled large swaths

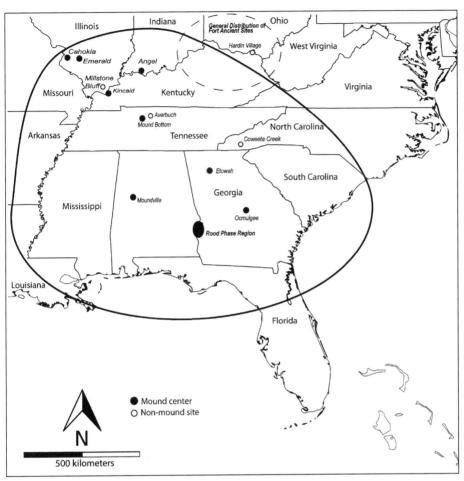

Figure 2.2. General boundaries of the Mississippian Southeast, with sites discussed in text.

of terrain for centuries after the first arrival of Europeans. Southeastern North America represented one such area.

For this reason, it is important to consider the nature of the so-called Mississippian cultures of the Southeast (figure 2.2). They had existed for five centuries prior to the arrival in 1513 of Ponce de León on the Florida peninsula at the head of the first official Spanish foray into the region. And for all practical purposes, Mississippian peoples greeted the expeditions of Hernando de Soto, Juan Pardo, and other major sixteenth-century explorers in the interior. The influences of the Mississippian lifestyle continued to play an important role in the landscape histories of the Southeast at least until the 1700s. It is, in fact, the Mississippian phenomenon that provides the geographic structure for this landscape study, as the general similarities expressed across the Southeast make for a useful point of departure for contrasting the general periods before and after the temporal threshold of European and Native American contact.

The term Mississippian is used hereafter in an admittedly somewhat normative sense to draw attention to a number of important shared attributes among the enormous variety of late prehistoric southeastern groups from about 1000 to 1600 CE. In no sense does this mean that this typological construct constituted some monolithic culture equally shared by all, merely that there was an extensive practice of differentially participating in certain traditions. These include the construction of mound-plaza complexes, certain lithic and ceramic technologies and styles (e.g., triangular projectile points presumably associated with the bow and arrow, shell-tempered pottery), ways of building domestic houses (setting vertical posts in wall trenches, wattle-and-daub-architecture), the practice of maize agriculture, and the manifestation of ranked social systems generally referred to as chiefdoms (Anderson and Sassaman 2012:152–190; Blitz 2010; Cobb 2003). These attributes were not universal, however, and they occurred in varied combinations in different localities as a geographic sweep of polythetic types. So, for instance, there was a somewhat spotty reliance on shell tempering and wall-trench houses in the south Appalachian region, whereas those traits are commonplace in the central Mississippi Valley. At the same time, there were very similar arrangements of mound and plaza complexes as the core of large towns throughout the Southeast (figure 2.3). During certain times in history, dispersed Mississippian communities also shared religious iconography. Further, by at least the 1200s to 1300s CE, regional conflict seems to have been endemic throughout the Southeast, manifested in fortified towns and a variety of bioarchaeological signatures of blunt- and sharp-force trauma (Bridges et al. 2000; Milner 1999; Milner et al. 1991; Smith 2003; Steadman 2008; Worne et al. 2012).

Within the boundaries that archaeologists use to outline the Mississippian Southeast, there was a considerable range of ethnic and linguistic diversity. Indeed, one of the challenges of the Hernando de Soto expedition as it wound its way through the Southeast for several years was identifying a succession of interpreters who could carve a linguistic path through the

Figure 2.3. Aerial view of the Kincaid site (Illinois) in archetypical Mississippian floodplain setting, showing mounds encircling the main plaza (courtesy of the state of Kentucky EPPC GIS Branch and the United States Department of Agriculture Aerial Photography Field Office).

jumble of languages that they encountered (Rankin 1993:211). Recognition of this diversity is to a large degree what has fueled the fascination with the so-called Mississippian Emergence (Marshall 1985; Smith 1990; Wilson 2017). In other words, what happened ca. 800–1000 CE that led such a disparate assemblage of societies, spread across such an expansive area, to develop the trappings of pan-regional identity while at the same time maintaining such distinctive local characteristics and languages? This remains a topic of lively debate.

Five to six centuries later, the end of the Mississippian phenomenon was a regional, time-transgressive process predicated by the indirect and direct consequences of interactions with Europeans. Certainly, there were many Mississippian chiefdoms that came and went well before the first arrival of Spaniards, since these entities could be relatively unstable (Anderson 1994b; Blitz 1999). Nevertheless, variations on these polities continued to thrive well into the sixteenth century. We even have evidence for groups who seemed to have maintained a semblance of Mississippian lifeways up until the late 1600s and 1700s (Brown and Steponaitis 2017; DePratter 1989; Hatch 1995; Neitzel 1965)—with the Natchez of western Mississippi perhaps being the last gasp before being scattered in the 1730s. During the seventeenth century, Spanish Florida pulled back from its attempts to colonize the interior north of the Florida peninsula, while

Figure 2.4. The general home territories of major Native American groups in the colonial era.

France and England did not begin their major colonization projects in the Southeast until the latter quarter of the century. As a result, we have few eyewitness European accounts of the Indigenous peoples in the interior for a significant portion of the 1600s.

When those chronicles finally do begin to appear in some number, they describe societies that had experienced sweeping alterations from their Mississippian roots. The erection of earthworks had all but disappeared, the ranked and powerful chiefdoms appear to have re-organized as sprawling confederacies, and there was a significant population decline as epidemic diseases increasingly took their toll. It is somewhat frustrating that we have relatively little documentary data on the critical period from the late 1500s through the 1600s, creating an interval of "forgotten centuries" (Hudson and Tesser 1994). Fortunately, our knowledge of this era is not restricted to European observations. A number of scholars have been staunch advocates of welding archaeological and ethnohistorical research to flesh out this poorly understood interval (e.g., DuVal 2006; Ethridge and Hudson 2002; Ethridge and Shuck-Hall 2009; Pluckhahn and Ethridge 2006). As a result, we have made considerable advances toward filling in the seventeenth-century lacuna in the years since Hudson's assessment. It is now possible to explore the landscape histories of the Southeast throughout the colonial era by relying on multiple forms of evidence, which also include Native American oral histories. This allows us to follow the fortunes of a wide variety of linguistic/ethnic groupings who were described in the rapidly accruing European accounts of the late 1600s and 1700s: familiar names such as Chickasaw, Choctaw, and Cherokee, as well as their predecessors who may have been known by other names (figure 2.4). These are their histories.

Introducing the Other Major Players

Even if one tends to view history as a process, it is hard to ignore the dramatic impact of four eventful dates on the calendar for their consequences on the landscape histories of all southeastern Native Americans. After decades of expeditions, explorations and failed colonies in the Southeast, in 1565 the Spanish Crown established St. Augustine as their first successful permanent outpost in La Florida. This set into motion the eventual formation of a widespread mission system with an influence felt well into the interior of eastern North America. A little over a century later, the English established Charles Town in 1670 as the first settlement in their new colony of Carolina. The Virginia colony was already well under way by this time, since Jamestown had been founded earlier in the century. However, by virtue of propinquity, Carolina would prove the major direct English rival to the long-term Spanish presence in the region, both in terms of its growing militarism and in its ability to win the affections of Native Americans once loyal to La Florida. The year 1699 represents our third red-letter date. After several disastrous attempts at establishing outposts in the Southeast in the late 1500s, France successfully made a beachhead at Biloxi (Mississippi) that would swell to become the enormous territory of French Louisiana. Sometimes an ally to the Spanish Crown but ever an implacable foe of the English, France would provide a third unsettling presence that encroached on Native American groups northward from the Gulf Coast as well as southward from Canada. Finally, in 1783, the Treaty of Paris would set the stage for the loose conglomeration of American colonies to evolve into the United States of America. Although the landscape histories of the southeastern Indians had already been dramatically transformed by this time, the birth of this aggressive republic would force a new wave of changes for Native Americans both within and without its nominal borders.

Generally speaking, the three major European players in the Southeast had different goals and methods of colonization. These cumulatively spurred a highly ramified history of landscape transformations for Native Americans. The Franciscan missions of Spanish Florida typically were built in established Indigenous towns, and friars were charged with both conversion and with using their outposts to support the economic well-being of the colony's capital. This was a model that was broadly, if not exactly, replicated throughout the Spanish empire in the Americas. But it must also be kept in mind that mission landscapes throughout North America also included ranches, presidios, and other communities articulated in a network of mutual support (Panich and Schneider 2014).

The English colonies to the north, in contrast, enjoyed far more autonomy in their relations with Native Americans. For some time, they operated under a principle of salutary neglect, later formalized under Prime Minister Robert Walpole in the early eighteenth century, whereby individual colonies tended to develop their own protocols for dealing with local Indigenous groups (Nammack 1969:9). From the perspective of the English Crown, economic development was abetted by providing some degree of latitude to local governance. For Carolina, and later, Georgia, this translated into a dichotomous strategy of pushing out Natives living within areas being actively settled by European migrants, while simultaneously attempting to attract groups to live on the frontier. Native American frontier towns were actively cultivated as partners in the lucrative trade in Indian slaves and deerskins, and conveniently served as barriers to potential incursions from Spanish or French forces. Following their initial founding on the Atlantic Seaboard, the colonies of Virginia, North and South Carolina, and Georgia began to steadily press westward, although they were stymied at numerous junctures by Native American interests.

The establishment and growth of French Louisiana followed a spatial pattern more akin to English colonies than to Florida. From 1699 onward, French communities spread out from Biloxi along the Gulf Coast, then began to infiltrate, slowly by comparison, into the interior. The early decades of Louisiana were difficult, as it was extremely marginal to the French empire and received little support and few immigrants; however, like Carolina, it was able to sustain itself with a lucrative trade in deerskins with Indians throughout the interior (Usner 1992:24–31). Nonetheless, the population of French citizens and attendant slaves grew very modestly in eighteenth-century Louisiana, fostering a more gradual encroachment than the English colonies at the same time (Usner 1998:59). As the colony successfully took root and expanded northward, the French Crown began to entertain a vision of linking up its vast holdings in New France (French Canada) and Illinois with Louisiana, creating a vast territory surrounding the English colonies to the east. Ironically, in some respects, French influence was even more extensive than that of the English because of their wide-ranging traders, or coureurs de bois, who pursued animal furs and hides throughout the vast drainage system of eastern North America. Although the coureurs de bois network was more prevalent to the north of the Southeast, these traders traveled down the Mississippi Valley and as far east as South Carolina (Crane 1916; Nassaney 2015). The French Crown provided strategic nodes in this system through the construction of forts and outposts. As one notable example, Arkansas Post was placed near the conjunction of the Arkansas and Mississippian Rivers to cement ties with the surrounding Quapaw villages, with the ambition of placing the entire Mississippi Valley under French control (DuVal 2006:76).

The powerful Chickasaws centered in northern Mississippi were major impediments to French interests. They controlled a key portion of the Mississippi Valley necessary to link the French holdings to the north and south. Even worse from the perspective of the French Crown, the Chickasaws were cordial with the English, especially the Carolina colony. The French and Chickasaw Wars of the mid-eighteenth century played a significant role in the landscape histories of both Louisiana and the Chickasaws, as France attempted to remove the Indigenous barrier to its imperial designs. Ultimately, the Chickasaws were able to stand their ground, and France eventually lost its North American holdings as a result of Great Britain's victory in the Seven Years War that ended in 1763. Although

France regained Louisiana in 1803, it rapidly turned around and sold it to the United States the same year (Vidal 2009:62).

With the continued growth of Louisiana, Carolina and adjoining English colonies, and Florida, many Native American groups would follow the path of the Chickasaws. They were consistently drawn into colonial wars between France, England, and Spain that would continue to transform Indigenous relationships to the landscape. One of the more dramatic examples occurred during the War of the Spanish Succession (Falkner 2015). In 1700, the ailing Charles II of Spain died without a child to assume the throne. Anxious to prevent the vast Spanish holdings from being divided up among a number of royal houses, he had bequeathed his empire to his grandnephew, Philip. Philip was both the Duke of Anjou and the second-eldest grandson of King Louis XIV of France. The union of the Spanish and French empires through the Bourbon dynasty would have effectively created the first superpower of the modern era, a prospect that was unacceptable to rival powers in Europe. England, the Dutch Republic, and Austria formed an alliance to support a rival claim to the Spanish Crown in the person of Archduke Charles of the Holy Roman Empire. They formally declared hostilities in May of 1702, initiating the War of the Spanish Succession and a conflict that would endure for 12 years.

Not content to let the war play out on European battlegrounds, some of the colonies of the involved powers pursued hostilities abroad. The extension of this conflict into eastern North America is known as Queen Anne's War. Governor Moore of Carolina tackled the hostilities on behalf of England with alacrity, leading assaults on Florida that decimated the colony (Arnade 1959, 1962; Hann 1988). Particularly damaging were his campaigns in 1702, when Spanish settlements and missions on the East Coast were overrun and siege was laid to St. Augustine, and in 1704, when his invasion of the panhandle region devastated the rich Apalachee mission system that had become key to the well-being of the economy. The net result of these and continuing attacks by English militia and Indian allies was the collapse of the entire mission system through most of La Florida—a process that was already well underway as a result of devastating slave raids that captured mission Indians for English plantations in both North America and the Caribbean (Ethridge and Shuck-Hall 2009; Gallay 2002).

Because of this conflict and others that were to follow, by the time the foundation was laid for the United States in 1783, the geopolitical map of eastern North America had been completely redrawn from that which existed at the beginning of the eighteenth century. Great Britain's domain was now limited to Canada. France had been effectively ousted in 1763, regaining Louisiana only to sell it to the United States in 1803. While Spain won back Florida in 1783 through the Treaty of Paris, this colony was a shell of its former self. Not only had a chronically fragile colony been greatly weakened by the military actions of Carolina at the start of the century, the establishment of Georgia in 1732 on the northern border of Florida provided an even closer English colony that was as equally aggressive as Carolina. Following the establishment of the United States, Spain bowed to repeated incursions and conflicts with its new neighbor to the north and eventually relinquished Florida in 1823, when it became an American territory.

The disappearance of colonial rivals did not reduce geopolitical tensions for Native Americans. Competing powers that could be played off of one another were replaced by a nation that, while not monolithic, was united in its aggressive ambition to secure more territory. Following the close of the Seven Years War in 1763, the English Crown issued a royal proclamation that established the Appalachian Mountains as a general dividing line between colonial settlements to the east and Native American settlements to the west (Nammack 1969:93). This putative boundary was an attempt to ameliorate chronic conflicts between Native Americans and the English colonies on the Atlantic Seaboard. While neither side strictly adhered to this line, after the Revolutionary War the new republic discarded altogether the fiction that two cultural worlds would coexist geographically. Daniel Boone had set one precedent when he first trekked across the dividing line into what is today Kentucky with about 20 settlers in 1763. Following the formation of the United States, waves of immigrants followed in his footsteps, pouring into the western flanks of the Appalachians and continuing to stream westward.

From the perspective of Native Americans, it can be argued that American independence unleashed damaging ideological as well as demographic forces that had been held in some degree of check by London. Within England, elements of the press and many intellectuals were anti-colonial and derisive of the treatment of Native Americans by their cousins in the colonies (Marshall and Williams 1982:208–209; Porter 2000:335)—although the British Crown itself ruthlessly subsumed the rights of Indigenous peoples to the interests of the empire (Bickham 2005). In response, many in the American colonies adopted the defensive philosophical posture, epitomized by the views of Thomas Jefferson, that Indians were corrupted by exposure to despotic regimes as manifested by the likes of the English and Spanish empires (Onuf 2000:26–27). As a result, direct intervention in Native American lifeways was justified as a corrective to this adverse "foreign" influence. One suspects that most Euro-American settlers were not overly concerned with polemics over their rights to penetrate the Appalachian boundary or to usurp Native American territory. Nevertheless, the beliefs of the founders of the American Republic had set the stage for the formalization of the rising notion of manifest destiny and the right of the United States to control the landscape fortunes of Indigenous populations that lay in the path of its expansion.

The Theoretical Lay of the Land

As is hopefully evident, the preceding overview of Native American and European trajectories in the Southeast emphasizes that landscape histories were mutual histories. Native Americans pushed to maintain their traditions of living on and through the land, while European interests sought to manipulate and control the resources and peoples of the Southeast. No party could hope to be completely successful in their endeavors without either countering, collaborating, or compromising with a number of other parties at the same time. For these reasons, the landscape histories of the Southeast provide an important lesson for the distinctively complex ways in which colonialism could play out locally, regionally, and globally.

This is not a book about landscape theory, but it is informed by theory. The bulk of the work on the archaeology and ethnohistory of southeastern colonial landscapes has had a political-economic cast, and for this reason, I will argue that the paradigm of historical anthropology is a useful framework for synthesizing that work and for demonstrating its larger salience to the field of anthropology. But this perspective by no means exhausts the range of provocative work on southeastern landscapes being carried out in the early twenty-first century. Thus, I will attempt to foreground alternative perspectives in various chapters where they have been brought to bear on human-landscape interactions.

I have characterized my theoretical viewpoint elsewhere as a neo-historical anthropology (Cobb 2014). This is to say that my perspectives are strongly shaped by the historical anthropology that came to the fore in the 1970s and 1980s and that was invested in a materialist perspective that privileged political-economic investigations of power and inequality. This approach, which gave rise to such seminal studies as *Europe and the People without History* (Wolf 1982) and *Sweetness and Power* (Mintz 1985), still has particular salience for a study on colonial landscapes because it was born in an attempt to understand—from an anthropological perspective—the causes and consequences of the rise of capitalism, market economies, and what would become referred to as the world system. European colonialism is one manifestation of this history, and many of the key scholars in historical anthropology, in addition to Wolf and Mintz, pursued research on colonialism and/or its immediate after effects (e.g., Leacock 1954; Stoler 1985). Naturally, there is more to the cultural experience than the exercise of power. But within the context of the colonial ambitions of the European states and the aims of Native Americans to maintain sovereignty, the history of the Southeast was in large part the history of a constant struggle over people, their lands, and their resources.

I refer to my perspective as "neo"-historical because it recognizes the important contributions made in the realm of post-colonial research, with post-colonial being understood as a theoretical outlook rather than an era or time period. Drawing on key figures such as Edward Said (1978) and Gayatri Spivak (1988, 1990), post-colonial theorists (including many who evolved from the historical anthropology paradigm) have focused on dimensions of power and inequality as phrased through rhetoric, discourse, ideology, and otherwise "cultural" perspectives that eschew strictly materialist causality and Eurocentric conceptions of the colonial experience (e.g., Gosden 2004; Liebmann and Rizvi 2008; Mignolo 2000; Stoler 2002). In the Southeast, Mark Rees (2001) advocates a melding of the material and ideological in the historical anthropology paradigm as "political culture," and Cameron Wesson (2008) likewise has promoted the integration of materialist and ideological perspectives in our pursuit of the past. This type of broader accommodation is necessary to avoid making a false divide in our exploration of the past that did not exist for those peoples who lived it. In other words, people lived in worlds that allowed them to recognize the need to extract stone from quarries to manufacture tools and to believe simultaneously that the stone was imbued with powers that could enter their lives in ways that transcended hunting game or preparing hides.

For their part, Europeans and Euro-Americans adopted a number of symbolic and ideological practices that served to foster a stereotype of Native Americans as beings who were inferior, were distinctly different from Europeans, and were ultimately subject to European control. We have already seen how Thomas Jefferson assumed a paternalistic attitude that justified the intervention in Native American lifeways as a kind of cultural uplift. This kind of domination was expressed in a variety of both subtle and overt ways, not the least of which was in the realm of language. It is noteworthy that the Fundamental Constitutions of Carolina—the founding philosophical document for the colony in 1670—consistently referred to Native Americans as "neighbors." While this term may connote an air of hospitality, it can also be viewed as establishing a semiotic landscape analogous to the 1763 Appalachian boundary whereby Indians would be framed as peoples who lived physically next to Anglo-Europeans—but not truly with them. In a similar vein, Robert Paulett (2012:10) observes that the common use of "neighborhood" in descriptions of the Indigenous landscape in the documents of colonial Georgia established a trope whereby Indians were a spatial obstacle to be eliminated rather than the friendly people next door.

The cultural relationships conceived of as material that molded the landscape histories of southeastern Native Americans was increasingly influenced during the 1700s by the Consumer Revolution that overtook the Atlantic World—and, indeed, the entire world. The Consumer Revolution was a major spike in the production and consumption of goods (including many luxury items) that many historians see as beginning sometime in the late 1600s (e.g., Berg 2004; Breen 2004; Carson 2017; Hodge 2014). In many respects, it continues today. Although an earlier genesis of this phenomenon can be seen materially in the tens of thousands of pieces of Ming porcelain recovered in early seventeenth-century Dutch shipwrecks (Berg 2004:85), there does seem to be a surge in the variety and volume of goods entering the Atlantic World that was associated with a major uptick in the British economy in the late 1600s. The Consumer Revolution in the context of the Atlantic World is often viewed through an Anglo lens, but a wide swath of nations and regions played a variety of roles in its formation and variable expressions (e.g., Kwass 2003; Martin 2008; Rönnbäck 2010). The American Southeast was one of these key areas. As we shall see in chapter 6, the massive trade in deerskins that reshaped both the social and ecological structure of the landscape was a response to aesthetic demand in Europe. With rising wealth and inequality in Europe and elsewhere, practices of display through clothing and other means became increasingly important as active markers of class and social division (Loren 2010).

What does this all mean in terms of an application to colonial landscapes? There are three dimensions of a neo-historical anthropology that are particularly pertinent, and which will guide the overall structure of this book: history, scale, and the lived experiences of people.

History Matters and Matters of History

Neo-historical anthropology privileges history; the deeper the better. Nevertheless, the history of colonial landscapes is not merely a linear narrative about the clashes and accommodations that disparate cultures had with one another. Indigenous landscapes must also be understood in terms of the structures of landscape meanings and practices that existed prior to the arrival of Europeans and how they continued to eddy through time at the intersection of shifting global interactions and local agency (Cobb 2005; Gallivan 2016). The deeply embedded historical practices of Native Americans did not disappear in 1492—they continued to shape the dynamic landscapes of the contact, colonial, and federal periods, and they continue to do so today. For this reason, every chapter of the book will consider how certain aspects of the Mississippian-period landscape set boundary conditions and possibilities for what would follow.

It must be emphasized that the emphasis on bridging between Mississippian and colonial-era societies in the search for continuities and discontinuities does not draw only from the precepts of historical anthropology. As is widely recognized, the longitudinal and holistic approach toward the study of southeastern Native Americans was pioneered by the ethnohistorian Charles Hudson. It has been carried forward by his students and the legions of southeasterners—ethnohistorians and archaeologists alike—who have been inspired by his long-term perspective on social history. This list is too long to cite here (although the names will crop up frequently throughout this work), so I suggest the interested reader consult the essay on Hudson's contributions and influences by Thomas Pluckhahn et al. (2006). Suffice it to say that the work by Robbie Ethridge,

Marvin Smith, Chester DePratter, and others in their cohort on dissolving the contact divide has deeply influenced my own thinking. Following their lead, one must appreciate how our knowledge of the Mississippian period has shaped our thinking about Indigenous landscapes, as well as vice versa. In this vein, I will take a brief detour to examine the history of research on late prehistoric settlement patterns in the Southeast to set the stage for what came after.

For the Americas in general, Gordon Willey's (1953) publication of his Virú Valley (Peru) research is often seen as the birth of a modern, scientific, and integrative perspective on the way that humans arranged themselves across the terrain. This study moved beyond viewing archaeological sites as isolated entities in order to develop the notion of a systemic settlement pattern. By assigning functional attributes to sites, Willey was able to create a regional perspective on the interactions of human communities, ranging from villages to forts. This approach became increasingly popular in the 1960s and thereafter, in particular when Howard Winters (1969) joined the settlement pattern methodology with the ecological emphasis of processual archaeology to create the settlement system model. In the Southeast, this approach reached full maturity with the publication of *Mississippian Settlement Patterns* (Smith 1978a), a compilation of case studies of late prehistoric regional settlement systems.

This research represented a landmark in ecologically focused research on southeastern landscapes. The predilection of many Mississippian communities for alluvial settings in many respects accounted for their demographic success, as they were able to take advantage of rich arable floodplain soils for maize agriculture while simultaneously exploiting the impressive diversity of plants and animals dispersed throughout a patchwork of oxbow lakes, sloughs, and swamps (Smith 1978b). Moreover, the studies had a strong political-economic bent as they explored the hierarchical organization of the settlement system as a sophisticated configuration of central mound centers, subsidiary towns, and numerous small villages and hamlets. These systems were typically viewed as held together under a chiefdom kind of leadership, characterized by flows of various kinds of tribute to leaders who held both secular and religious authority. Although this political-economic model was inspired to some degree by ethnographic research on Polynesian and other kinds of chiefdoms that had contributed to a neo-evolutionary paradigm, these insights were also informed by the documentary accounts of early European encounters with Native Americans pursuing Mississippian lifeways.

It is not always appreciated that many studies in the *Mississippian Settlement Systems* volume avoided a narrow, adaptive view of human interactions with the landscape. Several authors displayed considerable nuance concerning the social, economic, and ecological tensions and compromises surrounding the distribution of sites. Vincas Steponaitis (1978), for example, showed that the mound centers closest to Moundville (Alabama) seem to have seen their growth stymied compared to more outlying centers. He hypothesized that the demands for tribute from Moundville elites may have fallen most heavily on those who lived nearby, undercutting the labor that might otherwise have been available for earthwork construction at satellites. As Steponaitis (1978:449) further observed, variables such as warfare and regional alliance systems also needed to be factored into Mississippian settlement patterns. This was a marked departure from the stereotype of processual landscape research that was to be later critiqued for eliding agency and factionalism in favor of systemic, harmonious models of adaptation (Thomas 2008b).

Variations on this kind of political/economic/ecological landscape research continue to be pursued in the Southeast. In a widely cited study, David Hally (1993) showed that south Appalachian Mississippian mound centers were spaced with a considerable degree of regularity. He found that primary mound centers—interpreted as polity capitols—were never closer from one another than 33 km and that secondary centers—satellite towns—were never further than 22 km away from their capitol. This pattern led Hally to conclude that chiefdoms in this region, on the average, had about an 18 km effective political radius. Patrick Livingood (2015) took that research one step further with a geographic information system (GIS) analysis of Hally's data. This showed that the political radius corresponded with a half-day travel time, a distance that corresponded closely with certain other chiefdoms worldwide whose relatively compact size enhanced direct chiefly oversight and communal defense, among other factors. As seen in this study, the introduction of GIS to the study of community spatial patterns has been an important asset to landscape studies of a materialist persuasion in the Southeast. In this vein, Eric Jones (2010, 2016, 2017) has been an ardent proponent of what he refers to as "settlement ecology," an approach that weds the methodological advances of

GIS with the precepts of historical ecology to explore the key materialist variables underlying settlement choices and how they evolved among Native American societies in the Eastern Woodlands.

But more to the point: these recent studies as well as numerous others based in the late pre-European contact period of the Southeast have relied heavily on settlement and landscape data to address chiefly instability and cycling (Anderson 1994b; DePratter 1991), as well as conflict and factionalism (Anderson 1994a; Blitz 1999; Dye 2009; Milner 1999). From a political-economic perspective, the emphasis on volatility in Mississippian societies has dovetailed nicely with research on the colonial era. Europeans did not disrupt a peaceful, bucolic landscape; they were new parties who introduced further instability into a social environment with a deep history of unpredictability. Native Americans had already developed strategies for dealing with newcomers who might have friendly or unfriendly intentions. Europeans may have been a novel presence, but they were incorporated into a world that had already been shaped by long-standing extra-local relations.

Accommodating the Atlantic World

A traditional strength of historical anthropology is its broad-scale framework. Although it is important to privilege the motivations and practices that define human agency within local households and settlements, that agency over the past 500 years has been impacted and shaped by widely dispersed currents of colonialism, mercantilism, capitalism, and globalization. For this reason, the actions of agents and communities were often molded at the intersection of the global and the local, where long-term traditions of taste, desire, and need became increasingly intertwined with the demands and opportunities unleashed by the intervention of the Atlantic World. In Anthony Giddens's (1990) terminology, Native Americans in the Southeast were increasingly drawn into a process of modernity known as time-space distanciation: an unprecedented stretching of the fabric of social systems across space and time. By acting as proxies in regional variants of European wars raging across the Atlantic Ocean, by acquiring cloth from textile mills in England and beads from Venice, by providing deerskins for markets in Europe, Native peoples became intimately linked to peoples from far away whom they would never encounter face-to-face.

Even before the arrival of Europeans, Mississippian towns were engaged in far-flung relationships involving the movement of peoples, utilitarian objects, exotic goods, iconography, and ideas. Stone hoes made in southern Illinois and Tennessee by Mississippian manufacturers have been found over a large portion of eastern North America (Winters 1981); marine shell from southern Florida was traded into the interior and modified in various forms (beads, gorgets) to an impressively large number of Mississippian communities throughout the Southeast (Muller 1987); and even religious and cosmological beliefs seem to have emanated from the central Mississippi Valley and influenced widely dispersed communities from Oklahoma to Georgia (Brown 2007). The arrival of Europeans in the Southeast yoked Native Americans to a rapidly expanding world system that was not altogether foreign to their way of doing things.

Long-distance relationships would increasingly impact Native American landscapes by the 1700s, as shifting alliances among Europeans, among Native Americans, and between Europeans and Native Americans constantly threatened the existence of Indigenous and European communities and created ongoing pressures to uproot and migrate to safer havens. One of the more dramatic—and devastating—examples of this history is the 1704 attack during Queen Anne's War (alluded to earlier) by the Carolina colony on the Franciscan missions among the Apalachee in Spanish Florida (Arnade 1962; Hann 1988). A force of over 100 English militia accompanied by over 1,000 Creek allies literally laid waste to many of the missions and associated communities in the Florida panhandle region. Several thousand Native Americans, mainly Apalachees, were captured by the Carolina force. Over 1,000 were sold as slaves and ended their lives on plantations throughout the Caribbean, while over another 1,000 were settled along the Savannah River on the frontier of the Carolina colony. This attack, preceded and followed by others, effectively rolled up the mission system throughout Spanish Florida. Most of the survivors eventually settled within the perimeter of St. Augustine on the Atlantic Coast.

At a macro level, the landscape histories of these groups were inextricably tied to the cultural, political, economic, and religious ambitions pursued by complex alliances of colonizers, colonized, and groups who maintained a semblance of autonomy. The tragic case of the Apalachee missions is an example of what we might consider the butterfly effect in the political economy of colonialism and distanciation, whereby a seemingly modest event in one corner of the globe—a king leaves no direct heirs—cascades into a process with incalculable effects in another corner.

Human Experience

A focus on lived experience is central to historical and neo-historical anthropology. This emphasis is certainly shared by practice theorists, but draws its inspiration more from the likes of E. P. Thompson and Antonio Gramsci to, as Bruce Trigger (1993:176) put it, "stress intentionality and the social production of reality." Put another way, in recognition of the shortcomings of traditional political-economic approaches in anthropology in bridging from world systems to everyday lives, many adherents began to practice a "bottom-up" approach (Marcus and Fischer 1984; Roseberry 1988). From the perspective of landscapes, what this means is that despite the surrounding swirl of impinging processes and events, the focus must continually return to how actual people lived and worked together to create their own social relations and histories of landscape: "real people doing real things" (Roseberry 1988:163). This objective is necessary to decolonize the history of Native Americans, but it does not imply the complete free will of either Indigenous peoples or of those attempting to subjugate them. From the point of view of practice theorists, it can certainly be argued that people are active participants in the construction of their social and natural surroundings and institutions—that is, structure. However, while in the context of colonialism we are interested in real people doing real things, we can never forget the encroachments of others. It is possible to overplay the latitude that individuals have to engage in resistance (Roseberry 1989:141 passim). Despite their intentions, people are often coerced or manipulated by other interest groups who may have an outsized influence on the historical shaping of structure (Wolf 1990).

In terms of attempting to reproduce their conditions of existence on a daily basis, landscape relations for Native Americans played out in a dialectical way. On the one hand, Native American agency in the era of colonialism was defined by a singularly strong pursuit of autonomy (DuVal 2006; Ethridge 2010; Hahn 2004; Jordan 2013; Paulett 2012). The struggle over autonomy does not mean that it was achieved, at least completely, because self-governance was consistently entangled with the ambitions of colonial powers and neighboring Indigenous groups. Moreover, autonomy was pursued as a multi-scalar endeavor. For instance, at some points in history, the Creek Confederacy worked in concert to achieve some latitude from colonial interference in its affairs. At other points, certain Creek towns sought different paths of decision making and alliance formation than did others. In fact, as a basic social denominator, the drive for autonomy throughout the colonial Southeast was underscored by the centrality of the town as a unit of identity and governance. Even for those groups like the Creeks who achieved some level of regional or pan-regional organization, fundamental decision making typically emanated out of the town, or *talwa*. The *talwa* and its intrinsic institutions of household, clan, red:white organization, and other social formations structured the daily conditions of existence for most southeastern Indians.

Counterposed to this striving for autonomy and the continuity of tradition, Native societies in the colonial system were constantly beset by deterritorialization—a process whereby groups define their notions of self through the production of place but without static boundaries (Appadurai 1995; Yaeger 1996). The local is maintained through a complex web of interaction that is far reaching—that is, distanciation—and that may subvert long-standing local ties of authority, kinship, and other social bonds. The larger cultural landscape is thus a network of places defined relationally and contextually, as deterritorialized communities reproduce themselves by drawing on various scales and types of relationships (Appadurai 1995:204; Thomas 2001:173). In the modern era deterritorialization has been used specifically to describe the transmigration, fragmentation of space, and extensive flows that constitute globalization; however, "global" kinds of interactions characterize pre-modern settings as well. This is not to say that notions of territory or homeland disappear, but that the reproduction of those entities, or the ideas of those entities, is increasingly implicated in regional and global flows.

Conclusion

Some of the strongest proponents of landscape approaches in archaeology, drawing more on interpretive, subjective, or phenomenological frameworks, argue that there has been a tendency in processual, scientific archaeology to assume a top-down perspective on the landscape. This, in their view, flattens history by treating human actors and groups as dots or polygons that can be manipulated on maps (e.g., Dalan et al. 2003:35–36; Pollard and Gillings 1998; Thomas 2008b). They advocate a lateral or bottom-up perspective that attempts to understand landscapes as past actors experienced them. Although political-economic approaches typically do not attempt to interrogate meaning to any great extent, there is still an emphasis on a bottom-up approach to appreciate how agents and interest groups were buffeted by, and contributed to, the larger historical currents of colonialism.

This kind of approach also resonates well with post-colonial approaches that attempt to decolonize the past by removing Europeans as the primary lens by which we view the actions of Indigenous peoples (Ferris et al. 2014; Liebmann and Rizvi 2008). Working under rubrics such as "Native-lived colonialism," "decolonizing the past," "mutual histories," and "entanglement," archaeologists increasingly are seeking to integrate European texts, the archaeological record, oral histories, and the perspectives of Native peoples to try and achieve a plural perspective on past lifeways (Ferris 2009; Harrison 2004; Martindale 2009; Stahl 2002). In this sense, this book is incomplete in that its focus on landscapes is derived mainly from archaeology and ethnohistory, and it lacks the Native American voice that is now taken for granted in landscape studies in the southwestern United States (Fowles 2010). But hopefully, it is a step in the right direction.

From Cussita to Bears Ears

At a meeting held in 1735 between Creek leaders and colonial officials in Savannah, Georgia, Chekilly—the headman of the Lower Creek town of Coweta—recounted his people's origin story (Coleman and Ready 1982:381–387). After emerging from a mouth in the ground, they embarked on an extended journey marked by encounters with distinctive landscape features and other peoples. First moving westward, then turning back in the opposite direction, they came to a "red bloody River" that they lived alongside for two years. Traveling along this waterway, Chekilly's forebears found the "King of Hills," a source of sacred fire and the knowledge of important traditions and practices. Continuing their easterly migration, they discovered a white path that they followed for a number of years, continuing to cross many hills and drainages. This path eventually ended at the key Hitchiti town of the Pallachucollas (Apalachicolas), whose inhabitants welcomed the travelers with white feathers. Following this warm arrival, "they have liv'd together and shall always live together, and bear it in remembrance" (Coleman and Ready 1982:386). Chekilly's ancestors then split into two towns, Coweta and Cussita, that straddled the Chattahoochee River (figure 3.1).

The Cussita migration story, greatly condensed here, is so fascinating in its detail and context that it has spawned a cottage industry of commentary and interpretations from historians and archaeologists alike (Gatschet 1884:235–251; Hahn 2006; Hall 2009:14–16; Knight 1981:23–39). How could one not be riveted by a narrative that took two days to relate as it was simultaneously inked in black and red onto a bison hide that has subsequently disappeared? Less important for our purposes, though, is an exegesis of these various perspectives, and more that the towns of Cussita

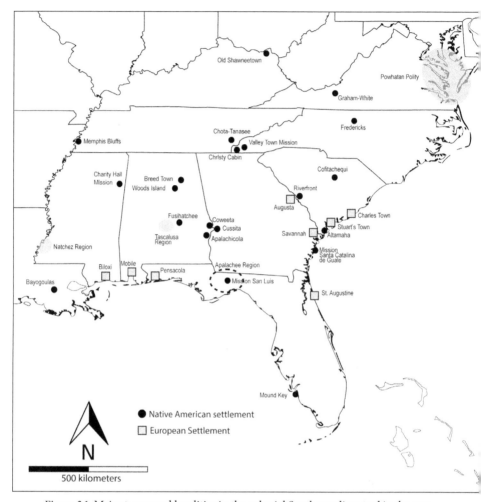

Figure 3.1. Major towns and localities in the colonial Southeast discussed in the text.

and Coweta deemed movement and the landscape as essential features of their origins, identity, and relations with other peoples. At one point in their journey, Chekilly's ancestors settled a dispute with the Chickasaws, the Alibamos (Alabamos), and the Obekaws (Abihkas) over "which was the eldest, and who should have the Rule" with a contest (Coleman and Ready 1982:383). Whichever group could first cover a stick from bottom to top with the scalps of enemies would be considered the senior people. At the conclusion of the challenge, the Cussitaws had emerged the winners, followed by the Chickasaws, the Alibamos, and finally by the

Obekaws, who "could not raise their heap of Scalps, higher than the knee" (Coleman and Ready 1982:383).

The Cussita migration story reflects a notion of space that is at the same time locational and relational. The landscape was a force that shaped the ancestors of Cussita and Coweta as a people and their larger social networks. Without question, some of the conclusions that could be pulled from this narrative would not sit well with some of their neighbors, especially the Abihkas. Moreover, there are other versions of Creek migration and founding that differ in significant detail (Gatschet 1884; Swanton 1922). But the mutualism of landscape, movement, and identity would be widely understood by any Native American. Like the stories of the Cussita people, the stories that various southeastern groups tell about their beginnings invariably invoke exodus. Chickasaws followed an oracular pole eastward before arriving in northern Mississippi (Gibson 1971:10–11), and the Hitchiti emerged from a canebrake before journeying past a lake and up a stream to establish their town (Gatschet 1884:78)—variations of these kinds of founding stories abound.

The fusion of landscape and culture, of course, is not unique to southeastern Indians. Scholars, perhaps Keith Basso most lyrically, have made this point emphatically for other regions and cultures of North America (Basso 1996; Deloria 1992; Momaday 1974; Nabokov 2006). Nor is this worldview restricted to Native Americans. Researchers working in varied settings have emphasized that the production of place and living in and through the landscape are foundational to building a sense of human belonging and identity (Appadurai 1991; Berleant 1997; Lovell 1998). Likewise, a number of landscape archaeologists have emphasized the experiential and sensual dimensions of topography (e.g., Bender 1993; Bradley 2000; Thomas 2001; Tilley 2004). Vine Deloria (1992) decried a compartmentalized and commodified notion of landscape divorced from these sensibilities that he believed permeated the Western values threatening Indian lands and cultures. In the eyes of many Native Americans, federal action taken on December 4, 2017, to greatly downsize the Bears Ears National Monument in Utah has been the fruition of Deloria's fears. The original monument size of 547,074 ha (1,351,849 acres) contained a variety of sacred places in addition to numerous important cultural and natural resources. Many Native Americans and their supporters maintain that the reduced monument size of 86,696 ha (201,876 acres) is a concession to political and economic interests in the region (for contrasting views for and against the monument, see Robinson [2018]). There are, for example, significant uranium deposits in the "de-monumentalized" zone. For those who argue for maintaining the enlarged boundaries, this is another example of the general lack of understanding of, and respect for, the fundamental underpinning of landscape to Indigenous lifeways.

The courts will have the final say on the outline of Bears Ears since a number of lawsuits challenging the legality of the monument's contraction have been launched since the action of 2017. Nonetheless, this controversy does raise the question of the priority of phenomenological versus materialist views of the landscape, perspectives that may occur side by side within a culture. Although many materialist-leaning archaeologists, such as myself, support the enlarged version of Bears Ears for all of the reasons put forth by its Native American supporters, Basso (1996:41, 66) has chided cultural ecologists and other materialists for adopting a perspective on landscape research in general that he sees as "one-sided and incomplete," particularly in the lack of attention to its symbolic character. Meanwhile, those of a materialist bent have cautioned against constructivist approaches whose minute attention to detail risks verging on the myopic, potentially eliding broader processes that contribute to the production of concrete social relations through the landscape (Albers 2002; Hirsch 1995; Yaeger 1996).

Ultimately, these arguments are a matter of emphasis rather than right or wrong. As I pointed out in the previous chapter, it is possible to appreciate the multivalent aspect of the landscape while at the same time emphasizing one facet that best illustrates a certain vantage point. My own viewscape is focused on the struggles over power, authority, and sovereignty as played out in the landscapes of the colonial Southeast. As illustrated by the Cussita migration story, even a narrative richly steeped in symbolism and metaphor may have overtly political ends. Steven Hahn (2004) has observed that the relation was conducted as a performance by Chekilly in front of powerful Creek headmen from other towns, as well as colonial officials. One of Chekilly's apparent goals was to promote and reinforce Coweta's leadership role in the Creek Nation. Although the paired towns of Coweta and Cussita had risen to prominence in the latter portion of the eighteenth century, both Chekilly's status and that of the towns were far from secure. While his telling of their migration gave due deference to Apalachicola's widely recognized status as a founding town in the region, it also naturalized the later ascent of the Muskogean Creek newcomers. In Joseph Hall's (2009:15–16) words, "Chekilly's account shows the belief that 'towns make history.'"

This chapter is in part an apologia. By illustrating some of the complex ways in which political and economic dimensions of the landscape are imbricated with religious, symbolic, and sensual dimensions, I am then asking the reader to allow me to forego an emphasis on the latter in the remainder of this book in order to focus on the former. For what it is worth, the kind of experiential landscape study favored by the likes of Keith Basso (1996) or Peter Nabokov (2006) has yet to be written for the colonial Southeast on a grand scale—an important subject for another day.

Persistent Places and Spaces

Persistent places are locations on the landscape that embody long-term and variable histories of residence, visitation, commemoration, and memory (Gallivan 2012; Rodning and Mehta 2016; Shaw et al. 2016; Thompson and Pluckhahn 2012). These settings are meaningful for generations of people, even if those meanings are not consistent through time. Meanings are always modified by humans, who are, if anything, far from consistent. Nevertheless, a general sense of power and importance may become attached to a location by virtue of recurring practices of visitation and even alteration of that spot. In a manner, persistent places may develop almost a character of spatial agency in that the values invested in them may retain or attract peoples eager to interact with them.

Although not explicitly relying on the term "persistent place" that has gained favor in the Southeast, a number of archaeologists have invoked the idea of citational practices to explore the nuances of how such landscape features come about and their larger, relational implications (Borić 2002; Jones 2005). This work shows that a so-called persistent place has both temporal and spatial dimensions. Repetitive rebuilding or remodeling "cites" that which preceded it, but never quite in the same way. As Hatley (1989:229) observes for the Cherokees, "[They] had an affection for individual places and townsites that cannot be evoked by statistics. . . . The repeated recolonization of the Keowee townsite reflected this continuing identification and understanding of local landscapes." We also see this practice in the archaeological record, where the layer-cake constructions of multiple townhouses—important ritual and public structures—at the same spot through time at the Cherokee site of Coweeta Creek were constantly altered in shape and size (Rodning 2009, 2010). In effect, residents were crafting history and deep time, where each building episode gained meaning from that which came before. But the practices and meanings potentially changed through time while still retaining the recognizable "oeuvre" (see Borić 2002) of a townhouse. Further, persistent places also act as key nodes that stitch together networks of places. They are locations that may draw together people at both intrasite and intersite scales through pilgrimage, busk (green corn) ceremonies, rites of passage, and a wide variety of other activities. Landscape features become persistent places because they are physical embodiments of memory. Repeated visits and activities surrounding them may evoke remembrances of events, peoples, and other significant facets of times past. The creation and reuse of these important places confers upon them a mnemonic role in the interpretation and reinterpretation of culture (Edmonds 1999; Jones 2007; Pauketat and Alt 2003; Wilson 2010).

The Southeast contains many examples of Mississippian persistent places where peoples engaged in the kinds of citational practices that harkened to deeper and broader histories. Brian Butler and I conducted research for a number of years at one such location in southern Illinois known as Millstone Bluff (Butler and Cobb 2012; Cobb and Butler 2002). This distinctive natural promontory (figure 3.2), coincidently or not, resembles a Mississippian mound and contains an unusual Mississippian village on its peak. The site, also known as Millstone Bluff, contains a stone-box cemetery, exhibits an arrangement of houses around a plaza, and has a suite of open-air rock art that references the multi-dimensional worlds of southeastern cosmology (Wagner et al. 2004) (figure 3.3): This world, which generally corresponded to the surface of the earth, was still complexly multilayered; an upper world of order and purity that resided above the sky vault; and an under world of change and chaos beneath the earth and waters (Hudson 1976:122–126).

These kinds of features, particularly occurring together, are somewhat remarkable for a community of modest proportions in the hilly interior away from the major mound centers of the Lower Ohio Valley. Importantly, this location has a history extending back into Woodland times, when it was one of a number of hilltop "stone forts" that are found in that region of southern Illinois, southern Indiana, and western Kentucky that surrounds the confluence of the Wabash and Ohio Rivers (Brieschke and

Figure 3.2. View of Millstone Bluff from the southwest (photograph by author).

Rackerby 1973). These site types, marked by stone enclosures, are widely thought to have some sort of ceremonial significance and were regularly visited for ritual purposes. Based on the radiocarbon date sequence at Millstone Bluff, Butler and I have argued that it was abandoned around 900 CE then reoccupied by Mississippian peoples in the 1200s as part of a migration into the hilly region of southern Illinois (Cobb and Butler 2002). By appropriating this symbolically powerful point on the landscape, the residents of Millstone Bluff appear to have made it into a nodal community in the locality, perhaps the locus of a modest polity.

In a parallel example, Timothy Pauketat and colleagues (Pauketat et al. 2015) have discovered what appears to be a Cahokian ritual outpost in the Upper Mississippi Valley (Wisconsin). Constructed in the eleventh century CE, the site of Trempealeau contains what are interpreted as religious buildings built in a typical Cahokian wall-trench style associated with ceramic and lithic objects also affiliated with the giant mound center in western Illinois some 900 kilometers to the south. This northern installation was built near a "storied landform"—Trempealeau Mountain—on a prominent bluff on the Mississippian River within a locality dotted by earthworks from the earlier Effigy Mound Culture. Pauketat et al. (2015:283) believe this may have been a type of religious mission, intended to convert locals to Cahokian belief systems. They see the economic fea-

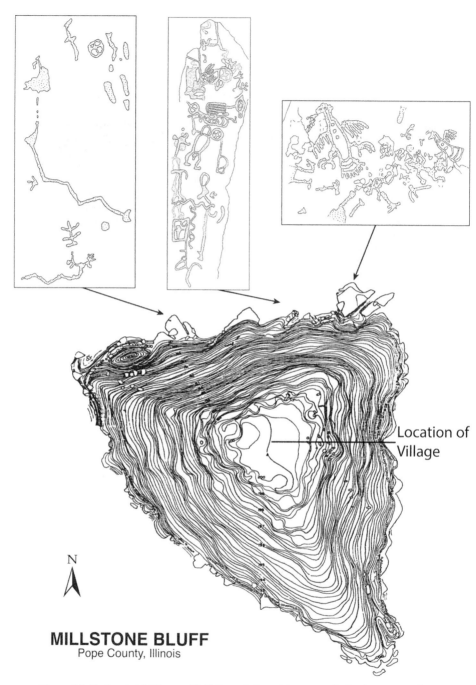

MILLSTONE BLUFF
Pope County, Illinois

Figure 3.3. Rock art at Millstone Bluff. From left to right are symbolic depictions of lower world, this world, and upper world (courtesy of Mark Wagner, Center for Archaeological Investigations, Southern Illinois University Carbondale).

tures of this settlement as, at best, secondary (e.g., it may have served as a Cahokian extraction point for valued local objects).

Similar acts of ritual landscape appropriation as an expression of political ideology are common elsewhere in the world. For example, certain Andean mountains were considered sacred places and the loci of pilgrimage, ritual, and special burials for hundreds if not thousands of years. Inka elites were quick to integrate these persistent places into their own cosmology of authority as they conquered new areas and new peoples who venerated the peaks (Besom 2013). Spaniards continued this tradition by building their early Catholic chapels on Inka spaces of state ritual (Wernke 2007a).

The phenomenon of persistent places emphasizes the false divide of space and place, or landscape and the built environment. As Severin Fowles (2009:449) maintains, "Even though most now acknowledge that landscapes are constructed no less than villages, there remains a tendency to contrast village and landscape as one would culture and nature." He urges that we push past the antimony that settlements are distinct from their natural surroundings and that natural surroundings are unmodified by human hands. Dispersed features such as paths, rivers, and ritual caves all constitute the larger world of individual settlements and, in turn, the landscape. Relying on landscape as a unit of analysis requires a consideration of how all of these kinds of locations mesh into a larger cultural, spatial, and temporal domain.

Persistent places are frequently these kinds of concatenations of natural landscape features and loci of human construction and dwelling. Millstone Bluff may have been an attraction because its natural shape and height made it a metonym for a constructed mound, transformed by humans first into an apparent Woodland ritual setting then into a Mississippian village whose residents may have been able to appropriate its symbolic character toward political ends. Trempealeau Bluffs and Mountain likewise were natural features of the landscape incorporated into the built environment, with the locality eventually becoming ensconced as a persistent place. One Cherokee narrative about the transport of a council house or townhouse by otherworldly beings underscores the isomorphism between space and place for many southeastern Indians: "They [the Nûñnë'hï, or immortals] steadied themselves again and bore the rest of the townhouse, with all the people in it, to the top of Tsuda'ye'lûñ'yï (Lone peak), near the head of Cheowa, where we can still see it, changed long ago to solid rock, but the people are invisible and immortal" (Mooney 1900:335).

Neill Wallis (2019) has floated the provocative idea that Middle Woodland Native American groups may have been inspired to build communities at locations where natural features of the landscape invoked the cosmos. He has documented that key features of the Garden Patch site (Florida) were placed on natural rises that described a U-shape—a common configuration for southeastern sites of that period. When paired with the strategic emplacement of mounds, the U-shape may also be linked to celestial alignments such as the summer solstice. By intimately linking human and natural features, aspiring elites could argue that the community layout, and their place in it, was "predestined."

Martin Gallivan's (2005, 2007, 2016) body of work on the Chesapeake region and the Powhatan polity represents one of the more in-depth explorations into the ontological blurring between so-called natural and cultural landscapes spanning late pre-Columbian to colonial times in eastern North America. His work strives "to shift the frame of reference from English accounts of the colonial era toward a longer narrative describing Virginia Algonquians' construction of places, communities, and connections in between" (Gallivan 2016:8). As Gallivan describes it, growing hostilities between the Jamestown settlers and the surrounding Algonkian towns can be attributed to a number of causes, but above all the insatiable appetite of English colonies for Native American land. Although Jamestown's encroachments on rich agricultural fields in and of themselves sparked a number of deadly conflicts, Gallivan (2016:182) believes that major Indian uprisings in 1622 and 1644 were precipitated by their angst over loss of "critical pathways and persistent places in the Virginia Algonquian landscape." These included burial grounds, feasting locales, and abandoned towns that were revisited for ceremonial purposes. As with Bear Ears, the colonials either could not, or refused to, comprehend how these places constituted the larger cultural landscape of the Algonquians.

The act of dwelling in itself may have contributed to imbuing places with special significance. Concerned about the inroads of English traders with the important Indian towns along the lower Chattahoochee River (groups who would form the nucleus of the Lower Creeks), Spanish Florida built a fort next to the town of Apalachicola in 1689 (Pavao-Zuckerman et al. 2018; Worth 2000:278–279). Within the year, the surrounding

Figure 3.4. Outward and return migration of groups between the Chattahoochee drainage and northern Georgia.

peoples abandoned the Chattahoochee River and resettled primarily along several drainages in north-central Georgia (figure 3.4). This action seems to have involved both a push—Spanish encroachments—and a pull—the establishment of the lucrative trading beacon of Charles Town on the Carolina coast by the English in 1670. With the onset of the Ya-masee War in 1715 that pitted these and other Native American peoples against the Carolina colony, most of the Creek settlements returned to or near the locations they had departed (Foster 2007).

The reasons for the reoccupation of the Chattahoochee Valley were complex, likely attributable to economic factors as well as those of mem-ory and nostalgia. After all, the effort that went into land clearing for towns and agricultural fields was considerable; such areas certainly would have been prime locations for resettlement even after a quarter-century of abandonment. When William Dunlop of South Carolina undertook a "southward" voyage in 1687, he observed that the once-thriving mission town of Santa Catalina de Guale on St. Catherine's Island (Georgia) was reduced to "the ruins of severall houses which we were informed the Spaniards had deserted for ffear of the English about 3 years agoe: the Setlement was great, much clear ground in our view for 7 or 8 miles together" (Dunlop 1929:131). It probably is no coincidence that many of the forts on the Carolina frontier were built at former Native American towns; these locations typically were along important routes and offered an open landscape conducive to reestablishing the agricultural fields necessary to support the military personnel (Cobb 2019). Indeed, European and Euro-American travelers throughout the Southeast often made reference to abandoned Indian cultivated parcels as "old fields" (e.g., Bartram 1793:52, passim; Romans 1999 [1775]:271). From their perspective, with the decline or removal of Indian populations, old fields became a highly desirable resource on the landscape that facilitated new colonial settlements.

Still, despite the allure of a landscape pre-adapted to resuming an agricultural lifestyle, the Cussita migration story shows that Creek towns, or *talwas*, and their locations were also viewed as important elements of the ritual landscape as well. As Thomas Foster (2017:3) notes, the Lower Creek town of Apalachicola had a "strong sense of homeland or origins despite frequent relocations." The union of *talwa* and landscape is a key reason that Creek "towns make history" (Hall 2009:15–16).

Mounds also make history. The practice of mound building in the Southeast extends back at least to the fourth millennium CE (Peacock et al. 2010; Russo 1996; Saunders et al. 2005). These artificial landforms oftentimes assumed the status of persistent places. At some sites, significant Middle Woodland mounds were incorporated within Late Woodland and/or Mississippian mounds (e.g., Pauketat et al. 1998), and both Woodland and Mississippian earthworks are known to have been placed on top of locations characterized by ritual activities even before the onset of mound building (Cobb 2015; Wright 2013). During the colonial era, the Cherokees are known to have placed townhouses on top of mounds that apparently had not been used since terminal Mississippian times (Steere 2015). These examples do not mean that the earthworks were apprehended in the same way throughout the generations, but they and their surroundings apparently were viewed as places that embodied a sacred aura. Indeed, in the colonial and even federal periods, Native Americans continued to occasionally bury their dead in mounds that had been built long before by their ancestors. It is no little irony that these later burials were typically referred to as "intrusive" by Euro-American observers who denied the connections between moundbuilders and historic-era Indians (R. Mann 2005). The reluctance of Americans to recognize monumental persistent places on the landscape of nineteenth-century Native American culture became a key rationale for the proliferation of bizarre theories attributing earthworks to Toltecs, Vikings, lost tribes of Israel, Romans, and other travelers who happened to find themselves in North America (Kennedy 1994).

In addition to earthworks, rock mounds dot the landscape of the Southeast as well as other portions of eastern North America. There is some controversy as to whether they were constructed by Native Americans or represent piles from farmers clearing their fields in more recent times (cf. Gresham 1990; Ives 2013; Moore and Weiss 2016). They usually occur in concentrations of several to several score, and they may be manifested as low tumbles of stone or well-crafted cones standing several feet high. Some rock piles or mounds may be of recent vintage. In the early eighteenth century, John Lawson (1967 [1709]:29) observed that Native Americans "have other sorts of Tombs; as where an *Indian* [italics in the original] is slain, in that very Place they make a heap of Stones (or Sticks, where Stones are not to be found;) to this Memorial, every Indian that passes by, adds a Stone, to augment the heap, in Respect to the deceas'd hero." There is earlier precedent for this phenomenon. The Middle Woodland Tunacunnhee site in northwest Georgia, for instance, had stone cairns overlying burials associated with Hopewellian-style artifacts, such as copper panpipes and platform pipes (Jefferies 1976). Whether or not we conceive of these locations as persistent places, they do seem to reflect a persistent landscape practice of honoring the dead with sanctified stone monuments.

Portable Places and Spaces

Relocation and migration became increasingly common features of the Native American experience during the colonial era. Writing of the Shawnees, travelers extraordinaire and justifiably famous for their widespread peregrinations from the 1600s to the 1800s, Stephen Warren and Randolph Noe (2009) make a provocative point: with so many groups pushed or pulled out of their territories and often buffeted across the Southeast without much respite, many traditional aspects of the landscape may have been lost—if not from memory, at least from routine encounters. Lacking the familiar touchstones found in a stable topographic setting, the town or *talwa* rose to a singular prominence in the Shawnee landscape. This was an entity that, regardless of place, manifested the essence of a people. So, after departing the Ohio Valley sometime in the early to mid-1600s and adopting a lifestyle of routine travel, by "the 1660s Shawnee towns were symbolic and portable rather than place bound and unmovable markers of identity" (Warren and Noe 2009:169).

Here, I think it is worth repeating an observation made by ethnohistorian Neil Whitehead (1992:139). Referring to South America during the colonial era, he has described how the encroachments and dislocations sweeping across Indigenous lands often disrupted regional and pan-regional connections. As a result, identity began to hinge more on the immediate locality, particularly the village or town, with an emphasis on language as a political marker. I am skeptical of cultural universals, but this is precisely what we see occurring in many parts of eastern North America. For this reason, at least for some peoples like the Shawnees, the built environment may have become foregrounded over the "natural" environment as permanent homelands dissipated. Along with this trend, portable and symbolic elements of the built environment may have gained particular value.

The plaza was one of these vital symbols. This open, central space, usually flanked by earthworks and/or houses, was a forum for important community events, such as ball games and busk ceremonies. During the Mississippian period, the plaza was a ubiquitous spatial, ritual, and social core of villages and towns (Cobb and Butler 2017; Kidder 2004; Lewis et al. 1998:15–16). This spatio-cultural centrality of the plaza is emphasized by the fact that southeastern groups have continued to make it a focus of their social and ceremonial life through the colonial period and up until the present. William Bartram observed that Creeks during the eighteenth century closed out their busk ceremony by building a fire in the town plaza (Bartram 1793:507–508), and the square or "stomp ground" continues in this same role in modern Creek communities in Oklahoma (Nabokov 2002:133–134). Because of the plaza's importance, Brian Butler and I

Figure 3.5. Reconstruction of council house at Mission San Luis de Talimali (courtesy of the Florida Division of Library and Information Services).

(Cobb and Butler 2017) have argued that its construction was the founding architectural event in the establishment of many Mississippian towns. They were particularly important to migrating groups for establishing, or reestablishing, a new place couched in familiar traditions and spaces—a role that would have gained even greater importance as migrations and forced relocations accelerated during the colonial period. In this regard, the plaza served as a portable mise en scène for reconstituting traditional social, political, economic, and ritual arrangements.

The formal plaza does have a deeper history in the Southeast, extending at least as far back as Middle Woodland times and perhaps earlier (Kidder 2004; Pluckhahn 2010). Perhaps owing to this history, it was one of the notable architectural constants during colonial times, when the built environment witnessed significant alterations in domestic house styles and the cessation of mound building. So too, the council house or townhouse seems to have been an important construction that conferred a sense of permanency during an era of dramatic change. These expressions of public architecture ranged in size from slightly larger than domestic houses (8 to 10 m long for rectangular structures) to monumental buildings like the one at Mission San Luis in the Apalachee province of Spanish Florida that measured 36 m in diameter (figure 3.5) (Shapiro and Hann 1990). Like plazas, townhouses or council houses hosted a variety of social, ritual, and political activities that fostered community identity and the reproduction of social relations. As a social and ritual focus of a community, Cherokee townhouses were typically one of the key pieces of architecture to be erected in a new town (Rodning 2009, 2010). Even with the conversions to Christianity occurring in the Spanish mission system, the council house remained an essential component of the Native American town (Thomas 1990:382–383).

As Native Americans began to uproot more frequently during the colonial era, the town became less of an anchor on the landscape and more of a buoy; its mooring could change but its general outline containing a plaza and council house was a constant. Notably, the portable permanence of the town was not limited to its material manifestations. Town names could also journey across the landscape. Appellations like "Great Tellico" and "Old Estatoe" were known to accompany relocated towns in Cherokee country (Smith 1979). Similarly, some Yamasee town names migrated with their frequent moves through Georgia, South Carolina, and Florida (Swanton 1922; Worth 2004).

Travel Corridors and Maps

Whether spaces and places are persistent or portable, the implication is that cultural landscapes are defined by locations keyed to community, ritual, memory, and other important aspects of cultural navigation. However, important nodes do not exist in isolation. A landscape is comprised of networks of places that are defined relationally and contextually (Appadurai 1995:204; Thomas 2001:173). Even nominally secluded locations of the sort associated with small-scale and secretive ritual activities may still be connected within a complex social field. This point is emphasized by the intriguing research of Simek et al. (2013), who propose that rock and cave art sites were symbolically linked on the Cumberland Plateau landscape in Tennessee. Open sites occurred at higher elevations and tended to contain more imagery associated with the upper world (e.g., sun circles) in Native American cosmology, whereas cave sites occurred at lower elevations and exhibited more under world symbolism (e.g., serpents, hybrid creatures). This structural relationship of sacred sites based on the topographic and cosmological antinomy of upper:under worlds extended across hundreds of kilometers.

For places to exist in a relational field, they must be linked logistically as well as socially and ritually. Here rivers and trails come into play. The

Southeast is crisscrossed by scores of constructed paths and hundreds of navigable waterways that were just as much a part of the landscape as were venerated mountains and beloved towns. Their efficacy for travel is reflected in an offhand observation by John Lawson in 1701 in the Carolinas region: "It is very odd, that News should fly so swiftly among these people" (Lawson 1967 [1709]:49).

Overland trails carved political, economic, symbolic, and phenomenological routes through the landscape. In a seminal study, William Myer (1928) documented at least 125 significant trails in the Southeast (figure 3.6). Although he referred to these as "early colonial trails," many of them must have been regularly tread for many generations before the colonial era. The region around the modern town of Nashville, Tennessee, for example, was effectively abandoned by its once-thriving Mississippian population by the end of the fifteenth century (Krus and Cobb 2018). Yet Myer's map indicates that this location was still an extant hub of trails hundreds of years later that resembled the intersections of multiple interstate and state highways around the city today. Even with the abandonment of central Tennessee, it is likely that these routes continued to bear travelers who were passing from one region to another or taking advantage of the surrounding hunting grounds.

With the dramatic rise in trade between colonials and Native Americans, certain trails began to assume particular prominence from the 1600s onward. After England established Charles Town as the capital of Carolina in 1670, this port city became an important conduit for moving Indian slaves to the Caribbean and deerskins to Europe. Vital trails soon radiated outward from Charles Town in all directions (Crane 2004 [1929]:134–136): to the north and northwest linking the city to the politically and militarily significant Cherokees and Catawbas in the Piedmont and Appalachia; south toward St. Augustine; and the so-called Upper and Lower Paths that extended to the powerful Creeks and Chickasaws to the west. By the turn of the nineteenth century, literally tens of thousands of enslaved Indians and millions of deerskins had moved along these and other paths to the markets of the Atlantic World.

Trails served as lines of ingress as well as egress. Beginning in the 1600s, Haudenosaunee (Iroquois) men began to follow the warrior path and other routes southward to raid Catawbas, Cherokees, and other groups (Cashin 2009; Fitts 2006; Merrell 1989; Perdue 1987). There is no solid archaeological data to suggest that long-distance raids over hundreds

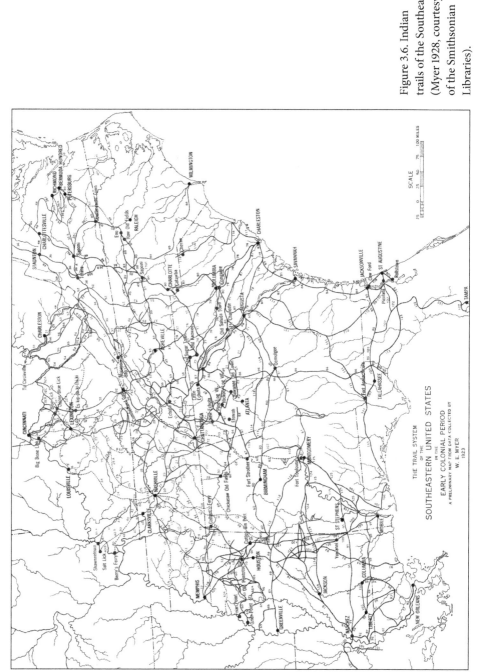

Figure 3.6. Indian trails of the Southeast (Myer 1928, courtesy of the Smithsonian Libraries).

of kilometers were a regular feature of Native American warfare in pre-Columbian times, although they may have happened on occasion. Thus, the almost-annual attacks from the northeast must be attributed to an expansion of the geopolitical landscape among Native Americans introduced by colonialism. Many southern Indian peoples found it necessary to adopt defensive strategies against Iroquois raids, such as reintroducing the nucleated, fortified towns of their Mississippian predecessors and distancing themselves from the north-south arteries regularly traveled by the Iroquois.

Trails also figured into the ceremonial life of southeastern peoples. A major route in Illinois extending from the Wabash River westward to Cahokia runs by the Emerald site, some 24 kilometers to the east of Cahokia (Koldehoff et al. 1993:340). This multi-mound site appears to have been a significant ritual center and point of pilgrimage during Mississippian times (Pauketat 2013). Likewise, a major trail running northward from the Ohio River in southeastern Illinois passes by the upland site of Millstone Bluff, discussed earlier in the chapter. This path runs by the north side of the site, and people exiting the trail to enter Millstone Bluff would have had to walk through and witness the bodies of rock art to enter the community, representing what appears to be a purposeful choreography of bodily movement from trail to site plaza (Cobb and Butler 2017).

What we do not know is whether these kinds of trails purposefully ran by important constructed features or settlements, or whether the features arose in response to the traffic on the trails. Further, even if sites like Emerald or Millstone Bluff were pilgrimage locations, it is possible that these routes ran by them but not necessarily to them exclusively. These centers may have been arrival points for some, while serving as cosmological caravansaries for others who could pause for spiritual refueling before continuing their journey elsewhere.

Trails themselves could carry metaphorical freight. In Chekilly's recounting of the founding of Cussita, his ancestors followed a white path. This references the familiar—but complex—red:white division among many Native American southeastern groups (Lankford 1993). Although the meaning behind the colors was not uniform or even stable across the Southeast, in general, white had connotations of peace and municipal order whereas red was associated with warfare, trade, and external relations (Dye 1995; Hudson 1976:234–239). Towns could be red or white, as could chiefs, as could age-grade associations. The white path followed by Chekilly's people presumably implies a route of optimism and moral certitude.

A vast network of waterways in the Southeast provided another important avenue for travel. The recovered remains of canoes and similar kinds of watercraft dating back to Archaic times attest to their long-term importance for navigation, particularly for rapid travel and for bulk transport (Newsom and Purdy 1990; Wheeler et al. 2003). During the Mississippian period, the proximity to a navigable drainage enjoyed by many major mound centers expedited access to the considerable volume of utilitarian and exotic goods that plied the waterways. Long-distance exchange networks are documented in eastern North America at least as far back as the mid-Holocene (ca. 5000 BCE) (Brown and Vierra 1983; Jefferies 1997), but Mississippian groups demonstrated an unsurpassed facility for trading raw materials and finished goods. Copper and marine shell were particularly valued, but the range of exploited raw materials is impressive and includes various cherts, salt, mica, galena, chlorite schist, fluorite, and green stones (Brown et al. 1990; Muller 1987). Likewise, there is an enormous variety of objects rendered from these materials, such as copper plates, shell gorgets, figurines, eccentric lithics, and digging implements, to name but a few (Cobb 2000; Muller 1997; Phillips and Brown 1978). Some towns, such as Cahokia near the Mississippi River, may have functioned as "gateways," relying on their strategic location and political muscle to funnel flows of goods in and out of their locales (Kelly 1991).

As Indian territories became articulated with the Atlantic World, the importance of water travel and trading paths to commerce became even more pronounced. Although French Louisiana and Spanish Florida engaged in the fur and hide trade to some extent, the English carried it to another level. After a modest start in the late 1600s, the Carolina deerskin trade rapidly accelerated to become the backbone of the colony's economy. Between 1699 and 1715, before a brief lull caused by the Yamasee War, Charles Town exported an average of 54,000 deerskins a year (Crane 2004:111). Many of these were ported by human or horse pack trains overland from the interior, before being transferred to pirogues (flat-bottomed, double-masted boats), at places like Fort Moore or Augusta on the Savannah River before final transport to Charles Town. Labor shortages in Carolina through the early decades of the 1700s made for a racially and economically diverse composition to the vitally important deerskin trade (Stewart and Cobb 2018). Indians and European traders did most of the work of transporting the hides to entrepôts like Augusta or forts that served as factors. Military personnel or individuals at trading houses directed the transactions of hides for goods and commodities. Finally, it was common for paradoxically autonomous indentured public servants and enslaved Africans to bring deerskins by boat for the last leg of the journey to Charles Town (Stewart and Cobb 2018:40–41). This kind of freewheeling racial admixture on the economic landscape of the Southeast would become increasingly constrained in the ensuing century.

One cannot emphasize enough the efforts made by Native Americans to take advantage of and control these avenues of trade and communication. The Chickasaws are a case in point. The Mississippi River was insinuated into the Chickasaw landscape in a complex manner that reflected both their sacred and pragmatic worlds (Mack 2018). The river was about 160 kilometers (100 miles) west of their core nucleus of settlements in northeast Mississippi, but it figured as a temporal threshold in their migration story. As they crossed the river from west to east, they also entered a new era of time as they settled in Mississippi. Like many Indigenous peoples, they also imputed cosmological powers to this waterway, figuring so importantly as a component of their cultural landscape that it was jealously guarded. As Europeans and other Native Americans traveling the river discovered, the Chickasaws monitored and controlled movement through a north-south stretch of the river roughly centered on modern-day Memphis, a city built on what was known to travelers as Chickasaw Bluffs. This example reinforces the notion that many Native American groups defined their sovereignty through extensions of their landscape that were cultural and conceptual, as well as politically and economically opportune.

While waterways and oceans were central to navigation in the Southeast, as seen with the Mississippi River, they also contained a variety of powers and both malevolent and friendly spirits. According to the English trader James Adair (2005 [1775]:248), the Cherokees "are also strongly attached to rivers,—all retaining the opinion of the ancients, that rivers are necessary to constitute a paradise." The Little Tennessee River, one of the major drainages in Cherokee country, was viewed as a helpful spirit known as "the Long Man," who restored health, conferred blessings, and whose waters provided the powers for important ceremonies (Hudson 1976:128; Nabokov 2006:56–58). Many southeastern Indians bathed every morning in rivers as a way of warding off both physical and moral pollution (Hudson 1976:324–325).

According to Paulett (2012:23–27), recorded accounts of Native American perspectives on travel in the colonial Southeast suggest that they followed a processional geography. Behind the objective of traveling between two locations was the knowledge that paths or waterways connected a sequence of places—usually towns—and that to follow a given route implied a series of interactions at all of these points along the way. Further, the control of trails was recognized as a source of power just as much as the control over waterways or other strategic elements of the landscape.

The modest number of surviving Native American maps seems to reflect this outlook. Both Gregory Waselkov (1998) and Patricia Galloway (1998) contend that these fall into two categories, what Galloway refers to as the sociogram and the event transcription. For the event transcription rendering, European cartographers transcribed geographical or social referents from Native American informants onto European-style maps. These are not fully Indigenous creations, but they do attempt to incorporate Indigenous knowledge and experience into the landscape. In the sociogram, a relationship of Indigenous towns or polities is represented by circles connected by lines or paths. Physical and social proximity tend to be equated on these diagrams, rather than metric distance. Further, the size of the circles corresponds with an ethnocentric view of the landscape (Paulett 2012:24–25; Waselkov 1989a, 1998); that is, a Catawba map depicts the Southeast with the major Catawba towns depicted as large central circles connected to other peoples (figure 3.7). These kinds of maps were notational rather than scientifically cartographic. On several occasions, though, Europeans constructed quite accurate maps—by their standards—by eliciting landscape features from Indian informants that conformed to Western notions of proper spatial relationships (Waselkov 1989a:293, 295).

Affective-Scapes

Landscapes are not defined solely by where things physically are and how people use those locations. Other senses may also define the cultural terrain. Viewscape research represents one of the more interesting recent advances in expanding our horizons about the ways in which places were spatially linked. Southwestern archaeologists have demonstrated that shrines related to the Chaco phenomenon (850–1150 CE) were placed on elevated locations to enhance the intervisibility of Chaco Canyon and its

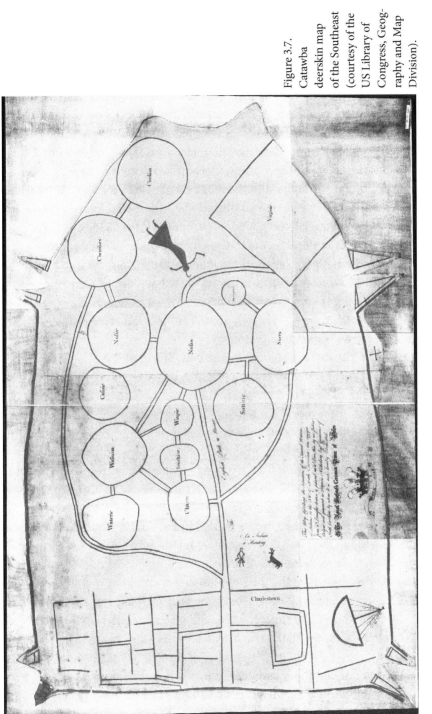

Figure 3.7. Catawba deerskin map of the Southeast (courtesy of the US Library of Congress, Geography and Map Division).

outlier communities (Van Dyke et al. 2016). These "symbolic umbilicals" created a spatial network of belonging across a large geographic expanse. Similar kinds of research have not taken hold widely in the Southeast, for various reasons. There seems to be a received wisdom in the Southeast that the wooded terrain likely hindered the open, sprawling viewscapes that typify the Southwest. However, it may be that the occupation of elevated sites like Millstone Bluff and Trempealeau was in part about gaining the higher ground necessary to enact a visual vantage point in this kind of setting. It is unclear how important such locations were in colonial times, at least with regard to the maintenance of viewscapes. Unlike the continuity of peoples in the Southwest, the widespread forced removal of southeastern Indians to Oklahoma Territory in the 1830s created a historical barrier in the ability of Indians to participate in daily engagements with the landscapes of their original homelands. Thus it is a challenge to recreate the kinds of landscape connections that may be taken for granted elsewhere. This is not to say that all of the oral accounts and memories of landscape have been completely erased in the Southeast, but we seem to have lost a considerable amount.

Sound also defines cultural landscapes. The crashing of a familiar waterfall or the bustling noises of a neighboring village may play important roles in the cultural and physical orientation of individuals. While there have been some novel forays into "archaeoacoustics" (Hultman 2013; Schofield 2014), this topic, like viewscapes, has not been systematically broached for the colonial Southeast. We do, however, have a few provocative examples of the ways in which missionaries attempted to impose Western notions of time discipline on Native Americans through the creation of new soundscapes.

Charity Hall was one of five Presbyterian missions to the Chickasaws built in the 1820s. Like most Protestant missions in Native American territory in the pre-Removal era, Charity Hall provided a school and vocational training where the missionaries endeavored to provide a Western education and job skills for Chickasaw youth. Under these auspices, the Reverend Robert Bell supervised his charges at Charity Hall (Mississippi) from 1820 to 1832 with the zeal of a factory head striving to make a quota:

About day-light the trumpet is blown—the signal for all to rise. In half an hour it is blown again, that all may attend family-worship in the dining-room. Within five minutes from the close of the worship,

Mr. Bell, with the boys, repairs to the field until eight or nine o'clock, and Mrs. Bell, with the girls, to sewing or other employments. They are then called to breakfast, where Mr. Bell is seated at the head of the table, with the boys on one side and the girls on the other. When breakfast is over, they repair to school until twelve o'clock. After an interval of an hour, they are called by the trumpet to dinner. After dinner, until four o'clock, they are at school. They then go to the field until night, when all are called to supper and family-worship. Throughout the whole, the scholars appear to be under strict discipline, which they observe with promptness and cheerfulness, except that they seem a little slow to start to work in the morning, but when at work they seem brisk and cheerful. (McDonnold 1899:139–140)

The use of sound to structure the rhythms of labor and recreation is familiar to most of us who attended school in the modern United States, with electronic bells or buzzers signaling the start and end of the work day and recesses and lunch in between. But it was a novelty for Native Americans more accustomed to organizing work by necessary daily and seasonal tasks rather than regimented time. The Franciscan missionaries in Spanish Florida used a similar system in the seventeenth century, giving rise to the term "living under the bell" (Bushnell 1994:96). The requirements of formal instruction in the Catholic faith, attendance at mass, and celebration of feast days were all marked by the peal of the bell in mission villages. Likewise, ringing marked the onset of more mundane activities such as construction events and the upkeep of mission buildings. This routinization of labor greatly altered the traditional daily schedules of Timucuas, Guales, Apalachees and other Indians incorporated into the mission system.

Due to the forced removal of the Chickasaws under the Jackson administration in the 1830s, Charity Hall was only in operation from 1820 to 1832. Given this brief interval, it is difficult to assess how successful the Rev. Bell and other missionaries were in their efforts to contribute to the reshaping of the economic landscape of the Chickasaws. Nor can we assess, appearances notwithstanding, how happily the children adapted to these circumstances. The same ambiguity applies to the Spanish missions. Like the Presbyterians, the Franciscans regularly reported an atmosphere of promptness, faithfulness, and cheerfulness at their missions (Gannon 1989:52–53)—except for the widespread revolts that broke out every few decades (Francis et al. 2011; Gannon 1989; Worth 1998). The archaeological remains of several missions in La Florida have yielded fragmented bells, apparently the target of Native Americans whose conversion may have been more apparent than real (Thomas 2017). These humble, "killed" bells are symbolic of the widespread struggles over how landscapes would be inhabited, used, and experienced by Native Americans throughout the colonial Southeast.

Conclusion

The preceding overview provides a point of departure for the path that will be followed in the remainder of this book. Landscapes are, and have been, integral to the worldview of many Native American and other cultures. For such societies, landscape is constitutive of culture. It is not a commodity, nor a simple network of exploitable resources, nor a simple aesthetic pleasure. However, the arrival of Europeans in the Southeast introduced a new set of beliefs about the landscape that clashed with Indigenous ones. Although Native Americans were not necessarily compelled to accept these beliefs, they were forced to act upon and against them. With Europeans encroaching from multiple directions and Native American groups adopting new strategies of movement and settlement, human-landscape relations were irrevocably altered. Writing about the Savannah River during the colonial era—a waterway that seemingly was abandoned in the 1400s CE and reoccupied during the 1600s—Paulett (2012:51–52) suggests that the shorter and episodic history of Indigenous occupation in the valley (discussed in more detail in the following chapter) may have led to a relationship with the river that was more "abstract" than the intimate meanings traditionally imbued in streams that may have been part of a community's life for hundreds of years.

I may be veering onto thin interpretive ice, but the replacement of thick meanings with more abstract meanings of the landscape may have become more common in colonial times throughout the Southeast as the regular shuffling of populations unsettled connections to persistent places with familiar histories. Whether that is true or not, it does seem that the political and economic dimensions of the landscape became increasingly foregrounded in the lives of Native Americans with the rise in conflict and increasing importance of trade relations with European colonies. My emphasis in the remainder of this book will be on how those kinds of material relations played out through and on the landscape.

The political and economic conflict between Native Americans and colonials over territory reached a culmination in the philosophy and policy of manifest destiny as expressed by the expansion of the United States into Native American territories in the late 1700s and 1800s. The idea that Euro-American peoples were entitled to lands that they knew best how to exploit not surprisingly has a deeper genealogy that was widely propagated by Europeans soon after Columbus first touched down. Various French Enlightenment thinkers such as Montesquieu and Turgot were instrumental in articulating an ideology whereby different types of subsistence systems were linked to a moral and legal structure manifested as an evolutionary progression from the familiar hunter-gatherer to agriculturist sequence, ideas that were adopted by influential Scottish philosophers such as Adam Smith and John Millar, who in turn popularized them in the larger English-speaking world (Heffernan 1999).

Aside from these broad rationales and ideologies, the landscape histories of the colonial Southeast ultimately were dictated at the local and regional level by transactions among and between Native Americans and Europeans. The imperial projects of Spain, France, and England each had varying objectives in North America. These shifted through time and across space, and they were continually rephrased by colonial actors "on the ground." For their part, the Native American peoples who already occupied this land were incredibly plural culturally, and their strategies of attempting to maintain authority over their landscapes likewise were diverse. What follows, then, is a twofold presentation: a series of microhistories that underscore the importance of parochial contestations and compromises, which are organized thematically to reflect how Native Americans frequently came up with common responses to European encroachments.

Migration and Displacement

There is a saying among families in the modern American armed forces—perhaps the most migratory social units in the nation since World War II—that three moves equal one fire. Even with the most careful packing and transport, at the other end of the line there is the inevitable, disappointing discovery of soiled furniture, smashed vases, and missing Matchbox cars. Because the objects and landscapes around us play a central role in mediating our worldviews and practices, their loss or alteration through recurring moves can literally rearrange our cultural and logistical surroundings. This perspective is particularly meaningful for the Native Americans of the Southeast, who experienced a tremendous number of dislocations, both voluntary and forced, with the arrival of Europeans. While some communities moved perhaps once in a generation, others found themselves constantly relocating every few years. This population churn involved both loss and gain, destruction and construction.

The waves of migration occurring during the colonial era were not an absolutely new phenomenon. Beginning with the Paleoindian (or earlier) journeys from eastern Asia some 12,000 years ago, to the forced relocations of Removal in the 1830s, southeastern Native American groups were always on the move. Still, it is hard to exaggerate the degree and frequency of displacement experienced by southern Native American tribes as an indirect and direct result of the imperial ambitions of Spain, England, and France. Destructive wars, the depredations of slave trading, and the incursions of colonial settlements undermined settlement stability to a historically unprecedented degree. Perceived opportunities provided yet another major stimulus for migration and relocation, as families and

towns moved to locations advantageous for trade, travel, and communication. Despite the surge in relocations in the colonial era, their structure
was nonetheless based on a deep history of multi-scalar migrations and
long-established relations with the landscape and with other peoples. To
fully appreciate the diverse strategies employed by Native Americans in
their widespread colonial migrations, as well as the myriad consequences
for living in the landscape, it is useful to consider first the nature of Native
American movements in the Southeast in the centuries immediately prior
to the arrival of the first Spaniards in Florida. Then I will consider three
different types of population movement that created distinctive Indigenous landscapes during the colonial era: serial migration characterized
by repeated displacement, widespread dispersals that we associate with
diasporas, and population flows that spurred the creation of frontiers and
borderlands.

Mississippian Patterns of Migration

Debates over the genesis and spread of the Mississippian complex beginning around 1000 CE have typically hinged on the question of migration.
The enduring question is whether there was a core area from which the
basic elements of the Mississippian complex (e.g., intensive maize agriculture, mound building) radiated outward via the movement of peoples,
or whether numerous groups across the Southeast were simultaneously
exchanging ideas and practices that quickly coalesced into this phenomenon (Cobb and Garrow 1996; Smith 1984, 1990; Wilson and Sullivan
2017). Although the argument has shifted back and forth, there are now
sufficient radiometric dates to support the thesis that the Central Mississippi Valley seems to have served as an important crucible for at least
a limited set of recognizably Mississippian practices that disseminated
rapidly in the eleventh and twelfth centuries CE (Anderson 1999; Brown
2007; Pauketat 2007). The follow-up question, however, is how exactly did
those practices move outward? It now appears that there was a complex
mix of migration and emulation involved, with different regions of the
Southeast experiencing varying histories of "Mississippianization."

David Anthony (1997) has proposed a "leapfrog" model for the spread
of the Neolithic in western Asia and Europe that may be analogous to the
dispersal of Mississippian lifeways. He has suggested that farming and related practices moved westward in a series of pulses, whereby colonizing

groups would make saltations of some considerable distance. Then, over a protracted period of time, other groups would backfill the middle terrain between the outposts and regions already following Neolithic lifeways. Applying this model to the Southeast, presumably that backfilled terrain already contained other, non-Mississippian communities who may have gradually adopted and altered Mississippian practices. Thus, the flow of the Mississippian phenomenon, like the Neolithic, likely entailed both the movement of peoples and the adoption of traits.

Southeastern North America does appear to contain widespread Mississippian outliers at an early date, that is, the eleventh century CE or slightly later. Well-known examples include the Macon Plateau site in north-central Georgia (Williams 1994), Rood phase sites in the Lower Chattahoochee drainage (Blitz and Lorenz 2002), the Mound Bottom site in central Tennessee (O'Brien and Kuttruff 2012), and the Trempealeau site in western Wisconsin, in the upper reaches of the Mississippi Valley, discussed in the previous chapter (Pauketat et al. 2015). Despite their far-flung nature, all of these complexes share some important traits with the Central Mississippi Valley, such as shell-tempered pottery, wall-trench style domestic structures, and mound-plaza arrangements. Aside from these and other compelling examples of migration, there was nonetheless an impressively rapid process of Mississippianization in the Southeast that clearly could not have been accomplished by the movement of communities alone. Extensive networks of trade, word of mouth, and perhaps even religious emissaries of some sort seem to have been influential to the spread of Mississippian lifeways.

At the other end of the spectrum are short-term moves very typical of small agricultural communities. There is strong evidence that after the establishment of the Mississippian phenomenon, a significant portion of the landscape was filled with relatively brief occupations, lasting a generation or two perhaps, comprised of farmsteads or hamlets containing one or a few families (e.g., Harn 1978; Kowalewski and Hatch 1991; Muller 1978; Smith 1995). It is quite possible that settlements relocated regularly as a function of exhausting local soils and resources (Foster 2016; Hatch 1995:154–155). In addition, social factors such as intrasite and intersite conflict likely instigated community fissioning and mobility (Blitz 1999). Most scholars would not necessarily refer to some of these types of movements as migrations; in many respects, practices of extensive agriculture are parallel to the somewhat scheduled moves that many hunter-and-gatherer groups make.

In between these kinds of repetitive relocations and the more dramatic colonizing efforts across the Southeast, there were many kinds of intermediate kinds of migration—a category of movement that does not receive much attention in the archaeological literature. Warfare, slaving, fissioning from social discord, demographic spikes or declines, and a host of other variables act to push and pull populations across the landscape at varying distances (Cameron 2013). Many such relocations can be haphazard and unplanned. These present a sharp contrast to longer-distance moves that may involve a considerable degree of organization.

We do have evidence in the Mississippian Southeast for this in-between category of population movement. For example, neighboring regions could witness back and forth movement due to oscillations in political, economic, and ecological conditions. Some communities apparently shuttled between the American Bottom and the upland area to the east as political fortunes shifted around Cahokia (Alt 2001; Koldehoff 1989; Pauketat 2003). This kind of to-and-fro dynamic has been documented in northern Georgia, too, where a recurrent population flow was associated with the rise and fall of mound centers. There may have been between 14 and 41 instances of chiefdom collapse in the region that would have been associated with migration episodes (Hally 1996:120). Dynamic growth and dispersion, propelled by factors such as internal factionalism and external conflict, may have been the norm for Mississippian chiefdoms (Anderson 1994a; Blitz 1999).

In short, the Mississippian landscape was decidedly not characterized by communities and polities that were enduringly stable. People uprooted on a constant basis for reasons related to demography, conflict, religion, ecology, and a variety of other push and pull factors. When Europeans first landed on the shores of southeastern North America, Native Americans already had a well-established repertoire of relocation strategies at their disposal. What they were not prepared for were the scale and frequency with which these strategies would need to be employed.

Contingent Grounds

Because many Indigenous groups simply disappeared in the upheaval of the colonial era, we will never have a fully comprehensive perspective on the movement and fate of all Native Americans in the Southeast. Nevertheless, a number of studies have provided important syntheses of the major population shifts among larger tribes throughout the seventeenth and eighteenth centuries. These provide a sobering portrait of the widespread dislocations—forced and voluntary—that seemed to have become an integral component of Native American lifestyles after the arrival of Europeans. These dislocations are what spurred an upsurge in the process of deterritorialization, as the movement of communities constantly reworked their ties to place and placed ever-increasing importance on forging new kinds of relations with different peoples and with those they had left behind.

Marvin Smith (1989, 2002) has helpfully translated the history of major population movements of southern Indians during the colonial era to a series of migratory maps (figure 4.1). His research shows that a handful of major dislocations during the early 1600s blossomed into numerous regional moves by around 1675–1700. In the early 1700s, this trend not only continued, due in no small part to slaving, but it was also marked by numerous long-distance migrations. As one notable example, a group of Shawnees traveled from South Carolina to join the Haudenosaunee confederacy in the Northeast early in the eighteenth century. To put this in perspective: the serial migrations of the early Coosa groups described in chapter 1 were on the order of 80 kilometers or less (Smith 2002); in the early eighteenth century, in contrast, the Shawnee journey from the Savannah Valley in South Carolina to the Susquehanna Valley in New York was about 1,200 km.

Population loss was the dark side of population movement. Disease, conflict, and slaving ravaged and destabilized Native American communities. The substantial body of research on the scale of demographic decline in the Southeast, while not entirely in consensus on details, is still in broad agreement that the numbers of Native Americans plummeted in the 1600s and 1700s before reaching some rough degree of stabilization at the end of the eighteenth century (cf. Cameron et al. 2015; Dobyns 1983; Kelton 2007; Muller 1997; Thornton 1990). Despite the debates over the numbers or percentages of the Indigenous population lost to pathogens,

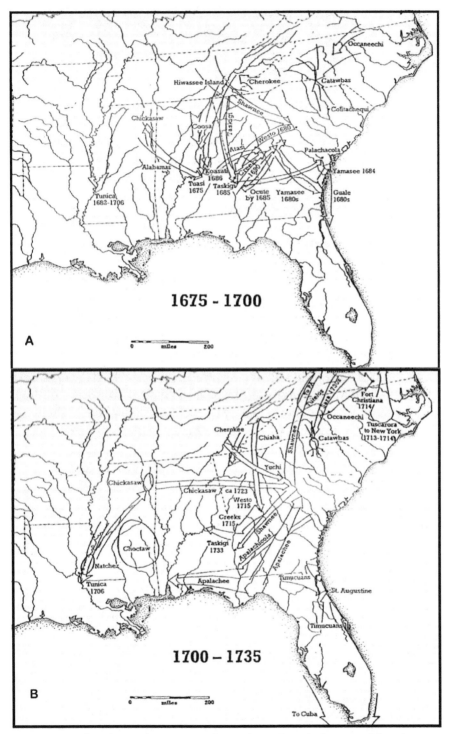

Figure 4.1. Two key phases of migration in the Southeast, from the late 1600s (*A*) to the 1700s (*B*) (from Smith 2002:Figures 4, 5; courtesy of Julie Smith).

one can go out on an epidemiological limb and assert that the toll was devastating. A description of a smallpox epidemic in South Carolina in 1698 gives some measure of the human cost:

> . . . in the mean Time we have no Reason to Expect any Mischeif from ye Indian Trade, the Small-Pox hath Killed so many of them, that we have little Reason to Believe they will be capable of doing any Harm to us for severall Years to Come, that Distemper having Swept off great Numbers of them 4 or 500 Miles Inland as well upon ye Sea Cost as in our Neighbourhood. (Salley 1916:104)

As the Europeans recognized, disease was constructing a landscape of clearance far more effective than they could have accomplished on their own.

Much of the impetus for population relocation seems to have been the recognition by many groups that their greatly reduced numbers made them increasingly vulnerable from attacks by Europeans and other Native Americans alike. Safe harbor was sought either by fleeing into the interior of the Southeast or by joining more powerful and welcoming communities. The dramatic demographic decline also invited migration by leaving uninhabited gaps strewn throughout the regional landscape of the interior. As the boundaries of powerful sixteenth-century polities shrank, communities were able to move into now-vacant localities formerly under the control of powerful chiefs.

To place these varying landscape histories into broader context, it is useful to consider contrasting models on European-Native American interactions by three prominent ethnohistorians. While not completely in opposition to one another, they do demonstrate somewhat different emphases on the ways in which Native Americans reorganized their relationship to their landscapes in the face of population loss and the steady encroachment of colonial powers.

In the first model, Robbie Ethridge (2006) relies on the metaphor "Mississippian shatter zone" to capture the tumult represented by the widespread and continuous dislocations throughout eastern North America (see also Ethridge 2010; Ethridge and Shuck-Hall 2009). As she has observed, by the mid- to late 1600s, the ubiquity of slaving and warfare, compounded by competitive trade in deerskins and other commodities with the colonies, prompted a prolonged period of continuous upheaval. Even for groups who enjoyed some sense of stability in their core regions, such as the Chickasaws in northern Mississippi and the Cherokees in the Appalachians, a secure life was never a given. Under the best of circumstances, continuous raids and European encroachments regularly chipped away at the edges of traditional territories. Under the worst of circumstances, towns that were unable to stave off slave raids or the excesses of warfare disappeared from history. Much of the population movement documented in the Southeast during the colonial era represents attempts to flee shatter zones, areas made all the more dangerous by the unpredictable nature of regional outbreaks of violence.

Shatter zones in a sense could be viewed as primary or secondary. In the former, the direct activities of Europeans had immediate impacts on a locality, leading to the dispersal and/or decimation of its residents. Examples of these are numerous. One of the more dramatic involved the Carolina invasion of western Florida and the destruction of the Apalachee mission system during Queen Anne's War in 1704, as described in the introductory chapter (Arnade 1962; Crane 2004; Wright 1981). Not only were many mission towns razed, but thousands of Apalachees were brought back to Carolina either to be resettled or else to be enslaved and shipped to the plantations of the Caribbean. Secondary shatter zones resulted from the indirect actions of Europeans, particularly as certain Native groups acquired firearms and began their own predations on neighboring peoples. Among these militaristic-slaving groups, to use Ethridge's terminology, the Westos are particularly noteworthy. They apparently represent a group of Eries from western Pennsylvania who headed south to Virginia in the 1650s to escape the internecine conflicts among Iroquoian groups (Bowne 2005; Meyers 2009). Taking advantage of being one of the first Native American groups in the South to acquire substantial numbers of firearms, they quickly set forth on a widespread reign of slaving that had wide-ranging repercussions. With their move to the Savannah River in 1659, the Westos' trail of devastation penetrated further into the South, reaching even into Spanish Florida. Some Southeastern groups, such as the Chickasaws and the Ocaneechis, soon became successful slaving societies in their own right. A brief observation about the Chickasaws by Thomas Nairne in 1708 encapsulates both the allure and extent of slaving throughout the Southeast:

Formerly when beavor was a commodity they sold about 1200 skins a year but no imployment pleases the Chicasaws so well as slave

Catching. A lucky hit at that besides the Honor procures them a whole Estate at once, one slave brings a Gun, ammunition, horse, hatchet, and a suit of Cloathes, which would not be procured without much tedious toil a hunting. They goe a man hunting to the Chicsaws [Choctaws], Down to the sea side along both sides of the great river [the Mississippi River], and 150 miles beyond it. (Nairne 1988 [1708]:47–48)

But all was not mayhem. Many regions in the Southeast did—at least for periods of decades—manage to achieve some level of stasis. As a result, they seemed to have been able to achieve an equilibrium with Europeans similar to what Richard White (1991), in our second model of European–Native America interactions, referred to as the "middle ground" for the Great Lakes region. There, French and English colonists were too thinly extended into the interior to forcefully implant a substantial infrastructure. This provided the Kaskaskias, Potowatomis, Miamis, Illinois, and other groups the leverage to assume a semblance of standing their ground even if severely weakened in numbers. In this setting, Native and European powers alike continually granted concessions and reached accommodations that ensured mutual survival. Many of the groups along the Coastal Plain region of the Southeast seem to have pursued this kind relationship with French and English settlements in the late 1600s and into the 1700s, only to fall back as the number of European settlements continued to expand inward from initial coastal settlements like Jamestown, Charles Town, Mobile, and Biloxi.

While the middle ground concept may be applicable to the Great Lakes and perhaps some other regions, it was not a universal condition. Joseph Hall (2009:9) believes that southeastern Indian communities were too transient—a response to the shatter zone phenomenon—to have established this kind of equilibrium. However, there is no minimum temporal threshold for what defines a middle ground: it could last for only 10 years or as long as 50. And there are certainly many instances throughout the Southeast of fragile and short-lived peacetimes. These periods are no less important for their brevity.

Nevertheless, there were other kinds of accommodations between Native American and colonials. In a third model of interactions, Kathleen DuVal (2006) emphasizes that Native inhabitants of the Arkansas River Valley, well removed in the interior and comprising sizable and militarily capable populations, had the power to construct a far more autonomous "native ground." Beginning with the polities who met Soto in 1541 and extending into the subsequent centuries, Pacahans, Quapaws, the Osage, and others along the Arkansas River consistently manipulated European colonials to their own ends. The French and English without question strongly influenced the history of the Arkansas Valley, but their ambitions were continually thwarted and molded by Indigenous powers. This kind of Native ground where Indians were far more in control of their land-scape destinies seems to have persisted well into the eighteenth century in many other regions as well, such as the homelands of the Cherokees in the Appalachians and various groups comprising the Creek confederacy along the Chattahoochee drainage (Rodning 2002; Waselkov 1993; Worth 2000).

It would be tempting, but far too simplistic, to argue that much of the Southeast witnessed a trajectory from Native ground to middle ground to shatter zone, with the timing of this sequence varying from one locale to another. Over the course of the long term, most significant contested landscapes in the Southeast did witness multiple variations on these themes. Even for those regions that did enjoy some degree of equilibrium with their neighbors, that period of respite was inevitably temporary. Overall, though, there seems to have been a series of much more unpre-dictable and provisional mini-histories where, for instance, a shatter zone could transform into a stable middle ground, only to become a shatter zone once again. There are many examples of these kinds of contingent grounds. I will consider them within the context of three categories of movement: shatter zones and serial migration, diasporic migrations, and migration to frontiers.

Shatter Zones and Serial Migration

Wesley Bernardini (2005) has proposed a model of serial migration for the southwestern United States, whereby the Hopi frequently moved in small social groups as clans. These groups would fuse occasionally as villages, then diffuse again as clans split off to resume migratory treks. Although some of this movement may have been underlain to some degree by eco-logical factors, the net result was a considerable degree of social fluidity within and between villages. On some occasions, the shatter zones of the Southeast likewise appear to have made relatively regular migrants out of some peoples who were unlucky enough to consistently land in localities that quickly came under assault. Although occurring under somewhat less benign circumstances than the Hopi, this form of conflict-driven serial migration nevertheless seems to have served as an important means for fostering novel and dramatic shifts in identity. The Yamasees represent one of the more striking examples of this process.

We are uncertain of where the term Yamasee comes from. It first appears in Spanish documents in 1663 referring to groups along the coast of South Carolina (Worth 1995). But they originally were composed largely of Tama peoples from north-central Georgia. The Tamas seem to have been survivors of the Ocute, Altamaha, and Ichisi chiefdoms who had been described by Hernando de Soto expedition chroniclers over a century earlier (Worth 2004:253). Westo slave raids spurred the demise of these significant polities, with the Tamas fleeing their territory in the interior sometime after 1659. John Worth (2004) defines a formative stage for the Yamasees from 1659 to 1665, during which the Tamas and other groups banded together for protection in the Port Royal sound region of South Carolina (figure 4.2). Beginning in 1663, they began to filter southeasterly to the Franciscan missions to the Guales and Mocamas on the Atlantic Coast. Then, in 1665, they appear on the *repartimiento* (obligatory labor) roles for service to St. Augustine. The Yamasees appear to have become prominent and numerous enough to warrant invitation from the Florida colony to establish settlements at St. Simon's Island, Georgia, and Amelia Island, Florida, where they were not subject to direct missionization (Ashley 2018:57–58). A 1675 census tallied 350 Yamasees dispersed across six towns on both of these islands (Worth 1995:28–29). Many Yamasees, often referred to as pagans, resisted conversion to Christianity throughout their stay in La Florida (Ashley 2018:58).

The next major move of the Yamasees was precipitated by the attack of the French pirate Michel de Grammont on St. Augustine and the coastal missions. Grammont, who had built a notorious career by ruthlessly raiding Spanish towns and shipping in the Caribbean and Central and South America, turned his sights on La Florida not long after sacking Veracruz, Mexico, in May of 1683 (Konstam 2008). Grammont's pitiless assault on the La Florida coastal mission towns the following October led the Yamasees to mass migrate north of the Savannah River, probably to around the vicinity of Hilton Head Island (Worth 1995:37). This move turned into

Figure 4.2. Overview of Yamasee migrations and homelands (adapted from Sweeney and Poplin 2016:Figure 1; courtesy of Alex Sweeney, Brockington and Associates).

a significant political as well as landscape shift; the following year, the Scots established a colony at Stuart's Town in Port Royal Sound to the north of the Yamasee towns, pulling the Yamasee into the larger English orbit (Roper 2004). In 1685 the Yamasees raided the Franciscan mission on Santa Catalina, returning with 21 enslaved Timucuans who were sold to the Scots. This action led to a dramatic reprisal from St. Augustine, which sent a naval force that razed Stuart's Town in two assaults in 1686. The ever-flexible Yamasees shifted their alliance to Charles Town.

If we consider the 1675 Yamasee census of 350 individuals as an estimate of the number who moved to Carolina from the coastal missions, the subsequent growth of their towns provides a fascinating insight into the workings of ethnogenesis, multi-ethnicity, and the landscape of migration. There are several accounts of masses of people flocking to the transplanted towns from multiple directions. The most impressive observation came from a trader by the name of Caleb Westbrooke (1685:5), who notified the Carolina government that

> a thousand or more Yamasees are come down daily from Cowetaws and Kusectaws, with whom they used to live. More are expected, and ten Cassiquas [*caciques*] with them. This day the Aratomahaw and other Indians are gone with canoes to bring them hither, besides three nations of the Spanish Indians that are Christians, Sapella, Soho, and Sapickays.

The groups deriving from Cowetaws and Kusectaws appear to have been Tamas who, rather than migrating to coastal missions, had fled southwesterly to the Chattahoochee drainage during the initial Westo raids after 1659. They seem to have been rejoining kin from whom they had been separated for several decades. The "Spanish Indians," however, were different peoples altogether, reflecting the widening amalgam that fell under the moniker of Yamasee.

With the destruction of Stuart's Town in 1686, the Yamasee again moved en masse, aggregating in five towns along the Ashepoo River (McKivergan 1991:49). This location moved them somewhat northward, presumably for ease of access to the markets of Charles Town. Sometime in the 1690s, the Yamasees returned to the Port Royal locality.

Here, the cultural landscape of the Yamasee underwent yet another significant transformation, again poorly understood. With their return to Port Royal Sound, the Yamasees established themselves into six Upper towns along the upper Broad River and four Lower towns to the south along the Colleton River. Aside from geography, the two clusters manifested several other important differences. They seem to have been autonomous political entities, with the Lower towns having a head town at Altamaha and the Upper towns having a head town at Pocotaligo (Green 1992). Perhaps most importantly, these were distinctive cultural entities as well. The Upper towns appear to have been dominated by Christianized

Guales whereas the Lower towns were dominated by non-Christian Tamas.

At this point, it is useful to step back and to ponder briefly: exactly who were the Yamasees? The incipience of this ethnic group, loosely construed, seems to be intimately tied to an initial Tama flight from the Georgia interior to the Carolina coast, where Spanish accounts accord them with the appellation Yamasee. It is possible, and even likely, that the Tamas joined with other groups as they arrived in the coastal region, but there are no references to Yamasees before the arrival of the Tamas. They continued to be recognized as a distinct entity during their tenure within the Spanish mission system, while at the same time apparently incorporating additional peoples. As the Yamasees returned to the Carolina region, their numbers continued to be augmented by a variety of peoples. They nonetheless retained an identity as Yamasee, a term commonly applied in both Spanish and English colonial records. Given the pervasiveness of the term Yamasee in the European accounts and the apparent absence of alternative terminology, we can presume that these towns self-identified as Yamasee despite their internal diversity—as opposed to reflecting a colonially imposed category such as "Creek."

Although anthropologists are far from universal agreement on what ethnicity is, most would probably agree that Barth's (1969) work on ethnicity was a turning point in emphasizing the cognitive and subjective elements of identity, rather than viewing identity as some kind of fixed entity. As Siân Jones (1997:64, passim) has observed, identity as phrased through ethnicity has both ontological (shared cultural tradition and practices) and situational (where membership may be fluid and shifting) elements, neither of which may be consistent through time. In this respect, the Yamasees appear to have been a highly situational group, united initially for reasons of security but thriving thereafter with a seemingly porous attitude toward group membership. Without a single core group, the Yamasees may have lacked the notion of a physical homeland (although we will always have to wonder about the landscape narratives passed from the elders to later generations), which in turn may have provided the cultural latitude toward the constant uprooting witnessed in their history. This entire cultural framework seems to have been instigated by an unrelenting exposure to shatter zones. In short, Yamasee ethnogenesis, like many forms of identity formation under colonialism, was an ongoing synthesis stemming from the intersection of the macro-scale disruptions of the Atlantic World and micro-scale strategies of persistence and survival (see Voss 2015).

The creation of another shatter zone, a massive one of their own contrivance, provided the basis for the next significant migration of the Yamasees. Life on the southerly Carolina frontier offered bounty and danger in similar measure with the mercurial English as neighbors. The Yamasees proved reliable and significant military allies, providing hundreds of warriors for the Carolina invasions of Florida in 1702 and 1704 during Queen Anne's War (Arnade 1959, 1962; Hann 1988). Yamasees also took advantage of the burgeoning deerskin trade, providing a steady flow of these valued commodities to Charles Town where they were exported to eager markets in Europe. However, English traders took advantage of advance credits on deerskins to heavily indebt the Yamasees (as well as other surrounding groups).

Yamasee anxieties over the implications of their debts (would they, too, be sold into slavery?), rising anger over repeated physical attacks and sexual assaults on Yamasee individuals by English traders, and a host of other disgruntlements came to a head in 1715. After plotting with the other Native American groups surrounding Carolina for months, in April of that year the Yamasees seized and killed several English dignitaries visiting Pocotaligo, the main Upper town. This action signaled a major uprising against the Carolina colony coming from all quarters: the Catawbas to the north, the Cherokees and Creeks to the west, a number of towns along the Savannah River to the southwest, and the Yamasees to the south (Oatis 2004; Ramsey 2008). Within short order, Carolina faced complete destruction with low country plantations in flames and citizens seeking refuge in Charles Town. The fragile Native American alliance was unable to hold, however, and the English marshaled an effective array of militia and rangers to turn the tide and effectively end the Yamasee War within two years.

The Yamasees, along with every other Native American group within relative proximity to the core of the Carolina colony, dispersed early in the war to protect their communities. As prodigal migrants, the Yamasees returned to Florida, where they were eagerly accepted home by Spanish officials. There they were settled upon a handful of missions within the immediate vicinity of St. Augustine. Even this did not guarantee safety, though, as the English made several concerted forays into the locality

Figure 4.3. Yamasee colonoware red-slipped rim sherd from a plate, a form associated with European ceramic traditions in this area of the Southeast (courtesy of Eric Poplin, Brockington and Associates).

with the express purpose of exacting revenge upon the perceived traitors. Due to these assaults, epidemic disease, and other factors, the numbers of Yamasee continued to decline steadily throughout the eighteenth century. When the Spanish Crown relinquished Florida to England in 1763 at the close of the Seven Years War, the Yamasees accompanied the Spaniard exodus from St. Augustine to Cuba. John Worth's (2004) fascinating archival work on this move has documented the location of their settlement in northern Cuba. Although it is unclear if anyone in that area self-identifies as Yamasee today, Yamasee communities do continue in the state of Florida (although they lack federal recognition).

The first major blossoming of archaeological research on the Yamasees began in the 1990s, when Chester DePratter at the University of South Carolina guided a number of graduate student projects on the settlements near the South Carolina coast (Green 1992; McKivergan 1991; Sweeney 2003). Although these involved mainly survey and relatively small-scale excavations, this work was important for locating some of the key towns and for clarifying some of the defining elements of material culture. Interestingly, one of the latter included a form of line-block paddle stamping as a ceramic surface treatment, a commonplace type within the Florida mission system. Other elements of the Yamasee history in Florida that were carried to Carolina include a variety of colonoware types, pottery displaying a fusion of Indigenous and European traditions (figure 4.3).

A wide range of items of European origin are recovered from Yamasee sites, including glass beads, kaolin pipes, iron kettle fragments, and armament objects such as musket balls and gunflints (Green 1992; McKivergan 1991; Sweeney 2003; Sweeney and Poplin 2016). Modified objects are also common, including rolled copper-alloy beads, presumably derived from kettles, and glass arrow points and scrapers (Sweeney and Poplin 2016:73).

The most extensive excavations on a Yamasee site have been carried out at Altamaha in South Carolina, the main town of the Lower Yamasees (Sweeney and Poplin 2016). These investigations in advance of a residential development revealed six roughly circular, single-post structures about 7 m in diameter. These are the best evidence we have of Yamasee domestic buildings. Their similarity to domestic structures in interior Georgia, the homeland of the Tamas who constituted the core of the Lower Yamasees (e.g., Hatch 1995), is a testament to the continuity of these lifeways even after multiple moves and the widespread incorporation of objects and materials of European origin. Like many southeastern Native American communities dating from the late 1600s to the 1700s, Altamaha, as well as other Yamasee towns, appears to have been very dispersed, with buildings separated 50 to 100 m (Green et al. 2002:19; Sweeney and Poplin 2016:75).

The Yamasees seemed to have moved about every 20 or 30 years throughout their history (Bossy 2018:9), but they were not the only people who experienced serial migration. The Westos, for example, with their journeys from the eastern Great Lakes region, to Virginia, to the Savannah Valley, are another example of how groups could successfully uproot themselves on multiple occasions and consistently adapt to changing circumstances. However, there are few groups who represent the chameleonlike quality of the Yamasees to shift and change in order to adjust to their surroundings.

The Question of Diaspora

The ability of communities to rely on cultural and social bonds to tether themselves together over huge expanses of the landscape is particularly impressive in the context of diasporas. The Jewish diaspora, of course, is one of the best-known in history. In archaeological circles, research on the African diaspora is a mainstay of historical archaeology (Barnes 2011; Fennell 2007; Orser 1998; Singleton 1995), while the Irish diaspora has received more limited treatment (Brighton 2009). Several ethnohistorians have referred to widespread Native American migrations as diasporas as well (Lakomäki 2014; Shuck-Hall 2009; Smithers 2015; Smyth 2016). It is useful to touch on this body of work because of its implications for a very different manner of living through the landscape. First, though, what exactly is a diaspora?

Diaspora specialists themselves are far from settled over what can properly be called a diaspora. Without running through every conceivable definition, a diaspora is a polythetic concept that implies at least four essential cultural processes related to place (Clifford 1994; Lilly 2006):

- a dispersal from a homeland
- the ongoing connection of multiple communities widely across the landscape
- ongoing ties of support between homeland and dispersed communities
- a group consciousness and solidarity defined in part by connections to a homeland

There are other criteria that have been forwarded as well, such as sustained feelings of nostalgia for a homeland as well as a sense of alienation in the host territory. While there is no universal definition for diaspora, broadly conceived it is a form of population movement that centers on various forms of sustained connectedness between communities with allegiance to a common home that may articulate vast areas of a cultural and geographic landscape (Clifford 1994:306).

Strictly speaking, the best candidates as Native American diasporas in the Southeast would seem to be those tribes who were forcibly removed as a result of the Indian Removal Act of 1830. By this time, the Chickasaws, Choctaws, Creeks, Seminoles, and Cherokees, who were living as autonomous political entities across the Southeast, were forced to move to the Oklahoma Indian Territory. But the ties between new and old homelands were never completely severed. For example, in the early decades of the 1800s, well before Removal, about 5,000 Cherokees moved to the Arkansas Valley to escape the encroachments and violence in their traditional homelands. These "Western" Cherokees still maintained ties with those they left behind, while still fostering "one version of a multidimensional, multi-regional Cherokee identity" (Smithers 2015:52). Dispersal continued with the Trail of Tears in the late 1830s, but a sense of Cherokee identity was forged through histories of memories of migration and an ongoing nostalgia for an ancestral homeland that continues into the twenty-first century. As seen in the case of Removal, diaspora is not just any form of far-flung dispersal; it also embodies a political struggle to maintain tradition and community within the context of displacement (Clifford 1994:307–308).

The Shawnees

In the colonial Southeast prior to Removal, the Shawnees would seem to be the people that best fit the parameters of a diaspora. Regarded as the most assiduous travelers in eastern North America by Euro-Americans and Native Americans alike, factions of Shawnees migrated to points as distant as upstate New York and the Deep South (Lakomäki 2014; Warren and Noe 2009). The irony is that there is no clear consensus on the Shawnee homeland and their antecedents. The most popular model is that the Shawnees are largely derived from the Fort Ancient (archaeological) cultures of the middle Ohio Valley, although even this is not universally accepted (Cook 2017; Drooker and Cowan 2001). The difficulty with resolving this issue is that the Ohio Valley witnessed considerable turmoil in the 1600s, from epidemics as well as from Iroquois raids and encroachments with the expansion of the Iroquois Beaver Wars and Mourning Wars (DuVal 2006:3). Moreover, there are no first-hand European accounts of the region prior to the upheavals of the mid-seventeenth century. As a result, there is no clear material lineage in the archaeological or ethnohistorical records that can be traced from Fort Ancient to a known Shawnee site.

The final, distinct Fort Ancient period is known as the Madisonville horizon, which begins about 1400–1450 CE (Drooker and Cowan 2001; Henderson et al. 1992). This would seem to be the appropriate place to seek the genesis of the Shawnees if indeed their roots are primarily in the Fort Ancient complex. There are significant changes during this period, such as an increase in dwelling size and more intensive intraregional and extraregional trade, but these trends seem to predate the arrival of Europeans (Drooker and Cowan 2001:100). Nevertheless, Fort Ancient sites dating from the early 1500s to the early 1600s have yielded a number of artifacts of European origin, including glass beads, copper-alloy tinklers, iron objects, and a Clarksdale bell (Drooker and Cowan 2001:101–102). The Hardin Village site, located on a bend in the Ohio River in northeastern Kentucky, has been one of the favorite candidates for a village displaying the attributes of a Fort Ancient to Shawnee transition (Hanson 1966). This site seems to date as late as the early 1600s and does have some copper-alloy ornaments of European origin, mainly beads and tubes of various sorts (Hanson 1966:168). However, the pottery styles and other artifacts are consistent with the terminal Fort Ancient period (Henderson et al. 1992:263). This does not rule out a Shawnee connection, but barring a clear sequence of dates until the mid- to late 1600s, the relationship cannot be unequivocally demonstrated.

A Fort Ancient to Shawnee link may potentially be made in the domain of architecture. The Hardin Village structures have been described as sizable rectangular buildings that were like "small Iroquoian longhouses" (Hanson 1966:172). When Indian agent Benjamin Hawkins made his initial tour of the Upper Creek towns in the 1790s, he visited the Shawnee village that was then part of the confederacy. He observed that their "town house differs from the Creek, it is an oblong square building 8 feet pitch roofed on the common mode of cabin building, the sides and roof covered with bark of pine" (Hawkins 1916:49). Here, at least, is one strong example of parallels between Fort Ancient and Shawnee forms of material culture.

The Shawnees seemingly departed the Ohio Valley sometime in the 1670s. Because of the scarce European presence in that region at the time, the earliest written accounts of likely Shawnee peoples occur well outside of the Ohio Valley (Drooker and Cowan 2001:104; Lakomäki 2014:24–26)—testament to a diaspora that "was so complex, rapid, and poorly documented that it is very difficult to trace in detail" (Lakomäki 2014:26). Maps from the late 1600s show that Shawnee peoples apparently had gathered into four widely dispersed settlement clusters (Warren and Noe 2009:169). One had landed among the groups that would become the Upper Creeks in Alabama, another had settled along the Cumberland River near modern Nashville, a third had traveled to the Savannah River near today's Augusta, Georgia, and a final group had moved northward to Illinois. Across these settlements, the Shawnees were further segregated into four divisions, with closely related language dialects and customs (Lakomäki 2014:14; Warren and Noe 2009:169). Although these peoples apparently maintained strong cultural ties with one another, linked by kinship and language, they acted as separate political entities. Tracing the continued movements of these communities is a fascinating challenge, as each cluster was prone to splitting, joining other groups of Shawnees or other peoples, then splitting again, all against the backdrop of eastern

North America. And this complexity does not even account for small contingents of Shawnees who dispersed in all directions. For example, Thomas Nairne (1988 [1708]:49) observed that a number of Shawnees ("Savanochs") accompanied French explorer Robert de la Salle on his visit to the Chickasaws in Mississippi in 1682. Several of them stayed with the Chickasaws for a few years after they "thankfully accepted of some feilds." In sum, mobile Shawnee communities are documented throughout the South, the Mid-Atlantic, the Northeast, and the Lower Great Lakes.

The Shawnee departure from the midcontinent was not complete. By the mid-1700s, many of their major settlements had gravitated to central Ohio, especially along the Scioto River, a major tributary of the Ohio River (Lakomäki 2014:89–91). Old Shawneetown, an informal capital and nexus of these Shawnees, was located at the juncture of the Ohio and Scioto Rivers and may have numbered over 1,000 people (Lakomäki 2014:90). The Bentley and Old Fort Earthworks sites appear to be the archaeological remains of this settlement (Henderson et al. 1992:271; Pollack and Henderson 1984). The re-analysis of some of the collections from this site cluster led David Pollack and Gwen Henderson (1984) to argue that Fort Ancient style artifacts, notably ceramics, occurred in historic Shawnee contexts, although the interpretation of this direct link has been challenged (Drooker and Cowan 2001:100).

The Riverfront site in South Carolina has yielded cord-marked, shell-tempered pottery that may bear some similarities to the Madisonville Fort Ancient tradition (Whitley 2012). This makes it a potential candidate for the Shawnee settlement on the Savannah River so often referred to in the historical records, although the strength of the pottery similarities between the two regions is "equivocal" (Cook 2017:20). Further complicating the picture, Riverfront is a complex, multi-component site that has a Mississippian component as well as another colonial-era Indigenous occupation that may precede the Westos' arrival in the valley (Whitley 2012). As a result, it is difficult to tease out any structures or features that are unassailably Fort Ancient/Shawnee. Nevertheless, the shell-tempered pottery is a new arrival to the ceramic traditions of this region that would seem to describe a site-unit intrusion of the sort one would anticipate in an era of displacement.

As Robert Cook (2017:8–23) emphasizes, to grasp the connections between Fort Ancient and Shawnee, it is first necessary to escape the mindset that "a" Fort Ancient phenomenon evolved into "a" Shawnee phenomenon. Since the Fort Ancient complex itself was likely some form of an extensive and heterogeneous merging, its evolution was a highly ramified process that drew on both external ties and internal developments. It is very unlikely that a single key site, or even sites, will provide the essential missing links of material culture to allow us to easily map out the braided cultural phylogeny of the Shawnees. The same could be said of any group addressed in this book.

Regardless of the nature of the connections between Fort Ancient and Shawnee, the reputation of the Shawnees as travelers without equal is well founded. Apparently opting to migrate from the Ohio Valley as it was transformed into a shatter zone, the Shawnees adopted a life of mobility as a response to the rapid changes occurring around them. They are an example of James Clifford's (1997) proposition that for many cultures, travel is so foundational to their way of life that it becomes central to their constitution of cultural meaning. In this respect, diaspora becomes part and parcel of how a people may come to define themselves. Even by the late 1790s, Benjamin Hawkins (1916:41) could still say of the Shawnee Upper Creek village (in Alabama) that "they speak the language and retain the manners of the countrymen to the N.W. [northwest]." By this point in time, the Shawnee diaspora "had conceptualized North America as a vast 'kinscape' crisscrossed by kinship networks that connected far-flung communities and individuals" (Lakomäki 2014:90).

The Natchez

In contrast to the nebulous origins of the Shawnee diaspora, we can assign an exact date and place to that of the Natchez diaspora: January 24, 1731, on the east bank of the Mississippi River about 270 kilometers north of New Orleans (Smyth 2016:54). At that time, the leader of the Natchez, the Great Sun, surrendered to an army of French regulars and Choctaw warriors. This episode represented the collapse of the erratically cordial relations between the Natchez and the Louisiana colony brought about by a series of increasingly aggressive French encroachments on Natchez lands in the first decades of the eighteenth century. In response, the Natchez had attacked the French Fort Rosalie on November 28, 1729, leaving hundreds of colonists dead and many captured. The French ambition to avenge this assault overthrew one of the major polities in the Lower Mississippi Valley, leading to a splintering of the Natchez people in many directions.

The Great Sun's contingent of 438 people was enslaved and shipped to plantations on the French Caribbean colony of Saint Domingue (Haiti) (Smyth 2016:54). Even though the English southeastern colonies were by far the most deeply implicated in the Native American slave trade, their involvement had largely abated at the close of the Yamasee War in 1715. So, somewhat ironically, the capture of the Natchez in 1731 may have represented the last major shipment of Native American slaves to the Caribbean. However, many hundreds of Natchez were able to escape in other directions.

For the average archaeologist invested in Mississippian-period research, the Natchez are perhaps one of the more fascinating peoples in the Southeast. Well after the time when most Mississippian chiefdoms had collapsed or transformed into qualitatively different entities, the Natchez retained the archetypical physical and social characteristics of a chiefdom: they still actively maintained a mound center, with a leader who resided on a platform mound; they displayed a complexly stratified political organization; and they encompassed a number of settlements in a site-size hierarchy. It is customary for archaeologists to pore over French accounts, especially the extensive narrative of Le Page du Pratz (1975 [1758]), who lived among the Natchez for a number of years, to glean insights into the kind of hierarchical structure that held this kind of polity together and which might serve as an analogy for chiefdoms of pre-European contact. Before their dispersal, the Natchez are known to have adopted a number of refugee groups fleeing violence and slaving, so they clearly were not a homogeneous entity themselves. Nevertheless, they are a fascinating example of the persistence of a Mississippian lifestyle eventually shattered by the actions of a colonial power. In conjunction with the Shawnees, the two cases also provide an important study of the very different ways in which diaspora could be lived.

In comparison to the repetitive wandering of the Shawnees, Natchez refugee groups found their settlement decisions structured by an avoidance of French-allied Indians. For this reason, a sizable number of Natchez were accepted into Chickasaw territory in northeast Mississippi in 1831. While the Chickasaws alternated between peaceful and hostile relations with the French, they were consistent allies with the English. Moreover, by the 1830s, hostilities with Louisiana were deteriorating into what would become known as the French-Chickasaw wars. Chickasaw territory therefore represented the closest safe haven for the Natchez.

The various European observations of the Natchez experience among the Chickasaws contain a number of contradictions concerning the cordialness or hostility of relations between the two groups (Lieb 2008; Smyth 2016). At the least, however, they seem to agree that the Natchez were allowed to establish a fortified settlement to the northeast of the Chickasaw communities, providing optimum protection from potential French attacks from the south and west. In addition, there are accounts of Natchez living among the Chickasaws, some possibly under conditions of servitude. By all accounts, there was some enmity between the two groups. An attack on the Natchez by the Chakchiumas in 1732, a group eager to placate the French, initiated an initial Natchez exodus eastward that continued for a number of years until most of them had departed Chickasaw lands. The Natchez town was still extant by 1736, however, because the French unsuccessfully attacked the Chickasaws that year from two directions in an attempt to reach and destroy the protected community (Cobb et al. 2017).

Although there are numerous accounts of Natchez residents throughout the Southeast, three major diasporic communities were established: one with the Overhill Cherokees, one with the Upper Creeks, and one in South Carolina at the invitation of the colonial government. Smyth (2016) makes the argument that this was a diasporic movement because there is evidence from the colonial accounts that these settlements were aware of one another, may have periodically been in contact, and maintained a strong Natchezean identity until, and after, Removal in the 1830s. On one occasion, for example, the South Carolina Natchez asked the colonial government to contact the Cherokee Natchez to send their people to assist in attempts to track down runaway slaves from Carolina—one of the tasks assigned to the South Carolina Natchez as a condition for their taking up residence in the colony (Smyth 2016:126–127).

The strong adherence to identity by the Natchez seems to be expressed clearly in their pottery. Some of their distinctive styles, such as Fatherland Incised, can be found at some of their refugee communities. Lieb's (2008) study of four Chickasaw sites found Natchez-style pottery at all of them. Interestingly, some of this pottery was made with traditional Natchez paste and tempers and may have represented the transport of vessels from their home territory. But a number of Natchez-style sherds were made with fossil-shell inclusions, a characteristic Chickasaw trait. Whether this represents a union of Chickasaw and Natchez families and communities of practice is unclear, but the occurrence of hybrid styles within Chicka-saw contexts is certainly a reflection of some sort of social interaction. Hundreds of sherds of Fatherland Incised also have been identified at the Overhill Cherokee town of Chota-Tanasee (Bates 1982:106–109).

Migration to Frontiers

Although Native Americans in the colonial era may have relied on long-standing social mechanisms to draw them together during times of need, the archaeological record also reflects a long-term history of inter-group conflict. Rivalry between chiefdoms is a recurring theme in the Hernando de Soto chronicles, where Native leaders are recorded as having consis-tently sought Soto's military assistance against neighboring enemies or to punish unruly subordinates in satellite communities. This seems to have been a widespread practice throughout the Americas as local leaders wel-comed a new and powerful ally into their settlements. "As in earlier times, the Europeans became the pretext for the settling of old scores" (White-head 1992:141).

By the time of the Soto entrada in 1539, the long-term landscape of chronic conflict had created a number of significant, depopulated buffer zones between sizable polities—areas that the Spaniards frequently re-ferred to as "deserts" (e.g., Elvas in Robertson 1993:69–74). Thus, the con-cept of a frontier, a contested zone between two or more polities, seems to have been well-entrenched in the Southeast long before the arrival of Europeans. Nevertheless, the Indigenous concept of a frontier and the co-lonial concept of a frontier were far from one and the same. For Europe-ans, a frontier was typically viewed as a presage to an eventual boundary demarcating limits of imperial authority. In practice, however, these were fuzzy zones of uncertain control, allegiance, and cultural composition.

Frontier studies have been a particular province of ethnohistory. In the past few decades, the New Western historians and the New Indian histo-rians became the most vocal proponents of the need to move away from the notion of a frontier as a distinct boundary and vanguard for a wave of advance and to replace it with a view of frontiers as dynamic and con-tested spaces (Adelman and Aron 1999; Barr 2006; Cayton and Teute 1998; Oatis 2004). As a result, North American colonial borderlands are now conceived of as regions of multifaceted power relations, ramified social change, and fluid categories of gender, race, and status. These approaches have taken the scholarship on frontiers a long way from Frederick Jackson Turner's Frontier Thesis (1920), which, on the one hand, has been lauded for foregrounding the frontier as an important organizing principle for comprehending the evolving nature of colonial relationships, and on the other, has been vilified for its evolutionary and triumphal treatment of the spread of manifest destiny.

Frontier and border research in social anthropology has arrived at a similar place as ethnohistory, where frontiers and boundaries are widely viewed as shifting zones of meaning, practice, and territory at the interstices of political and cultural systems (Alvarez 1995; Donnan and Wilson 1999). These theoretical trends have also been felt in archaeology, where the material record has been used to address how the constitution of frontiers was an ongoing process emanating from cross-cutting relationships between groups, rather than merely an outcome dictated by a dominant group constantly pushing against another, less powerful neighbor (Lightfoot and Martinez 1995; Naum 2010; Parker 2006).

There are several regions in eastern North America that not only exemplify this vision of plural and porous frontiers, but also demonstrate that Native Americans oftentimes played an equally strong role in their creation as did European colonies. In this regard, the Susquehanna River drainage in the Northeast and the Savannah River drainage in the Southeast provide a provocative study in contrasts. I include the Susquehanna frontier within this study because, as will be made clear, its formation can be attributed directly to events in the South in the early eighteenth century. As these examples illustrate, "When borders gain a paradoxical centrality, margins, edges, and lines of communication emerge as complex maps and histories" (Clifford 1997:7).

The Upper Susquehanna Valley Frontier

Even at the time of the American Revolution, the Haudenosaunee (Iroquois) Confederacy still controlled a significant portion of what is now New York state (figure 4.4). In addition to the military prowess of the various members of the metaphorical Longhouse, the success of the Haudenosaunee was fostered by a long history of playing off Dutch, English, and French colonial interests against one another. Nevertheless, by the early 1700s, the ever-expanding English colonies of New York and Pennsylvania continued to apply steady pressure to the southern and eastern portions

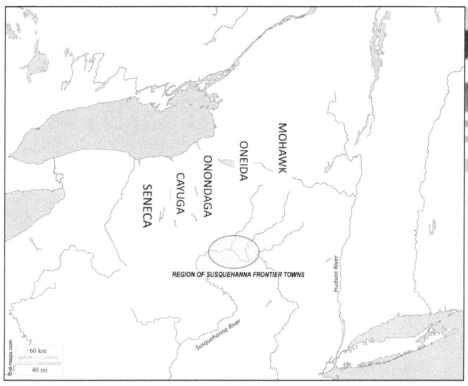

Figure 4.4. Traditional Haudenosaunee culture areas and major frontier towns on the Susquehanna River (adapted from d-maps.com/carte.php?num_car=7478&lang=en).

of traditional lands, even after significant portions of territory had been ceded west of the Hudson River.

One of the novel responses to these encroachments by the Haudenosaunee was the deliberate creation of a southern frontier along the Upper Susquehanna River (figure 4.4). Over the course of several decades, this became a dividing line between the heartland of the Haudenosaunee to the north and west and English colonials to the south and east (Cobb 2008). The initial formation of this boundary was directly related to events in the South. Following a bloody war of attrition with colonials in North Carolina that began in 1711, the Tuscaroras began filtering to the Northeast by at least as early as 1713 (Boyce 1987). The Tuscaroras are an Iroquoian-speaking tribe who may have split from the core Haudenosaunee before the time of European contact. The Haudenosaunee still recognized these ties in the eighteenth century and had already begun negotiations with Pennsylvania before the close of the war to allow the Tuscaroras to reenter the Longhouse. Thus it was that with the cessation of hostilities that the Tuscaroras moved to the Upper Susquehanna drainage, where they were settled under Haudenosaunee supervision (Richter 1992:238–239). Although the Tuscaroras were to later move to western New York, the success of this experiment encouraged the Haudenosaunee to adopt a stream of refugee groups who were "settled under Iroquois guidance and protection at strategic spots in the Susquehanna watershed" (Richter 1992:239). These included a variety of groups from surrounding regions, such as the Mahicans, Delawares, Conoys, and Nanticokes. As described previously, even a group of Shawnees from South Carolina traveled northward to join this multicultural frontier.

For reasons unknown (perhaps climatic change), it appears that the Upper Susquehanna Valley had been abandoned by proto-Iroquois Owasco groups in the 1300s CE (Rippeteau 1978). As a result, the Valley provided the perfect setting for settling a series of migrant groups: it represented a depopulated region with rich, arable soils for arriving groups with a history of agriculture; it contained a major waterway that afforded easy travel; and geographically it was a very convenient dividing line between the colonies of Pennsylvania and New York on one side and the Longhouse Confederacy on the other.

Far from feeling threatened by this development, the English Crown encouraged the growth of this frontier. Recognizing that it represented a convenient barrier to possible French incursions from the north, William Johnson, the British superintendent of Indian Affairs for the northern colonies, channeled the relocation of friendly Indigenous groups toward the Susquehanna Valley before and during the Seven Years War (Hauptman 1980:131–132). Christianized Indians also moved to the region at the prompting of missionaries (Hauptman 1980:132). In another important link with the South, the New York frontier was viewed as a free zone by black slaves in the American South, and there are accounts of runaways making their way to the Native American settlements along the Susquehanna River (Hart 1998).

From an ecological perspective, the towns we know by such names as Oquaga, Chuggnuts, Unadilla, Tioga, and Otsiningo were placed at locations with access to large and rich tracts of flood plain; these settings led them to become some of the most productive communities among the Haudenosaunee Confederacy (Hauptman 1980:134–135). Because the sizable towns received considerable attention in colonial documents, archaeologists have been able to use those descriptions to relocate them. Yet there are also numerous allusions to surrounding modest hamlets and villages as well, and one gets the impression that overall, a considerable number of refugee communities large and small could be found along the Upper Susquehanna River (Seeber 2011).

Internally, the towns were far from homogenous, representing a mix of diverse groups that had come together at these locations, complemented by Haudenosaunee representatives. At the town of Oquaga, the Tuscaroras who had migrated from North Carolina lived alongside Cayugas, Mohicans, Mahicans, Delawares, and Nanticokes (MacLeitch 2011; Seeber 2011). If the town of Otsiningo can be used as a guide, the various groups that gravitated together to form a town continued to live in distinct enclaves that seemingly stretched for miles along both sides of the river (Elliott 1977). Despite their internal diversity, however, town leaders from a diplomatic perspective often referred to the towns as a single entity.

Unfortunately, only a very modest amount of systematic archaeology has been carried out at these fascinating communities, and most of that has focused on Otsiningo. As a result, we have a very poor grasp of what the frontier towns looked like materially. Otsiningo has yielded smudge pits, along with diagnostic artifacts of the eighteenth century, such as glass beads, gunflints, and kaolin pipes (Prezzano and Steponaitis 1990; Seeber 2011), but the investigations have been too restricted in scope there and at contemporary sites to make any fine-grained assessments of the impacts of migration and coalescence. The Susquehanna Valley towns were abandoned before advancing American troops during the Revolutionary War, who put most of them to the torch (Mintz 1999:111–113).

The Savannah Valley Frontier

Like the Susquehanna Valley, the Savannah drainage was abandoned sometime in the 1300s to 1400s CE after serving as a home to numerous Mississippian towns and villages (Anderson 1994b). In addition to the archaeological absence of Mississippian sites after the fifteenth century, we have complementary documentary evidence for abandonment. In the 1540s, Hernando de Soto's army passed through the valley, which was described as "an uninhabited region" (Elvas in Robertson 1993:80). Again, climate change may have been a central factor in the exodus, although conflict and factionalism may have played important roles as well.

A relocation of northern Indians as a prelude to the formation of the Savannah frontier mirrored the migration of southern Indians to initiate the Savannah frontier. The Westos, so central to setting off waves of shatter zones throughout the Southeast, were seemingly the first Indigenous group to resettle in the Savannah Valley in the Colonial era when they established their town on the banks of the river in 1659 (Bowne 2005:21–23, 76). In another parallel with the history of the Upper Susquehanna Valley, the Savannah Valley was rapidly settled by numerous groups from widely diverse regions once a precedent had been set (figure 4.5). Many came of their own volition; some were settled forcibly.

There the parallels between the two regions largely end. In contrast to the Northeast, there was no centralized Indigenous group or confederacy that controlled large tracts of land on either side of the Savannah Valley. By the 1600s there were still some regional Mississippian-like polities of some note, including Cofitachequi in South Carolina and some modest Lamar chiefdoms in Georgia, but none of these approached the size and power of the Haudenosaunee Confederacy. Moreover, the depredations of the Westo and other slaving groups quickly fragmented the cohesiveness of those Mississippian chiefdoms that did remain by the mid-seventeenth century.

It is uncertain exactly where the Westos settled on the Savannah River or why they chose that location. We do have a frustratingly brief description provided by Henry Woodward (1911:132–133) in 1674 of their village, which he referred to as Hickauhaugau:

I viewed the Towne, which is built in a confused maner, consisting of many long houses whose sides and tops are both artificially done with barke, uppon the tops of most whereof fastened to the ends of long poles hang the locks of hair of Indians they have slaine. The inland side of the town being duble Pallisadoed, and that part which fronts the river having only a single one. Under whose steep banks seldomly less than one hundred faire canoes ready upon all occasions. They are well provided with arms, ammunition, trading cloth and other trade from the northward for which at set times of the year they truck driest dear skins furs and young Indian slaves.

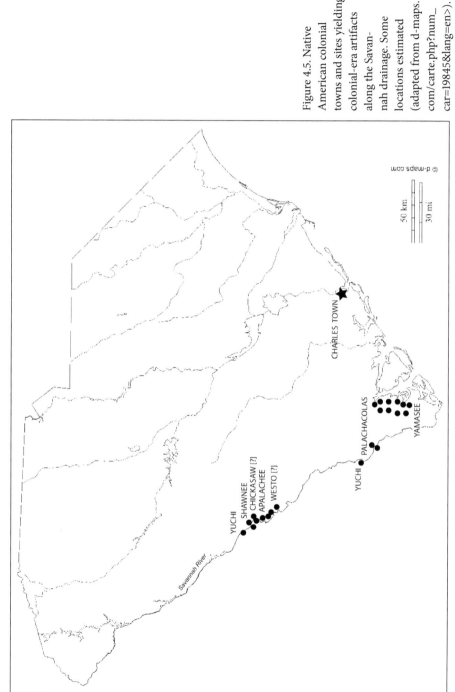

Figure 4.5. Native American colonial towns and sites yielding colonial-era artifacts along the Savannah drainage. Some locations estimated (adapted from d-maps. com/carte.php?num_car=19845&lang=en>).

Despite a number of competing hypotheses for the town's location, it has yet to be identified (Bowne 2005:22–24).

Following the arrival of the Westos in the valley, a procession of groups followed. Lacking a central Indigenous authority to orchestrate the movement of peoples, the ensuing settlement history was far more punctuated and uneven than that witnessed by the Upper Susquehanna Valley towns. A dramatic shift occurred when the Lords Proprietors of England established Charles Town as the capital of the Carolina colony in 1670. With Carolina now the southernmost of the English colonies, the Westos, other southern Indians, Spanish Florida—and even Virginia—found a new potential rival in the region. The Westos were the first victims of the whimsical loyalties of the Carolina colony. Originally, each side recognized the importance of the other and quickly moved to form a regional alliance. As a result, the Indian slave trade that the Westos had formerly funneled through Virginia was now redirected to Charles Town. Increasingly concerned about the might of the Westos, the English moved to eradicate them. Carolina allied with a group of newly arrived Shawnees, perhaps the residents of the Riverfront site and active players in the slave trade. Together, they set forth to destroy the Westos in 1680; by 1683, they had effectively dispersed them (Bowne 2005:99–102).

With the feared Westos gone and the lucrative trade potential with the English well known—thanks in large part to a robust history of Indian trade with Virginia—a succession of Indigenous groups moved into the Savannah Valley in the last half of the 1600s and well into the 1700s. Although there was no formal treaty establishing the Savannah River as a frontier, by suggestion, cajoling, force, and economic opportunity, Carolina found the valley eventually populated with a number of friendly Native American towns. The best evidence we have for this outcome derives from occasional censuses of Indigenous towns made by Carolina officials from regions both within and without the general frontiers of the colony (Headlam 1933:302) (table 4.1).

The summaries from the censuses indicate that there were, or at least the Carolina officials were aware of, 11 Native American towns representing four Native American groups along the Savannah River in the early eighteenth century. Thanks to descriptions from the colonial archives, in conjunction with archaeological investigations through the years (Cobb and DePratter 2016; DePratter 2003; Elliott 1991), we have a fairly solid sense of the locations of many of these towns (figure 4.5).

Table 4.1. A 1715 Carolina Census of Native American Towns in the Southeast (Savannah Valley towns in boldface)

Distance from Charles Town	Indians	No. of Vill	Men	Women	Boys	Girls	Totalls
90 miles S.W.	Yamasees	10	413	345	234	223	1215
130 """"	**Apalatchicolas**	**2**	**64**	**71**	**42**	**37**	**214**
140 "W.	**Apalatchees**	**4**	**275**	**243**	**65**	**55**	**638**
150 "W. by N.	**Savanos**	**3**	**67**	**116**	**20**	**30**	**233**
180 "W.N.W.	**Euchees**	**2**	**130**	**270**			**400**
250 "W. & by N.	Ochesees or Creeks	10	731	837	417	421	2406
440 "W.	Abikaws	15	502	578	366	327	1773
390 "W.S.W.	Tallibooses	13	636	710	511	486	2343
430 "S.W. by W.	Albamas	4	214	276	161	119	770
			3032	3446	1816	1698	9992
	Cherokees, vizt.						
450 miles N.W.	The Upper Settlement	19	900	980	400	480	11530
390 "N.W.	Middle Settlement	30	2500	2000	950	900	
320 "N.W.	Lower Settlement	11	600	620	400	480	
640 "W.	Chickesaws	6	700		1200		1900
200 "N.N.W.	Catapaws	7	570		900		1470
170 "N.	Saraws	1	140		370		510
100 "N.E.	Waccomassus	4	210		400		610
200 "N.E.	Cape Fears	5	76		130		206
70 "N.	Santees	2	43		60		125
20 "N.	Congerees	1	22				
80 "N.E.	Weneaws	1	36		70		106
60 "N.E.	Seawees	1					57
Mixed with ye	Itwans	1	80	160		240	
English Settlements	Corsaboys	5	95	200		295	5519
							28041

Note: Spelling follows the original table. "Vizt." Stands for the more common "viz.", or "namely."

It must be borne in mind that this accounting was made before the onset of the Yamasee War in 1715, which dispersed all of the groups living in the valley. In this regard, it coincides with a phenomenon like Richard White's (1991) "middle ground," when a fairly stable relationship existed between the frontier towns and Charles Town. However, the census was reset to zero, practically speaking, as a result of the Savannah Valley frontier transforming into a shatter zone during the war. This period of tumult was short-lived. After a few years, the valley again became home to a number of Native American towns, though greatly reduced in number and variety.

The founding of each of the Savannah Valley towns followed a unique trajectory. As we have seen, the Westos arrived from Virginia after initially being pushed out from the region of western Pennsylvania. The peripatetic Shawnee likely originated in the Ohio Valley and founded Savano (Shawnee) Town on the South Carolina side of the river sometime in the mid-1600s (Whitley 2012:88). This became the major Indian settlement on the Savannah River for decades, rapidly attracting English traders and other Native American groups. Like the Westos, the Shawnees were largely drawn by the lucrative slave trade. The Yuchis (Euchees), probably from eastern Tennessee, were also attracted by the slave trade and immigrated in the early seventeenth century. Some portion of the major Hitchiti town of Apalachicola (Apalatchicolas) arrived from the Lower Chattahoochee Valley in the late 1600s, simultaneously fleeing the incursions of Spaniards in their home region and seeking the lucrative trade market of Carolina. The Apalachicolas founded the town known by the English as Palachacolas along a major trade route between Charles Town and the interior. Finally, as noted in the second chapter, many Apalachees ("Apatchees" in the census) were forcibly moved to the Savannah Valley by James Moore after his infamous raid on their mission system in the Florida panhandle.

In addition to its rich soils, the Savannah Valley provided Native American towns easy access to hunting grounds to the west, north, and south, while the markets of Charles Town to the east were easily reached by well-established trails. The river settlements further provided a convenient buffer to the threat of invasions from Spanish Florida to the south. With the founding of Mobile on the Gulf Coast in 1702 as the capital of French Louisiana, a third colonial power had entered the south Appalachian region. As a result, the importance of a secure frontier region became even more pressing to leaders in Charles Town—thus their continued encouragement of settlement there by friendly Indigenous groups.

For a number of decades, the valley was mainly populated by Indians who were discouraged from moving closer to Charles Town by the colonials. The main European presence there before the 1730s consisted of only a handful of small forts or garrisons, most built in reaction to the Yamasee War that devastated the Carolina colony (Cobb and DePratter 2016; Cobb and Sapp 2014; Elliott 1991). For a significant period of time, most of the colonials clustered along the coast; origin points for the Indian groups were typically scores to hundreds of kilometers in various directions from the valley, and considerable expanses of somewhat sparsely settled land occupied the gap between the frontier and these two extremes. In short, the Savannah drainage was at once a frontier linking colonials and Indians and a distant rim to large numbers of people from either side who were invested in its stability.

When conditions settled after the Yamasee War, the only former inhabitants of the Savannah Valley to return in significant numbers were the Yuchis. They seem to have first occupied the locality of the now-deserted town of Palachacolas before moving westward across the river and establishing a town of unknown name (referred to by archaeologists as the Mt. Pleasant site) (Elliot and Elliot 1997). The major new arrivals in the postwar period were the Chickasaws, who migrated in 1723 from northern Mississippi (Cashin 2009). As a result of longstanding amicable relations between Charles Town and the Chickasaws dating to the early decades of the colony, there had been continued attempts by the English to lure their strong ally to the Savannah drainage. A faction finally departed to settle near what is today Augusta in 1723.

The return of the Yuchis and the arrival of the Chickasaws were the result of a concerted effort by Carolina to lure allies to a critically strategic region that was now vacant. Although the Yamasees in Spanish Florida and the Carolinians continued their struggle for several more decades, most of the remaining groups party to the Yamasee War made their peace with the colonials. The waxing and waning and waxing of Indigenous settlement in the Savannah Valley can best be described as a dialectical relationship between numerous southeastern groups and the Carolina colony. Charles Town officials greatly desired the economic benefits afforded by the Indigenous trade in slaves and deerskins. They were thus anxious to have Indian settlements in some proximity to the colony—especially because these sentry towns also presented the hope of slowing down any potential incursions by French or Spanish forces. But the colonials did not want the towns so close that they potentially represented a threat to the well-being of English settlers.

In the eyes of Europeans, this threat was viewed as existential as well as physical. Both the deep woods and the inhabitants of this New World were thought by many to represent a dangerous allure to an intrinsic desire of European men to abandon civilization and return to their primeval roots (Merrell 1999); Indian towns thus were always a potential source of moral contagion. These feelings were mutual. Native Americans benefited from the logistical benefits of proximity to Charles Town for the purpose of transporting commodities. But as the colonial records attest, those who lived closest to the colonials—especially the Yamasees—were constantly seeking redress for grievances related to the abuses of English traders and encroachments on their territories (Oatis 2004:99, 115–120).

Archaeologists at the University of South Carolina initiated a multiyear project in 2010 dedicated to locating some of these towns and exploring the lifeways of those who occupied them (Cobb and DePratter 2016). This work showed that the colonial maps of the era were fairly accurate in terms of settlement locations. Not surprisingly, some of the field investigations revealed that the reality on the ground was more complex than that recorded by Europeans. Although the towns are defined largely by the predominant group that occupied them (see table 2.1), it is likely that they were somewhat plural. For example, explorations of the Palachacolas town vicinity in the lower part of the valley also demonstrated the existence of an adjoining community with a very different ceramic tradition, likely representing a different migration episode (Cobb and DePratter 2016). Because of the ebb and flow of Native American settlements out of the valley, though, it is difficult to ascertain whether these were contemporaneous.

Excavations at the Yuchi village at Mt. Pleasant, the southernmost Yuchi site in the Savannah Valley, emphasize the difficulties of gleaning a fine-resolution understanding of the inhabitants of these towns, because they were often next to, or succeeded by, European settlements that took advantage of the strategic locations and open landscapes created by the Indigenous inhabitants (Elliott and Elliott 1997; Elliott 2012). The Yuchi settlement was situated next to a Georgia Rangers military outpost, while Palachacolas was in proximity to, and perhaps overlain, by a Carolina fort. The favorable landscape locations created by Native inhabitants thus became the footprints for the wave of Euro-American settlers who were to follow.

Further complicating matters, it is difficult to address the sites that do lack a clear link to the colonial records—particularly if their material culture seems foreign to the Savannah Valley and also lacks clearly diagnostic features of other regions. We have already seen how the Riverfront site may be the remnants of a Shawnee settlement, but the supporting data are ambiguous. The Rae's Creek site is another site in this category. Located on the outskirts of modern Augusta, the site shares some similarities with the Riverfront site in that it contained a large percentage of shell-tempered, cord-marked ceramics with some gross similarities to types in the Ohio Valley, eastern Tennessee, and other regions (Crook 1990). It also has yielded ceramics similar to both Cherokee and Creek traditions. As has been documented elsewhere in the Southeast, many of the locally distinctive ceramic types disappear in the colonial era, to be replaced by technological and stylistic traits widespread throughout the region (Foster 2017). This trend is reflected by factor analyses of ceramic metric and surface attributes of pottery from three different sites in the Savannah Valley, which indicate a strong degree of inter-assemblage similarity (Needham 2011). Given the complexity of the Savannah Valley cultural landscape, these kinds of complex patterns indicative of the flow of ideas and peoples should perhaps be expected.

Conclusion

Left unexamined in these overviews of the landscape of population movement are the kinds of social arrangements that made migration possible. One intriguing possibility is that various kinds of political, social, economic, and ritual extraregional relationships extending back into the Mississippian period continued to forge relationships between neighboring groups even as their worlds were upended by the interventions of colonials. Joseph Hall (2009:79) suggests that the tributary relationships that existed among Chattahoochee chiefdoms before the arrival of Europeans may have continued in diminished form afterward, and "the paths that carried beads after 1639 were the same ones that carried migrants before 1663." Perhaps even more importantly, clans and other forms of extensive kinship networks linked communities across considerable distances during the colonial era (DuVal 2006:25; Rodning 2002; Saunt 1999:21; Warren and Noe 2009:169). Other social mechanisms of hospitality may have been widespread. In the following chapter, I will explore how these processes worked to bring people together in different ways across the landscape.

Arrival and Emplacement

Soon after establishing a beachhead at Biloxi (Mississippi) in 1699 for what would become the colony of Louisiana, the French were firsthand witnesses to the turmoil instigated by epidemic diseases and the Indian slave trade well before they had arrived. In 1700, Jesuit priest Paul du Ru arrived from Biloxi at the Native American town of the Bayogoulas on the west bank of the Mississippi River, hoping to establish a mission (Usner 1998:45–46). He described a community of several hundred individuals who, according to Pierre Le Moyne d'Iberville, who had visited the previous year, had already lost one-quarter of its population to smallpox. Du Ru was nonetheless impressed by the size and orderliness of the village, which contained a very large plaza with a temple at each end. Notably, one of these temples belonged to the Mongoulachas, a neighboring group that had recently integrated with the Bayogoulas.

The Mongoulachas were just one of multiple groups fleeing disease, warfare, and slavery that ended up joining the Bayogoulas. Du Ru describes the Quinipissas being accepted into the Bayogoulas town after his arrival, followed by the Taensas in 1706, who had been driven from their villages to the north. These kinds of aggregations did not always turn out well, as the Taensas turned on the Bayogoulas, killing a number of their people. Nevertheless, the main town of the Bayogoulas was a microcosm of a widespread pattern throughout the Southeast in the 1600s and 1700s, where diverse peoples congregated in places they viewed as safe harbors. For many, this choice seems to have been the alternative to extinction, or, at best, extirpation.

Given the Indigenous population upheavals of the colonial era, it is easy to imagine a vast landscape in constant turmoil. Yet as exemplified by the Bayogoulas, those groups that were able to maintain some degree of cohesiveness also served as islands of (relative) stability for less fortunate neighbors fragmented by conflict and disease. Some well-known groups, such as the Chickasaws, Choctaws, and Cherokees, regularly accepted refugees into their ranks. Various strategies of hospitality and gathering by these and other peoples during the colonial era created a regional landscape of settlements and localities of impressive plurality. Some towns and polities were not only stable, they were even able to expand their geographic range and might. In the Northeast during the 1600s and 1700s, Haudenousaunee groups in the New York region began to range in an arc from the Ohio Valley to the Deep South in their quest for furs, prisoners, and scalps (Abler 1991; White 1991). Similarly, the Osage in the Missouri region exerted their military and economic might over Europeans and their Indigenous neighbors during the eighteenth century to create a polity of impressive scope across portions of Missouri and Arkansas (DuVal 2006).

Southwestern archaeologists Stephen Lekson and Catherine Cameron have remarked that studies of regional abandonment, a perennial topic of interest in their study region, must be complemented by a consideration of migration (Lekson and Cameron 1995:184). The preceding chapter on population movement was an elaboration of their observation: how can one possibly scrutinize the process of uprooting without considering how people on the move reached their new destinations? However, there is still another variable in the equation of population movement and the landscape. The study of relocation should, in turn, lead to questions concerning the reestablishment of place. In the gymnastics of migration, once there was a decision to make a leap, how did groups stick a landing?

Social anthropologists have used the term "emplacement" to refer to the notion of socially producing place—an especially important process today given the huge upsurge in migration and displacement in the twentieth and twenty-first centuries (e.g., Appadurai 1991; Gupta and Ferguson 1997; Lovell 1998). Under this conception, people physically and culturally construct their own histories through social decisions concerning settlement location and the development of the built environment and surrounding landscape. Following from Marx's dictum that people do not just create history from whole cloth because they are also a product of history, so too do clusters of people living together through time become products of landscape decisions made from previous generations and in their own lifetime. The construction of place is central to the establishment of human belonging through that history. Identities are spatialized through ongoing processes of inclusion, exclusion, and the construction of difference.

These identities are not necessarily unvarying. Perhaps in localities of high stability and modest population circulation cultures may assume a considerable degree of conformity. But expanding flows of things, ideas, and people undermine homogeneity between and within localities. Places then become increasingly culturally plural or hybridized as peoples from different backgrounds converge and negotiate accommodations—not always cordially—for living in proximity to one another. This is the type of cauldron that gives rise to ethnogenesis and other forms of amalgamation and serves as a complement to migration in the formation of strategies of deterritorialization. The heterogeneous outcomes of producing and reproducing locality in an arena of pan-regional migration and flows associated with modern globalization also can be found in premodern and colonial settings (Cobb 2005; Wernke 2013).

Emplacement, however, is a very broad rubric that potentially encompasses a variety of ways of socially producing place. In the colonial Southeast, it is possible to detect several variations of emplacement that contributed to novel constellations of Native settlements across the landscape. In this chapter, I will address coalescence, the mixing of peoples of different backgrounds in a community or locality, as a complex process that could split in many directions. Colonization is another phenomenon of emplacement that can be distinguished from coalescence by the strategic or predetermined establishment of satellite communities. Finally, I will consider the Spanish mission system as a peculiar form of a resilient region, an area that displayed a greater continuity through time than was the norm for much of the colonial Southeast. As with displacement, variations on these forms of emplacement can be readily discerned during the Mississippian period.

Mississippian Emplacements

Surely, "coalescence" must be one of the more important linchpins of landscape studies in Southeast ethnohistory and archaeology since the 1990s. This notion refers to the convergence of multiple peoples, often due to external stressors like warfare, demographic decline, or climate change, who then develop strategies for shared histories of survival and persistence—although the ties that bind may vary widely in their strength. Robbie Ethridge and Charles Hudson (2002) deserve much of the credit for highlighting the importance of this practice in the Southeast, although Steven Kowalewski's (2006) overview of the concept of coalescence shows that the term, or ones very much like it, go back for several decades of scholarship in various areas of the world. Given how common coalescence seems to be, Kowalewski, as well as Robin Beck (2013:7), has concluded that it is an example of a general social process, albeit not a social type, that occurs under periods of extreme regional duress followed by population movement. Although I agree with this assessment, I prefer a somewhat broader rendering of the sort offered by Kathleen DuVal (2006:26) that does not see duress as a necessary condition for what she refers to as a history of Mississippian "inclusivism," which set the stage for colonial era coalescence:

These centuries [of the Mississippian period] set patterns that would continue into later times. Inclusivism would color how natives dealt with newcomers who brought new customs and beliefs. Diversity would continue to demand that different kinds of people figure out ways of living together, and some forms of diplomacy, exchange, and conflict would last. Incorporating alien peoples proved to be an effective means of maintaining and increasing power.

Several studies have suggested that Cahokia and the surrounding American Bottom region were more coalescent than formerly recognized. Diversity in architectural, mortuary, and technological styles and practices indicates that the early growth of this huge center during the eleventh century CE involved the immigration of peoples from a wide surrounding region (Alt 2006; Emerson and Hargrave 2000; Pauketat 2007:149–151). Stable isotope analyses of human burials from the American Bottom further support the idea that peoples from many localities had converged in this region during the Mississippian period (Slater et al. 2014). Evidently, Cahokia and its environs were a nexus of population flows for hundreds of years. The question is why. One possible response is religion. As discussed in chapter 2, Cahokia and other centers in the larger region, like the Emerald mound site, may have been ritually charged places that became regular places of visitation or pilgrimage. In some cases, people may have opted to settle within the halo of these cosmologically powerful places rather than return to their various homes.

If one wishes to emphasize coalescence as a particular form of fusion occurring under extreme social and/or natural pressures, rather than voluntary migration, such cases can also be found during the Mississippian period. The Middle Cumberland Valley region of Tennessee, among many other areas of the Southeast, appears to have experienced a surge in conflict in the fourteenth century (Moore and Smith 2009; Worne et al. 2012). The large burial sample from the Averbuch site in that region, numbering over 800 individuals, displays evidence for interpersonal trauma as well as adverse health consequences from living under crowded conditions (Berryman 1984; Eisenberg 1991; Worne 2017). Some of the skeletal expressions of poor health include infectious disease (e.g., tuberculosis, treponemal infections) and a relatively high incidence of nutritional deficiencies and bouts of severely reduced access to foodstuffs (e.g., porotic and cranial lesions, linear enamel hypoplasia). An epigenetic study of the human skeletons suggests that the residents of Averbuch came from many different backgrounds, quite likely as refugees from endemic warring (Vidoli and Worne 2018).

The coalescence, or coming together, of different peoples seen in the American Bottom and the Middle Cumberland regions revolved around localities with established histories of occupation. There also seem to be examples during the Mississippian period where places were purposefully colonized with the aim of spreading influence from a home base. This seemingly fostered a kind of side-by-side coalescence where the insertion of new groups into a region eventually led to interactions between the two. These include, for instance, the apparent site-unit intrusions discussed in the previous chapter; Trempealeau (Wisconsin), Mound Bottom (Tennessee), and Macon Plateau (Georgia), among other sites, seem to suddenly appear as islands of Central Mississippi Valley characteristics in a sea of regional Woodland traditions. If these were indeed established by founding populations from Cahokia or elsewhere, they seem to be suggestive of orchestrated attempts from one or more major centers to extend their influence elsewhere through the founding of satellite centers.

Some of the best direct evidence we have for intrusions of Mississippian peoples derives from several sites in the Fort Ancient tradition, the eastern neighbor of the Mississippian cultural area in the central Ohio

River Valley. Strontium isotope analyses of human bone suggest that individuals from the Cahokia and Angel Mounds localities were buried in certain Fort Ancient communities (Cook 2017:114–118). These sites have also yielded artifacts (Ramey knives, Cahokian-style pottery) and features (wall-trench houses) typical of Mississippian complexes. The mechanisms to account for these occurrences potentially include captive taking, marriage, and other kinds of alliances (Cook 2017:143). In sum, the archaeological record suggests that Mississippian peoples practiced both subtle and overt strategies for strategically emplacing both small numbers of individuals and entire communities over an extensive region, physically and culturally laying claim to the Southeast.

Multiple Pathways to Coalescence

The reason that coalescence has stoked the theoretical fancy of students of the colonial Southeast is not hard to fathom. The population upheavals of the Native landscape were so widespread and sustained that one would be hard pressed to throw a dart randomly at a map of the region without striking a location that witnessed coalescence. All of the larger, well-known Native groups in the Southeast—the Choctaws, Chickasaws, Creeks, Cherokees, and Seminoles—were outcomes of various forms of coalescence (see contributions to Ethridge and Hudson [2002]). In her work on the Choctaws, Patricia Galloway (1995) has conducted one of the more detailed interrogations into the genesis of a modern Native American group and was led to conclude that the process was fairly rapid, occurring between about 1550 and 1650 CE, and was very murky—conditions that seem to apply to many peoples in this enigmatic interval. Nor were coalescent communities limited to the Southeast. All of the accounts available for the Susquehanna frontier towns under Haudenosaunee oversight were multiethnic (see chapter 4): Otsiningo (New York) in 1766 was reported to contain discrete Nanticoke, Onondaga, Mahican, and Conoy settlements; in 1749, Shamokin (Pennsylvania) contained Delawares, Senecas, and Tutelos, and Wyoming (Pennsylvania) had Shawnee and Nanticoke enclaves (Elliott 1977; Schutt 1999:381).

Despite the provocative evidence for peoples of different backgrounds living alongside one another, coalescence as a process still lacks precisely defined parameters among anthropologists. It is a layered and multidimensional phenomenon that was practiced in a variety of ways and had numerous manifestations (Beck 2013; Kowalewski 2006). Further complicating the landscape, examples of compounded or serial coalescence also occurred. The Natchez, who took up residence with many other peoples after being routed by French and Indian forces in 1731, themselves had already taken in a number of refugee groups before their own dispersal (Brown 1982; Milne 2009). When the Chickasaws accepted a number of Natchez into their territory, these guests may have included families from the Yazoo Valley and other areas who had already been integrated into Natchez communities. The Southeast provides an important setting for exploring the many ways in which groups socially and physically aggregated on the landscape. Here I will focus on the well-known Creeks, Cherokees, and Catawbas as three studies in contrasting coalescences.

The Creeks

Given the extensive archaeological and historical research on the Creeks, they provide one of the richer portrayals of the complex and nuanced ways in which large-scale, regional coalescence could occur and change through time. The term Creek is an English imposition on a diverse array of ethnic and linguistic groups who by the eighteenth century were distributed in two geographic clusters: the Lower Creeks who inhabited the lower Chattahoochee drainage that divides Alabama and Georgia, and the Upper Creeks found along several major river valleys in eastern Alabama (figure 5.1).

The well-known Creek Confederacy of the eighteenth and early nineteenth centuries in essence was a "territorial assemblage of many small groups" (Knight 1994:373) that seems to have emerged in the first part of the 1700s under somewhat hazy historical circumstances. As this congeries continued to grow in numbers and might during the 1700s and into the 1800s, they became a major political player in the late colonial and early federal periods of the Southeast. But the seeds of this process go back to the earlier migrations in the 1600s that filled the Creek landscape. In the early contact period, Apalachicola and other Hitchiti-speaking towns appear to have dominated the Lower Chattahoochee Valley. Then, waves of Muskogean migrations into the valley in the 1630s and later may have swelled the population to as many as 10,000 persons (Hall 2009:79–80). After an apparent population decline in Creek country in the latter 1600s, the numbers increased through the 1700s (Muller 1997:174–175; Wood

Figure 5.1. General distribution of Upper and Lower Creek towns.

1989), presumably because of the continued inflow of people seeking refuge within a confederacy of growing size and power.

Despite the power inherent in their numbers, the Creeks were split
among many cultural, political, and economic cleavage planes. Knight
(1994) has shown that the Creeks expressed coalescence in a multidimensional, nested fashion. As an evolving confederacy, by the late 1700s the
Creeks developed an assembly known as the National Council, which
was headed by a National Chief. This confederacy conjoined the Upper
and Lower Creek divisions. Each of these divisions incorporated mixes
of Yuchis, Alibamos, Apalachicolas, Shawnees, Natchez, Chickasaws, and
other peoples. These groups in turn assembled in varying mixes within
towns, or *talwas*, which were the core unit of governance and loyalty. To
add to the complexity, cross-cutting dimensions of social units such as

clans and the red:white/war:peace divisions created additional competing allegiances. But historical accounts consistently refer to the *talwa* as the nucleus of Creek society. As Thomas Nairne (1988 [1708]:32) observed during his time with the Creeks in their formative, migratory stage in north Georgia, "Each town of the Ochessees tho not of 40 fameillies is a sort of petty republic, and hath all it's Officers within it self." Yet even the *talwa* was not a homogeneous entity. A town may have been dominated by a particular people, but it may have contained residents from many cultural backgrounds. From the perspective of scalar coalescence, the confederacy and the *talwa* were opposing ends of a spectrum; they were geographic and social entities that were both cause and consequence of diverse peoples knitting together on the landscape.

A number of archaeologists have filled the gap created by the relative lack of documentation on the genesis and early growth of the Creek amalgamation. Early Creek coalescence may have been instigated in part by the arrival of the succession of Spanish expeditions in the late sixteenth century. An early movement in this direction can be found in the Upper Creek region, where the downriver movements of the Coosa people described in chapter 2 appear to have led them to join with another group on the Coosa River that is known only as an archaeological entity, the Kymulga phase. The Abihka people described over a century later are likely a fusion of the two, and in the eighteenth century they were joined by Chickasaw, Natchez, and Shawnee refugee villages (Waselkov and Smith 2000:244).

The Lower Chattahoochee Valley contained a number of thriving chiefdoms before the arrival of Europeans. During the Stewart phase (1475–1550 CE), there were several mound centers and a number of village and farmstead sites (Worth 2000). There was a dramatic decline in sites after this period, presumably reflecting the collapse of several polities. Only two mound centers appear to have persisted into the 1600s (Knight 1994:383). The simultaneous increase in the size of several sites, which often appear as tightly packed villages, in the Lower Tallapoosa Valley (Alabama) potentially reflects the incorporation of peoples from the Chattahoochee drainage and other, surrounding regions (Knight 1994:384; Waselkov and Smith 2000:252).

The successive landscape biographies of Creek towns are summarized by John Worth's (2000) attempt to correlate pre-Yamasee War (1715 CE) archaeological sites with known Lower Creek towns and Thomas Foster's

(2007) book-length treatment of Lower Creek archaeology post-dating 1715. As described in Spanish accounts, the Apalachicolas dominated the lower Chattahoochee drainage during the 1600s, although two major Muskogean towns, Cussita (Georgia) and Coweta (Alabama)—the protagonists of Chekilly's narrative (chapter 3)—straddled the Chattahoochee River near the Fall Line between the Piedmont and Coastal Plain. As the work of Worth (2000) and Foster (2007) shows, based on diagnostic artifacts and European accounts, it is possible to place some of the well-known identified towns with some degree of confidence. In many cases, though, there are documented archaeological sites that date from the 1600s to the early 1800s that cannot be assigned to a historical place name with any confidence. These include scores, if not hundreds, of smaller hamlets and farmsteads that have received at best only passing mention in the eye-witness accounts of the era.

Following these early forms of regional coalescence, two significant events played a major role in the evolution of the landscape histories of the various peoples who would merge as the Creek Confederacy in the 1700s. First, the English founding of Charles Town in 1670 introduced a rival to the Spaniards. The new colony and its traders quickly gained a reputation for having a far greater wealth of goods than the Spaniards. The English colonials were anxious to trade their commodities for enslaved persons and deerskins to rapidly enhance the economic autonomy of Carolina. Not surprisingly, this kind of beacon led many groups along the lower Chattahoochee to move easterly to facilitate access to the Carolina trade (Waselkov 1989b:119). Second, as noted in chapter 3, the migration away from the Chattahoochee River accelerated when the Spaniards built a fort in the Apalachicola locality in 1689 (Pavao-Zuckerman et al. 2018; Worth 2000:278–279). The eastward flow of at least 10 towns settled primarily along the Ocmulgee River (referred to as Ochese Creek by the Carolinians), the Oconee River, and the surrounding region (it is one of these towns that is described in the quote by Nairne, above). One group from Apalachicola moved further eastward and founded the town of Palachacolas among the string of settlements along the Savannah River on the Carolina frontier (see chapter 4). It is unclear if the broad, eastward migration of these towns was a total evacuation. Worth (2000:275, 279) believes that this move may have been fairly complete, as a Spanish garrison commander claimed that the entire lower Chattahoochee Valley had been abandoned.

The appellation "Creek" seems to have been coined by the English for the Indians who had migrated from the west during this interval. "Creek Indians," then "Creeks," became common shorthand for the diverse peoples settled along Ochese Creek and in the surrounding north-Georgia region by the early 1700s. After the Yamasee War, the term became a common reference by English colonials for all of those groups occupying the major drainages in east-central Alabama and the Lower Chattahoochee Valley—an exercise in arbitrary ethnic lumping further solidified by the commissioners of the Indian trade in South Carolina when they designated a single representative to the Creeks in 1718 (Hall 2009:137). The period "in exile" continued to foster coalescent practices as many of the Creek towns accepted immigrant groups from other regions (Worth 2000:282). This interval of displacement was brief, brought short by the Yamasee War of 1715. In an episode of return migration, many of the groups now falling under the designation of Creek returned to their homeland. A Spanish survey in 1716 indicates that many of the named towns returned to their respective localities occupied before the late seventeenth-century departure (Hahn 2004:92). Foster's (2007) mapping of archaeological sites along the Lower Chattahoochee seems to confirm this supposition. These reestablished communities continued to be joined by Yamasees, Natchez, Shawnees, and other peoples.

As the Creek Confederacy took shape after the Yamasee War, it experienced, and would continue to experience, a multitude of forms of coalescence. Some communities underwent an organic ethnogenesis into a new group identity, as seen in the early formation of the Abihkas in Upper Creek territory as a conjoining of Coosa and Kyamulga phase peoples. At another level, the Creeks were geographically organized into their Lower and Upper divisions. As a larger confederacy, they were held together by weak, but occasionally effective, political institutions developed in the eighteenth century.

So far, I have avoided a direct encounter with the question of the origins of the Creek Confederacy itself. One camp (e.g., Braund 1993; Corkran 1967; Swanton 1922) has favored the idea that it predated European contact, whereas another has argued that it was an artifice that emerged in the 1700s (Ethridge 2003; Hahn 2004; Knight 1994). Keeping in mind the multidimensional complexity of this loose-knit federation, it might be suggested that we need to distinguish the Creek "Coalescency" from the Creek "Confederacy." Going back at least as far as the late fifteenth to early sixteenth centuries, there are signs of diverse peoples aggregating in the major drainages of what would become the Lower and Upper Creeks, but the historical and archaeological records to date are not very forthcoming about the manner in which these communities were organized internally or with one another. But they do display signatures of coalescence. The more formal political trappings of a confederacy that could periodically act in a large-scale and concerted fashion seems to have emerged in the 1700s.

The Cherokees

Cherokee territory displayed a history of some degree of coherence and stability throughout much of the colonial era (relative to many localities), although it was hardly immune from the ravages of warfare, slaving, and European encroachments. One of the reasons for this perseverance may have been geopolitical. Cherokee towns were located in the rugged Appalachian region and its perimeter, well away from the coast. Although they were regularly visited by explorers and traders as far back as the 1600s, mounting significant settlements beyond the occasional outpost was beyond the logistical scope of European powers well into the 1700s (Marcoux 2010). As DuVal (2006) argues for the Arkansas Valley, this kind of interior setting helped confer some groups with considerable autonomy, as well as the ability to dictate terms to colonial leaders. Likewise, Choctaw settlements were some distance from the primary English and Spanish colonial outposts on the Atlantic seaboard, removed from consistent contact with European powers until the establishment of Biloxi on the Gulf Coast by the French in 1699.

Rodning (2002) emphasizes another key similarity between the Cherokees and Choctaws, one that may not be completely divorced from geopolitical distance. Their persistence and even growth can be attributed to a complex process of coalescence very early in the colonial era, where populations from regions surrounding the Choctaw and Cherokee homelands moved in and intermixed with the core areas. In fact, it is this early cultural bricolage that gave form to what became recognized as Choctaw and Cherokee in the late 1600s to early 1700s—which is to say, a veneer of similar language and practices in each region overlaying a considerable degree of variability and factionalism. We know much more about the Cherokees than the Choctaws from the perspective of archaeology, so

I will focus on this group as an example of the ability of an Indigenous group to bend but not break over an interval that continues into modern times.

In the colonial period, the Cherokees were arranged in five distinct geographic clusters across Tennessee, Georgia, and South and North Carolina (Rodning 2002; Schroedl 2000). These constituted the Lower, Middle, Overhill, Out, and Valley towns (figure 5.2). Because the English colonials were eager to establish relations with the various Cherokee groups after the founding of Charles Town, the Cherokees have a robust documentary and ethnohistorical record compared to many other contemporary Native peoples. This evidence has been buttressed by a significant amount of archaeological research. As a result, we have a good if not perfect grasp on the location and arrangement of many of the major towns of the late sixteenth through seventeenth centuries. Marshall Williams (2009) does sound a cautionary note about settlement location and place names for archaeologists in his overview of the town of Estatoe; the *South Carolina Gazette* of 1760 referred to the propensity of Cherokee towns to frequently fission, and an Estatoe, Old Estatoe, and New Estatoe appear to have overlapped temporally to some degree. The movement of town names through space and time, as well as the elaboration on the same name synchronically, can wreak havoc with attempts to pinpoint southeastern towns in many regions.

The precolonial roots of the various Cherokee subregions are murky. The historic period Cherokee are known to have engaged in occasional modest mound construction of the sort that is associated with Mississippian sites. There is also a possible, punctuated link to some Late Mississippian-period mound centers that appear to have been deserted in the late 1400s and were then occupied by later Cherokee settlements (Rodning 2002, 2015; Steere 2015). It is unclear whether these were recognized as ancestral sites or whether the Cherokees were reappropriating locations that, because of their mounds, were venerated landscapes. In some of the Cherokee subregions, there are apparent continuities in pottery styles from the Late Mississippian to Historic periods (Hally 1986). Overall, the larger Cherokee culture area contained a number of significant towns of Late Mississippian vintage. To some degree, the colonial-era Cherokees are part of this heritage. But as we saw with the Fort Ancient to Shawnee evolution, the lines are not necessarily direct, and they are further obscured by population flows into and across the Cherokee regional clusters

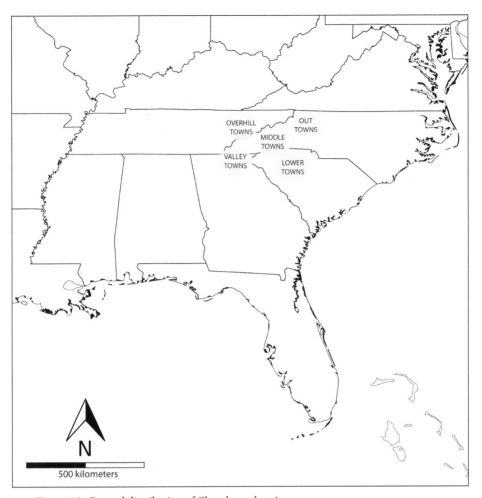

Figure 5.2. General distribution of Cherokee subregions.

throughout the colonial period. Further, the muted documentary record of the 1600s contributes to a biased view of the first emissaries from Virginia and Charles Town scaling the Appalachians in the late 1600s to encounter the Cherokees in a form that the colonials presumed had a deep history.

The ensuing Cherokee landscape history is a genuine testament to resiliency within a period of increasing volatility. With the French making overtures in the early eighteenth century and the deerskin trade growing increasingly prominent, the southern colonies of the English Crown were eager to ally with the powerful and numerous Cherokees. The eventual success of this alliance was marked by the construction of two English forts in the Cherokee homeland, Fort Prince George in western South Carolina (Ivers 1970:70–72) and Fort Loudoun in eastern Tennessee (Kuttruff 2010). As with the Yamasees, the Cherokees learned that living in close quarters with English colonials led to two outcomes: more consistent access to the wealth of the empire and more consistent misunderstandings that led to disastrous conflicts. As one example, a massacre of several Cherokees in 1758 by disgruntled colonials escalated into a trade-off of massacres on both sides followed by a larger scale war (Oliphant 2001). English forces destroyed all of the Lower towns and many of the Middle towns in 1760, leading to a flight of many of the Cherokee refugees from the homeland perimeter to the Overhill towns that were more protected in the interior (Schroedl 2000:218; Smith 1979:49).

Cherokee towns came under assault from other directions as well. Chronic conflicts with the Creek Confederacy to the south proved to be costly. Even before the devastation of the war with the English, a conflict with the Creeks in the 1750s led to the abandonment and/or destruction of many of the Lower towns (Smith 1979:48). Further, the increasing circulation of peoples from all backgrounds led to the familiar recurring outbreaks of devastating epidemics. A smallpox epidemic in 1738 may have reduced the Cherokee population of 20,000 by half (Thornton 1990:79) and may have been a key factor in the abandonment of the Lower towns (Schroedl 2000:214). Another major smallpox epidemic in 1783 led to another precipitous decline in numbers (Thornton 1990:79).

The welcome peace that was worked out with the English in 1761 proved to be short-lived. When the Revolutionary War broke out, the Cherokees maintained their alliance to the British Crown. The conflict with the colonials continued into the federal period, not coming to a close until 1794. During this interval, most of the towns of the Valley, Out, Lower, and Middle regions were destroyed, with populations aggregating in the Overhill towns. Limited excavations at the Townson site, possibly the Cherokee Valley town of Chowa, provide a small, poignant window into the devastation wrought by General Griffin Rutherford's campaign to destroy the Middle and Valley towns in 1776. There, archaeologists uncovered a completely burned cabin and the charred remains of an older male (Ward 2002:85–86). In just six short days, the military expedition had transformed a landscape of coalescence into a landscape of clearance.

Continuing encroachments from federal and state governments on Cherokee lands prompted a major push southward into the region of northeast Georgia that became the new and prosperous core of the homeland. This proved to be a penultimate large-scale relocation, as Removal in the 1830s forced much of the population to Oklahoma along the infamous Trail of Tears. Cherokees who were able to avoid federal bureaucrats and troops were able to recoalesce as the Eastern Band of Cherokees in western North Carolina.

Despite the occurrence of distinct Cherokee subregions and their frequent upheavals, a rich history of archaeological investigations of these sites reveals a duality analogous to that of the Mississippian phenomenon: considerable spatial variability overlain by a facade of similarity, suggesting strong cultural connections between the traditional subregions (see Dickens 1976; Keel 1976; Marcoux 2010; Schroedl 1994). Circular townhouses or council houses are invariably found in towns of any size; domestic occupations focused on a paired circular winter house and summer rectangular structure (with the summer structure becoming obsolete later in the 1700s); and ceramic traditions are very similar, if not identical (Rodning 2002; Schroedl 1994). Jon Marcoux (2010:131–133) has shown that the Cherokees did make one significant architectural concession to the repeated patterns of displacement and emplacement. Compared to Mississippian-period houses, Cherokees built houses of similar size but with fewer posts. Marcoux attributes this trend to a diminishing investment in durable houses as the Cherokees recognized the unpredictability of long-term occupations. Another shift occurred in the federal era, as traditional constructions were typically forsaken for European-style cabins at the same time that the custom of individual farms was replacing the tradition of communal towns. This housing style shift occurred elsewhere in the Southeast as well.

The Catawbas

Town or group names that resemble the term "Catawba" have a written history going back to the first Spanish accounts of the Carolina Piedmont in the 1500s (Moore 2002:1). As seen with the Creeks, however, the name seems to have been imposed in part by the English in the 1700s on diverse groups that had been coalescing for some time. This process seems to have begun in earnest with a southward move of Siouan groups from the upper Catawba Valley in western North Carolina. James Adair (2004 [1775]:246) in 1743 described the impressive diversity of those who came together under this rubric: "their nation consisted of almost 400 warriors, of above twenty different dialects." With the continuing acceleration of displacement, even distant non-Siouan groups such as the Natchez and the Coosas added to the eighteenth-century Catawba mix. David Moore's (2002) research demonstrates that, prior to this amalgamation, there was a strong continuity in cultural patterns in the Catawba River Valley from the late pre-European contact to early colonial eras. As he further points out (Moore 2002:19–29), both the Spanish accounts from the Pardo expeditions of the 1560s—describing encounters with established chiefs—as well as the archaeological record of mound building indicates that variants of Mississippian chiefdoms inhabited the region.

Archaeological and ethnohistorical research suggests that the depopulation of the upper Catawba Valley was followed by a move to the border region of North and South Carolina sometime in the late 1600s (Moore 2002:194). It is there, in the opening decades of the 1700s, that the Esaws, Kadapaus, Sugerees and other regional groups came together in the Lower Catawba Valley. At this early date, though, there still was no overarching Catawba group or polity of that name. John Lawson did report being hosted by the king of the Kadapaus in 1701 (Lawson 1967 [1709]:49–50), the first English reference to what likely was a rendering of Catawba. However, the term likely referred to just a single town at the time. In fact, the Catawbas seem to have migrated to the north of the Sugarees, who were an established polity composed of several towns in the valley (Beck 2013:255). Likewise, the Esaws were described as a numerous people with many villages in the same locality. So one can even question the prominence of the Kadapaus in what would become the Catawba coalescence. In any event, the usual suspects of disease, colonial encroachments, and the repeated incursions of Iroquoian war parties fostered a coalescence of peoples in the early 1700s who, by the time of the Yamasee War, began to be consistently referred to as Catawbas (Beck 2013; Davis and Riggs 2004; Fitts 2006; Merrell 1989).

Robin Beck (2013:255) maintains that the structure of the Catawbas in the first part of the 1700s differed significantly from either the contemporary Creeks or Cherokees. The latter two were more far-flung spatial entities, with towns and their outliers spatially segregated from one another.

In contrast, the Catawba towns were a "continuous chain of occupation" that still maintained distinctions between peoples and towns. This pattern is similar to the Haudenosaunee towns along the southern Susquehanna drainage, where entities like Otsiningo and Oquaga contained a string of diverse settlements living alongside one another (chapter 4).

During the eighteenth century, the Catawbas, whose traditional lands in the Carolinas were by now well populated by white settlers, transitioned into a somewhat unusual history for Native Americans living cheek by jowl with European colonies: an extended period of relatively cordial relations that did not end in abrupt disaster (as it did for the Yamasees and the Natchez).

Their success was due in part to two interrelated factors (Fitts 2017). First, they rose to prominence as a reliable ally by regularly serving as military auxiliaries for North and South Carolina. Second, they nucleated and fortified their settlements, in contrast to the more dispersed patterns that had become commonplace elsewhere in the Southeast. This pattern provided a defendable built environment in addition to allowing for the rapid mobilization of warriors.

The internal nucleation of towns was accompanied by an increasing aggregation of towns such that by the mid-1700s, they were all within five square kilometers of one another (Davis and Riggs 2004). This nested compaction did not provide complete stability, however. Epidemic diseases and geopolitical events spurred several moves throughout the century. In 1759, a major smallpox outbreak reduced the nation by more than half. This was followed by a move of the survivors to the South Carolina settlement of Pine Tree Hill (today Camden, SC). The Catawbas moved back north in 1761, but in the interim had formally ceded their traditional territory in exchange for a 24-square-kilometer area (Merrell 1989:197–198). By the 1770s, most of the Catawba population of 600 resided in a single town.

The long-running Catawba Project by the University of North Carolina's Research Laboratories of Archaeology has provided some of the more systematic research to date on a southeastern Native American group during the colonial era. The work is particularly important because it has investigated towns spanning the colonial and federal periods, revealing the major changes occurring among the Catawbas during this volatile interval (Davis and Riggs 2004; Fitts 2017; Riggs 2010). These investigations confirm the evidence from maps and narrative descriptions that the

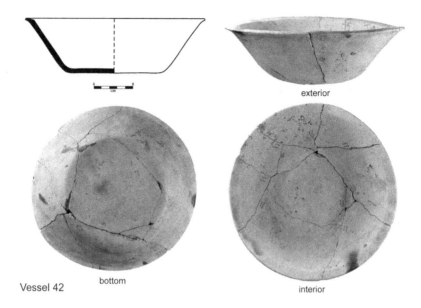

Figure 5.3. Catawba colonoware vessel. The flat bottom is atypical of Native American ceramics (Davis et al. 2015:461; courtesy of the Research Laboratories of Archaeology, University of North Carolina at Chapel Hill).

villages were typically nucleated and fortified. Frequent uprooting of villages is reflected in the built environment, as there is rarely evidence for the rebuilding or repair of domestic structures after the initial settlement was established. The ceramics from the first part of the 1700s are unusual in their regional consistency. In other words, rather than exhibiting the expected amalgamation of several groups with distinct pottery traditions, the ceramic attributes (e.g., notched applique rim strips, complicated stamping surface treatment) conform comfortably with the Lamar tradition extending back several centuries in this area (Riggs 2010:32–34).

This is another variation of the pottery homogenization described in the last chapter for the Creek and Savannah Valley regions, and it can be seen elsewhere in the colonial Southeast. The Altamaha (also known as San Marcos) pottery style that is characteristic of coastal Georgia and Florida in the 1500s was widely adopted by mission Indians and their neighbors in the 1600s and 1700s within a large swath running from South Carolina to the interior of central Florida (DePratter 2009; Saunders 2000). The adoptees of this type included, at the least, Guales, Mocamas, Timucuas, and Yamasees. Why certain ceramic lingua franca styles rose to prominence in certain regions of the colonial Southeast is a fascinating question that has yet to be satisfactorily answered by archaeologists. But this pattern is clearly linked to widespread processes of displacement and coalescence.

In the mid-eighteenth century, the Catawba potting tradition took a sharp turn. With the move to Pine Tree Hill in 1759, they completely reengineered their ceramic traditions to take advantage of the colonial market economy. In place of their typical Lamar-like wares, they began to manufacture high-quality coarse earthenware, characterized by thin vessel walls, highly burnished surfaces, and a new variety of forms such as plates and pedestaled bowls. The vessels often have European attributes, another variant of the colonoware manufactured by the Yamasees, Florida mission Indians, and other Native peoples in the Southeast (figure 5.3). These were traded and sold widely throughout South Carolina (Davis and Riggs 2004:4–5). This ceramic industry still thrives today.

Colonization

With communities pushed and pulled by conflict and slaving across the colonial landscape, it is easy to arrive at the misconception that Native Americans were always playing a rearguard action in terms of controlling their landscape histories. Nothing could be further from the truth. Centuries before many of their communities were buried by modern real estate developments, Native Americans had already learned that the value of economic relations was often dictated by location, location, location. Accordingly, many societies leveraged proximity to European colonies to accumulate considerable wealth and power.

Some groups ended up in advantageous and lucrative positions by simple virtue of the historical location of their home territory. An early example of this is the Apalachicola province in the Lower Chattahochee Valley, just north of the Spanish missions to the Apalachees in the Florida panhandle. Although out of the direct Spanish orbit, they and adjoining groups were clearly of long-term interest to St. Augustine for purposes of conversion, exchange, and pacification. It is for these reasons that the governor of La Florida brokered a peace between the warring Apalachees and their neighbors the Amacanos, the Chacatos, and the Apalachicolas in 1638 (Hall 2009:65; Worth 1993a:46). The cessation of hostilities allowed the Apalachicolas to position themselves as middlemen, transferring

European goods from the mission system deep into the Southeast while moving Native goods back into the colony (Hall 2009:92). The Apalachees, who were pulled into the northwest quadrant of the mission system in the 1630s, also became intrepid traders into the interior. The 1630s thus represents a kind of threshold, during which there seems to have been a significant upsurge of goods of European origin appearing on sites throughout the lower Southeast, apparently mediated by a number of groups on the margins of the orbit of the Spanish mission system (Smith 1987; Waselkov 1989b).

There are numerous examples of these kinds of serendipitous landscape histories throughout eastern North America. During the first half of the seventeenth century, the Susquehannocks along the Susquehanna Valley were important intermediaries between the European coastal settlements along the mid-Atlantic Coast and Iroquoian groups of the interior (Richter 1992:53–54). Likewise, during the same timeframe, the Quapaws used their strategic location at the confluence of the Mississippi and Arkansas Rivers to control French access into the interior to the west (DuVal 2006:67). Modest Native American towns or polities around the colonial settlements of Biloxi and Mobile were referred to by the French as *petites nations*. These typically were coalescent communities that had either aggregated to form new towns that could take advantage of trading opportunities with the French, or had supplemented established towns already on the margins of the colonies (Usner 1992:45). Archaeologists have been able to identify some of the material expressions of coalescence on the edges of French colonial society. When the Apalachees were dispersed by Governor Moore of South Carolina in 1704, many fled westward to Mobile. Some of the pottery fragments recovered from Old Mobile excavations display the typical paste characteristics of standard Apalachee types. A number of these are colonoware forms, such as pitchers and brimmed vessels with foot rings (Cordell 2002).

While some groups were able to finesse a natural advantage in the location of their territory, others played an even more forceful role in exerting control over their strategic landscapes. In a powerful symmetry to the encroachments of colonial powers, some Native American peoples manipulated their ties with Europeans and other Native Americans alike to extend their sphere of influence well beyond their core homelands. One of the more prominent examples of this was the ability of various Haudenosaunee groups to range widely across eastern North America. It is difficult to overestimate the impacts of their raids on patterns of displacement in the Southeast (Abler 1991; White 1991). Closer to their home range, the Haudenosaunee were very successful during the colonial era in establishing extra-regional satellite communities well outside of the core region of New York (Jordan 2013). A number of these were in what is now Pennsylvania to the south and along Lake Ontario to the north, with several more in Ohio to the west and the St. Lawrence drainage to the east.

Kurt Jordan (2013:13) provocatively refers to these as colonies. But he differentiates colonialism from colonization based on a distinction made by Gil Stein (2002), according to which colonialism relates to intercultural relations of domination and colonization refers to the process used by groups like the Haudenosaunee to implant migrant communities for the purposes of controlling trade and for protecting core home territories. The latter process reflects attempts to maintain autonomy or extend influence rather than to subordinate local groups. Examples of this kind of long-distance emplacement can also be found in the Southeast. When the Hitchiti and Muskogean towns along the Chattahoochee River moved eastward toward interior Georgia in the 1690s, some towns in the traditional Upper Creek river valleys dispatched satellite communities to join them on the Ocmulgee River (Hall 2009:102). Perhaps not feeling directly threatened by the Spaniards to the degree that the Chattahoochee communities were, this strategy allowed the proto-Upper Creeks in Alabama to split the difference of maintaining parent towns on home soil while placing an advance guard closer to Charles Town. In fact, the town of Abihka established a satellite town in the abandoned Upper Chattahoochee Valley as a way of overseeing the important trading path that ran between their home territory and the new Ochese Creek lands in Georgia (Hall 2009:102).

The Chickasaws appear to have established some of the more far-flung and enduring splinter communities in the Southeast. The early accounts of French and English explorers and traders in the late 1600s to early 1700s describe the Chickasaws as comprising a vibrant cluster of towns in what is today northeast Mississippi (Adair 2005 [1775]:354–355; Nairne 1988 [1708]:36; Stubbs 1982). This group played a continuously prominent role in the formation and transformation of colonial landscapes for a number of reasons: they already seem to have constituted a significant presence politically and demographically in the late seventeenth century when Europeans first began to arrive in force; they occupied a particularly strategic position that gave them regular access to the Mississippi Valley (and which also allowed them to interdict river traffic); and they parlayed an early alliance with the English into a role as one of the first groups to widely own European firearms in the mid-South. The latter success quickly made them a feared slaving group in the late 1600s to early 1700s, responsible for creating a number of shatter zones throughout the Lower Mississippi Valley (Ethridge 2010; Gallay 2002; Johnson 2000). Johnson (2000:94–95) observes that early Chickasaw access to European firearms and the corresponding military advantage conferred on the Chickasaws somewhat of a landscape paradox: although their numbers were considerably smaller than other major nations of the Southeast such as the Choctaws and Cherokees, they controlled territories almost as large as their contemporaries.

The Chickasaws were remarkably successful at maintaining a great degree of autonomy until Removal in 1837, but they too found themselves under continual assault from many directions throughout the 1600s and 1700s. Their most implacable foes were the French and their close allies, the Choctaws, to the south. Although not always at war, and while at times some Chickasaw factions favored the French, the enmity between the two sides was constant enough to flare up in a series of major confrontations during the 1730s to 1740s known as the French and Chickasaw wars (Atkinson 2004; Early 2011). The shift in locations of Chickasaw archaeological sites from the mid-1600s to the mid-1700s provides a compelling visual perspective on the impacts of these conflicts on the spatial contraction of the settlement system (figure 5.4) (Cegielski and Lieb 2011). As the conflicts worsened, southerly Chickasaw communities—those closest to French Louisiana and Choctaw territory—took the brunt of the fighting and casualties. The southerly ridge systems were largely abandoned by the 1750s, with most of the population concentrating on a large ridge system to the north around what is today Tupelo, Mississippi.

Although the Chickasaws were closely allied with South Carolina, they found themselves positioned the furthest west of the various Native American polities that maintained sustained contact with the Atlantic seaboard in the first half of the eighteenth century. Despite the distance, many of the Yaneka Chickasaws, those occupying one of the primary ridges exposed to attacks from the south, dramatically left Mississippi en masse in 1723 for South Carolina under the guidance of a headman with the title of Squirrel King (Cashin 2009). They resettled in the Savannah

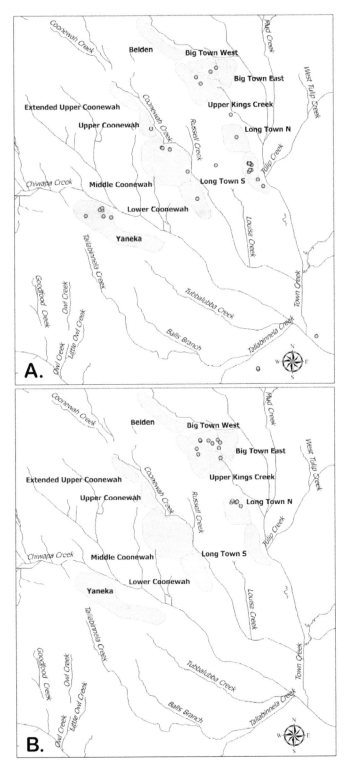

Figure 5.4. Chickasaw settlements prior to (*A.* pre-1680) and following (*B.* 1721–1736) French attacks (Cegielski 2010:Figures 10, 12; courtesy of Wendy Cegielski).

Valley on the Carolina frontier, originally on Horse Creek to the north of the important English military outpost, Fort Moore. Due to longstanding amicable relations between Charles Town and the Chickasaws, the English had lobbied them to move to the Savannah drainage for a number of decades—a request that received greater urgency as Carolina grew concerned over the security of its frontiers following the Yamasee War (Cashin 2009:9–10). The damaging conflicts between the Chickasaws and the French and their Indian allies provided the impetus for a portion of the Chickasaws to accept the invitation.

The Savannah Chickasaws maintained links with their parent population courtesy of established trade routes that ran from Charles Town to Savano Town and Fort Moore on the Savannah River, and from there splitting several directions into the interior. The so-called Upper Path was particularly important because it was a direct avenue toward the Upper Creek towns; from there it ran northwesterly and into Chickasaw territory (Crane 2004 [1929]:134–136). Importantly, the Savannah Chickasaws seem to have played a key role in keeping that conduit open. As Cashin (2009:6) notes, "While serving his Savannah River neighbors, Squirrel King also served his own people, those who accompanied him and those who remained behind in the homeland, by protecting the trading lifeline that ran from Charlestown through Savannah Town to the Indian nation."

The Chickasaws anchored in Carolina may have proven critical to the survival of the parent group in Mississippi for military as well as economic reasons. The most noteworthy example is represented by the battles of Ogoula Tchetoka and Ackia in 1736. This attempted pincer movement by the French to eliminate the Chickasaw nation led to two disastrous defeats of the colonial-led forces (Atkinson 2004:43–58). One English trader reported that the so-called eastern Chickasaws warned those in the heartland of the French plans, providing them sufficient time to prepare for the impending attacks (Atkinson 2004:44; Cashin 2009:27). There are also accounts of members of the eastern Chickasaw contingent returning west to aid the towns in Mississippi during other French assaults (Cashin 2009:87). At this critical point in their history in the mid-1700s, the friendly English frontier of the Chickasaws served as a critical offset to the hostile French frontier.

Archaeological investigations of the sites of Ogoula Tchetoka and Ackia underscore the damaging harvest of continuous conflict on the landscape of Chickasaw towns and point to why the Chickasaws were so eager to maintain long-distance ties with the English. Armed engagements between colonials and Native Americans typically involved attacks on communities rather than set-piece battles of the sort carried out on the battlefields of Europe. Ogoula Tchetoka and Ackia were no exception, and in both cases, French-led forces attempted to overrun both of the towns (figure 5.5). As a result, battlefield and living areas overlap one another (Cobb et al. 2017). Identifying areas of actual engagement is largely a matter of attempting to link settlement locations to maps and documents (when available) and/or discerning concentrations of lead shot and other forms of military artifacts amid a larger welter of domestic debris.

Proximity to Carolina still was insufficient to provide a complete safe haven for the Chickasaws on the Savannah River. The long-distance Iroquoian raids that plagued the Catawbas also targeted Chickasaws. Following their original settlement near Horse Creek, there were repeated movements by segments of the Chickasaw migrants to New Savannah and to the Ogeechee and Oconee Rivers in Georgia on the south side of the Savannah River, as well as continual returns to points on the north side (Cashin 2009:74 passim). Although one would think the distinctive Chickasaw material culture would stand out in their new environs on the Carolina frontier, efforts by archaeologists at the University of South Carolina to relocate their migratory settlements so far have been unsuccessful.

No other Chickasaw groups comparable in size to the one on the Savannah River departed the homeland. However, smaller strategic contingents were established in several other locations. One of the more important was the so-called Breed Camp, founded in 1741 on the Coosa River among the Upper Creeks (Cashin 2009:7). This served as an important way station on the Upper Path linking Savano Town and Fort Moore with Chickasaw territory in Mississippi. South Carolina, recognizing the importance of this outpost, reimbursed trader Thomas Andrews, who had provided ammunition and supplies to the Chickasaws for its establishment (Cashin 2009:54). There are also numerous offhand accounts of dispersed Chickasaw settlements outside of their traditional territory. For example, coureurs de bois from French Canada encountered a Chickasaw town on the Tennessee River in northern Alabama in 1701 (Riggs 2012:50). Another small Chickasaw settlement further upstream on the Tennessee River may have been established to help ward off raids from Illinois groups (Crane 1916:14–15).

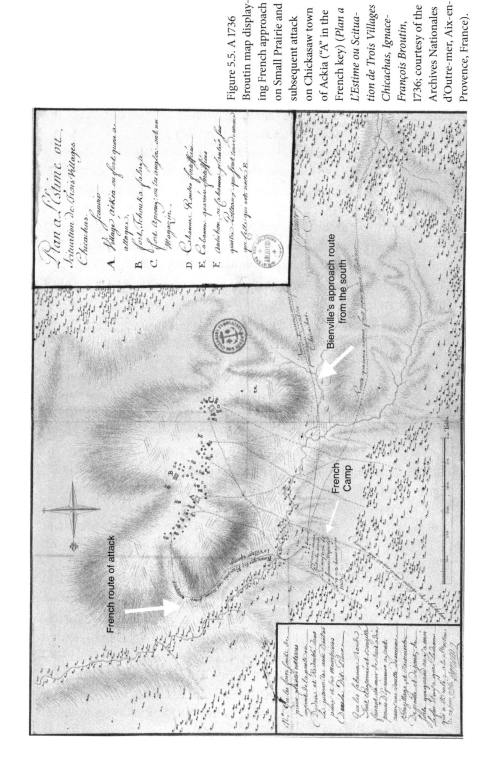

Figure 5.5. A 1736 Broutin map displaying French approach on Small Prairie and subsequent attack on Chickasaw town of Ackia ("A" in the French key) (*Plan a L'Estime ou Scituation de Trois Villages Chicachas, Ignace-François Broutin*, 1736; courtesy of the Archives Nationales d'Outre-mer, Aix-en-Provence, France).

The Breed Camp, the Savannah River villages, and other stations were not part of a structured system of regional control on the part of the Chickasaws in Mississippi. The degree of deliberation from the home territory that went into the development of these towns is problematic. The Yaneka exodus seems to have been a splintering from the other Chickasaws for reasons of survival, whereas one English agent claimed that the Breed Camp residents were despised by other Chickasaws (Braund 1993:6). Strictly speaking, these settlements cannot be viewed as a variation of centralized colonialism as practiced by European powers. But neither were they isolated outposts. Together, they comprised a network that projected Chickasaw influence far beyond the boundaries of the homeland and contributed to a significant geopolitical and economic presence for this people that belied their modest numbers.

The Mission System of La Florida

I treat the Franciscan mission system of Spanish Florida as a separate category of emplacement because there are no parallels for this phenomenon among other areas of the colonial Southeast. Certainly, there were Catholic missionaries who accompanied French administrators and soldiers. In addition, a number of Protestant missionaries attempted to convert Native Americans to Christianity. One of the more notable individuals in this regard was John Wesley, one of the founders of Methodist theology, who spent an unsuccessful stint in Georgia attempting to spread the Gospel to Creeks and other groups (Wright 1981:207–208). The Moravians also had a few outposts in the Southeast (Engel 2009:83; Wright 1981:197, 209). But only the Spanish empire successfully implemented a cohesive mission system as a combined religious and geopolitical arm of colonialism on a wide scale. As we shall see, the mission towns were distinguished by a long-term emplacement preceding the permanent arrival of Europeans in the late 1500s that was maintained for well over a century afterwards. The primary new arrivals during the early phases of the colonial era were European clergy, who constructed mission complexes that were integrated into the surrounding built environment.

The Jesuits were the first Catholic order charged with spreading the Catholic faith in La Florida. Their arrival in 1566 was quickly followed by several years of failed efforts across an ambitiously large south-north swath. Jesuits attempted to establish missions in far southern Florida among the Tequestas and Calusas, the Chesapeake Bay region, and points in between (Hann 1991; Milanich 1999). Facing small numbers of conversions, indifferent or hostile Native American leaders, and the deaths of nine of their missionaries, the Jesuits withdrew in 1572.

Loath to leave a religious vacuum, the Spanish Crown directed the Franciscan order to resume the missionization process in La Florida. The first Franciscan friar landed in 1573, and the arrival of 13 more priests in 1587 marked the beginning of a widescale effort to convert Indians (Gannon 1989:36–38). The fortunes of the Franciscans were a stark contrast to those of the Jesuits. Their success in developing an extensive network of missions throughout the colony of La Florida—with minimal logistical support from the Crown—is a testament to the ability of a religious order to play a pivotal role in mapping out a landscape of colonialism. After establishing two missions at St. Augustine upon their arrival, Franciscans continued to add religious outposts northward along the coast in the 1580s and 1590s among the Guales, Mocamas, and other peoples. With these early successes, the Franciscan friars next turned their attention to the Timucuan interior, rapidly building a number of missions in the period from 1595 to 1633 (Worth 1998:35). The final jewel in the Franciscan mission system, the thickly settled Apalachee region in northwestern Florida, was incorporated in the 1630s (Hann 1988). By the mid-1600s, the Franciscans had 70 friars established across 40 principal missions overseeing the lives of perhaps 26,000 Indians (Gannon 1989) (figure 5.6). Even if the latter number is a somewhat optimistic projection on the part of the Franciscans, it does not discount their rapid and widespread success (Thomas 1990:377–378).

The importance of the mission system to the survival of St. Augustine and La Florida cannot be overestimated. Many of the societies that were incorporated into the system had a long history of cultivating maize. Their mission surpluses became the lifeblood of the colony. And despite the transformations being experienced by the mission Indians, they, more than any other group in the Southeast, sustained to a considerable degree the political structure of their pre-European forebears. Several interrelated factors promoted a continuation of the chiefly hierarchy in Spanish Florida as it collapsed elsewhere in the Southeast (Worth 2002). First, St. Augustine itself sat in an unproductive setting and was unable to provision itself. Second, Florida's setting in a relatively unattractive margin of the empire failed to attract the stream of colonial farmers to occupy the

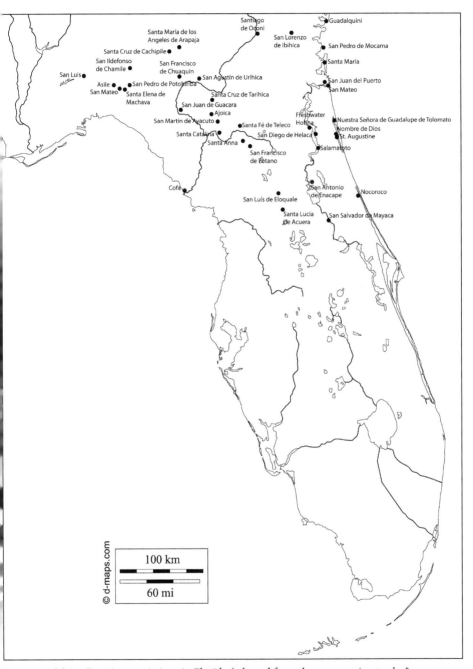

Figure 5.6. Major Franciscan missions in Florida (adapted from d-maps.com/carte.php?num_car=6851&lang=en).

hinterland and provide the needed surplus that potentially could have supported the capital. Finally, the Spanish system of annually supplying underperforming colonies, the *situado*, was predictably unpredictable given the oscillating fortunes of the Spanish Empire. As a result, Indians in the mission towns exercised considerable autonomy in sustaining their traditional sociopolitical structure. Quite simply, the colonial administration in Florida did not have the wherewithal to intervene in local affairs to the extreme degree seen elsewhere in the Spanish Americas. Whereas regions like Peru uprooted and aggregated into mission towns literally hundreds of thousands of Native peoples in a process known as *reducción* (VanValkenburgh 2017), Florida at most implemented an attenuated *reducción* (Hann 1986:371).

In return for their relative independence, traditional leaders in Florida mission towns merely needed to declare their fealty to the Spanish Crown and intensify agricultural production sufficiently to ensure a regular supply of foodstuffs to St. Augustine and the colony's troops. This system of support, known as the *sabana*, also expanded the repertoire of traditional crops to include traditional Old World plants such as wheat (Bushnell 1994). In effect, the Spanish colonial infrastructure upheld the statuses of chiefs by providing a new variety of European wealth items in exchange for their support. Following an age-old pattern, the leaders used these goods to leverage power in their home towns through gifting and other means.

Compared to the upheavals and migrations occurring in the landscape of the Southeast during the first three-quarters of the seventeenth century, the Franciscan missions supported an unrivaled degree of stability of place that corresponded with the continuity of traditional sociopolitical roles. Because St. Augustine officials lacked the resources to establish a secular infrastructure within La Florida, the missions filled this void admirably. The core missions, or *doctrinas*, were installed at major Indigenous villages by one or two friars who took up permanent residence after building a church, living quarters (*convento*), and outbuildings such as a kitchen (*cocina*) (Gannon 1989). The mission towns then became hubs for the conversion of satellite communities, where *doctrina* friars would establish *visitas*, or churches lacking permanent clergy that would be called upon regularly by the priests residing in the larger towns. The productivity of established *doctrina* towns, in turn, encouraged a stability of place and a certain latitude to Native Americans to control their own destinies.

In other respects, though, the stability of landscape was a physical veneer. Traditional patterns of labor had to be restructured significantly in order to sustain the *sabana*. Despite the persistence of the trappings of chiefly power, the demand for surplus to support St. Augustine required significant adjustments to the traditional subsistence cycle. Like agricultural societies elsewhere in the Southeast, prior to the arrival of Europeans, Florida Indians historically followed a broad-spectrum diet consisting of both wild and cultivated plant foods, not to mention a variety of animals. This meant that certain portions of the year required intensive gathering forays, particularly in the winter as stored maize supplies ran low. In his expedition to northeastern Florida in the 1560s, French explorer René Laudonnière observed how local groups regularly dispersed into the woods from January through March, "during which time you do not see an Indian anywhere" (Laudonnière 2001 [1587]:121). The mission system imposed restrictions on mobility because the expanded commitment to agriculture required sustained Indian labor in and around the villages. Moreover, for purposes of religious indoctrination and regular access to the sacraments members of the community were expected to live *bajo campana*, under the bell, defined as no more than half a league from the church bell (Bushnell 1994:96).

The demand for labor was felt in other important ways as well. The most productive mission lands among the Guales along the Georgia coast and the Apalachees in northwestern Florida were some distance from St. Augustine. Indians were thus impressed into a *repartimiento* system in which a portion of the village population was required to provide labor annually to port food to the capital (Worth 1998:190–195). This labor pool consisting of unmarried males was additionally essential for the physical maintenance of the capitol and other colonial infrastructure projects. The impressive fort, Castillo de San Marcos, at St. Augustine, for example, was built from the exertions of Indians quarrying and stacking thousands of blocks of coquina, a locally available variant of limestone (figure 5.7).

Town chiefs (*caciques*), directly managed the *repartimiento*, so the institution was a hybrid of Spanish expectations and Indigenous agency. Nevertheless, the labor demands seem to have had a high physical cost. The Franciscan Fray Jesus reported in 1630 that long-distance porting of goods to St. Augustine was causing widespread exhaustion and death among missionary Indians (Hann 1996:186). In addition, the restrictions on the seasonal round disrupted traditional diets (Bushnell 1990:476).

Figure 5.7. Castillo de San Marcos (photo by author).

Bioarchaeological studies of the remains of mission Indians reflect these physical tolls with notable increases in proxies of nutritional deficiencies (such as porotic lesions) and osteoarthritis associated with heavy workloads (Hutchinson and Larsen 2001; Larsen et al.1990; Stojanowski 2013).

Because of their relative stability, missions as persistent places were often coalescent places. As we have seen, when the Westo Indians began their deep South slaving campaigns in earnest in the 1660s, interior groups like the Tamas often fled to the coastal mission system. The spike in intercolonial conflicts following the establishment of Carolina in 1670 made the larger mission settlements even more desirable to refugee groups inhabiting newly forming shatter zones between English and Spanish, and later French, territories. Many of these zones, such as the Apalachee region, were once thriving mission regions themselves before their inhabitants moved toward more protected missions in the interior. This kind of turmoil often intersected with waves of pathogens, causing profound drops or oscillations in mission populations. For example, archival data suggest that in the mid-1600s, there was a decline in the populations at San Francisco de Potano and Santa Fe de Toloca in the interior due to disease, but their populations rebounded in the late 1600s, likely due to the arrival of refugees from other missions (Milanich 1978:78–79). Some of these patterns of mixing can be detected in the archaeological record. San Francisco de Potano, one of the more successful refugee missions in the interior, endured for a century, from 1606 to 1706 (Waters 2006). Investigations there in the 1960s revealed that 30% of the pottery was non-local (Milanich 1978:79). Most of these types appear to derive from eastern Timucua and Guale regions well to the east and northeast. There are also types typical of Apalachee territory in the Florida panhandle.

The great bulk of the work on missions in Florida as well as elsewhere in the Spanish borderlands of North America has focused on the ecclesiastical complexes containing the church and living quarters of the friars. The relative lack of attention to Native domiciles in Florida has led to a patchy understanding of the daily activities of Native Americans under the mission system (Hann 1996:87). Jill Loucks's (1993) work at the Baptizing Spring site (likely the mission San Augustín de Urica) in the late 1970s attempted to remedy this void by focusing intensively on two Native American structures. She found little evidence of change in traditional material culture from pre-European times, reflecting the autonomy of mission villages. Reminiscent of San Francisco de Potano, however, the house contexts did contain a surprising heterogeneity of non-local and local ceramic types—the kind of pattern we would expect with coalescence and the arrival of migrants or refugees. Equally interesting, Loucks (1993:205) identified two categories and contexts of colonowares. A finer colonoware that seemed more akin to European types was concentrated around the likely church and *convento*. Coarser colonoware variants were associated with the Indigenous structures. As with the Catawbas, the mission Indians seemed to be making some forms of pottery to conform to European tastes.

Investigations at the Fig Springs site (either mission San Martín de Timucua or San Martín de Ayacuto) likewise discovered a similar discrepancy in the spatial segregation of objects of European origin versus Native American ones (Weisman 1992). However, Worth (1998:195) has observed that 95% of the glass beads at Fig Springs occurred in Indigenous contexts away from the mission buildings. This might suggest that Native Americans were exercising some selectivity in their adoption of non-local goods. The *repartimiento* may have supported this kind of agency in consumption habits since seasonal laborers in St. Augustine were paid (through their chiefs) a daily wage in trade goods.

Missions were not isolated outposts. They were closely tied to ranches that employed Indians, presidios, and Indigenous communities lacking missions or *visitas*. For this reason, scholars have begun to widen the horizon on mission landscapes to encompass the variety and number of other types of settlements that were essential to the integration of Spanish colonies (see contributions to Panich and Schneider 2014). This kind of perspective has not been broached systematically in archaeological studies of Spanish Florida, but it is clear that entities such as the *repartimiento* system and large ranches like La Chua south of San Francisco de Potano, which also employed Indian laborers, led to a widespread circulation of peoples throughout the colony.

One of the paradoxes of the mission system is that its successful integration into a regional network of empire was simultaneously offset by the concomitant rapid spread of pathogens, exacting an even higher toll on populations who already were physically taxed. During the first major interior expansion of missions into the interior from 1612 to 1616, up to half of the Indians may have died from disease (Hann 1996:174). These losses would continue to mount later in the century with major blows from slaving and colonial wars.

The retreat of the mission system accelerated in the 1680s when earlier slaving expeditions by the Westos were replicated by the Yamasees and other groups eager to fill the slave market at Charles Town. These early major raids were largely directed at coastal missions. They had the effect of spurring the southward retreat of important missions like Santa Catalina de Guale, situated on fertile St. Catherine's Island and a breadbasket for the colony. After the predecessors to the Upper and Lower Creeks began their migration to the Ochese region in the 1690s, they turned to raiding the Timucuan missions in the interior. The first major incursion took place in 1691, when a group of Ochese Creeks, Yamasees, and English Carolinians attacked mission San Juan de Guacara in north-central Florida (Hahn 2004:53). The tempo of slave raids increased in the ensuing decades, culminating in the devastating raid by Carolina's Governor Moore on the Apalachee missions in 1704 (described in earlier chapters). Population relocation became a veritable flood of peoples fleeing the northerly missions.

The archaeological site known as Harrison Homestead offers a window into the growing instability of the mission system in the latter part of the seventeenth century. This was the location of three successive missions from 1675 to 1702 that served three different groups (Worth 1995): Santa Catalina de Santa María (Mocamas), Santa Catalina de Yamasee (Yamasees), and Santa Catalina de Guale (Guales). The volatile history of repeated occupations can be attributed to their placement on a barrier island (Amelia Island) well to the north of St. Augustine. This location left it vulnerable to slaving expeditions, pirate raids, and attacks from Carolina, prompting its history of abandonments. The final mission, Santa Catalina de Guale, was destroyed during Governor Moore's 1702 invasion of Florida (Arnade 1962). Archaeological investigations revealed two of the church core areas adjacent to one another (Saunders 1993, 2000). This is a combined European and Indigenous variant of a persistent place, perhaps because of the fact that this may have been considered sacred ground (burial areas were located there) and that there was a nearby Native American village (Hemmings and Deagan 1973).

The tattered remains of the mission system were decimated by a series of Ochese Creek raids in 1705 and 1706. The regional stability of the mission system, already crumbling, was effectively erased as most of the surviving Indians were placed in missions surrounding St. Augustine (Hann 1996:300–303; Worth 1998:142–146). This led to the somewhat astonishing situation of effectively clearing Florida of most resident Native Americans. Indian allies of the English on slaving missions in the early 1700s purportedly were traveling as far south as the Florida Keys to capture the few remaining peoples in the peninsula (Hann 2003:179; Worth 1998:146). A territory that in the early 1600s boasted tens of thousands of Native Americans saw its population now largely restricted around St. Augustine.

In contrast to the in situ mission towns that characterized the traditional Franciscan system in Florida, the missions on the periphery of St. Augustine were colonially structured coalescent communities. In an attempt to maintain missions with viable numbers, Spanish administrators were compelled to place peoples of different backgrounds together. Ironically, these numbers were significantly augmented when the Yamasees, for several decades a major thorn in the Florida colony, were allowed to return following the Yamasee War of 1715.

There have been some limited archaeological investigations at a few of these later missions. Most of these have been in advance of modern building construction and related projects, the result of cultural resource management mitigation work mandated by the city of St. Augustine's preservation ordinance. Work at Nuestra Señora del Rosario de la Punta, on the south side of the city, revealed typical Indigenous, single-post circular structures and pottery consistent with Yamasee types (Boyer 2005). Likewise, a partially excavated domestic structure at San Antonio de Pocotolaca had single-post construction with features containing pottery typical of Yamasee assemblages elsewhere (Hall 2016). Kathleen Deagan's (1983) research on St. Augustine households where female Native Americans had married men of Spanish descent demonstrated a strong persistence of Indigenous crafting traditions. Parallel to her findings, Indians at the later missions surrounding St. Augustine maintained many aspects of their domestic lifestyles.

Following demographic decline from disease and continued attacks from the English colonies to the north, the remaining Indians around St. Augustine were aggregated into two missions in the 1750s, Nuestra Señora de Guadalupe de Tolomato and Nombre de Dios (Hann 1996:323). When the Spanish Crown ceded Florida to England and St. Augustine's residents departed for Havana in the aftermath of the Seven Years War in 1763, 89 Indians opted to accompany them—the remaining members of a mission system that once numbered in the tens of thousands. What had been one of the more stable Native American landscapes in the Southeast became, first, a contracting web of coalescent refugee towns, and, ultimately, a devastated shatter zone.

A group of Lower Creeks migrated into the relative emptiness of Florida in the late 1700s, coalescing with the remnants of the surviving groups and eventually becoming known as Seminoles. At the time he visited them in the 1770s, William Bartram remarked, "The Siminoles are but a weak people with respect to numbers. All of them, I suppose would not be sufficient to people one of the towns in the Muscogulge. . . . Yet this handful of people possesses a vast territory; all East Florida and the greatest part of West Florida" (Bartram 1793:209). Not for the first time, what constituted a shatter zone for one group of Native Americans became an opportunity for another.

Conclusion

The complexity of the emplacements and aggregations witnessed in the preceding case studies exemplifies the difficulties with extracting even general modalities in the landscape histories of the Southeast and treating them as categories. Except for those rare instances when groups inhabited unoccupied terrain like the Savannah River Valley, diaspora or displacement were followed by emplacement or coalescence of some sort. As a result, when one people, such as the Natchez, were compelled to leave their homeland, they typically found themselves living with or around other groups, such as the Chickasaws, who were willing to take them in. The extensive, plural cultural terrain fostered by these practices gained even further complexity when some powerful groups decided to purposefully expand their geographic reach by installing new towns in regions outside of their traditional homelands.

Despite the attempts by the Spanish Crown to isolate Florida from the upheavals of slaving and warfare, its settlements were increasingly victimized by the predations of English colonials and their allies. But influence did run in both directions, particularly in the first half of the seventeenth century. During that period, the European goods entering the expanding mission system were traded by Christianized Indians to families and friends in the interior, fostering a dramatic upsurge of European objects throughout the Southeast (Waselkov 1989b).

As the late 1600s and 1700s progressed, the ongoing patterns of displacement and emplacement lent the southeastern landscape an increasingly fractal quality. Households were often composed of people of mixed backgrounds, where Chickasaw men might have Natchez spouses or an English trader may have married the daughter of the local leader. Marriage between Spanish citizens and Indian women was commonplace in St. Augustine (Deagan 1983). In turn, towns themselves may have incorporated distinct enclaves of newcomers, while nominal culture regions (e.g., Cherokee, Creek) could contain discrete settlements of migrants forced out of shatter zones. By the mid- to late 1700s, the Cherokees, Creeks, Choctaws, Chickasaws, Seminoles, Catawbas, Creeks, and other surviving Native American communities of the Southeast were all multidimensional coalescent entities.

Eruptions and Disruptions

The year 1453 ushered in turmoil at a number of locations around the globe. On May 29, Sultan Mehmed II breached the massive defensive walls of Constantinople, bringing an end to the last formal political vestiges of the Roman and Byzantine Empires. The sweeping cultural, political, military, and economic repercussions of the fall of this storied metropolis constitutes a major inflection point in Mediterranean history, marking the end of the Late Medieval era. Although Europeans at the time viewed this event as an alarming blow to Christendom, the many Catholic states and principalities continued their own internecine conflicts without pause even as the Byzantine emperor desperately sought help from the West. Notably, one of the bloodiest conflicts of the era, the Hundred Years' War, drew to a close in October of 1453 soon after the fall of Constantinople as French forces recaptured Bordeaux, leaving Calais as the primary remnant of English aspirations on the continent.

Mississippian landscapes also were undergoing considerable upheaval in the same time frame, perhaps due to climatic perturbations and perhaps even precipitated by an enormous volcanic eruption that may have taken place—as fate would have it—in 1452 or 1453 CE (Gao et al. 2006; Witter and Self 2007). This volatility was manifested by an atmosphere of political oscillations, population relocation, and warfare, conceivably prompted by a series of severe droughts that began centuries earlier in the 1200s to 1300s CE.

Could the turmoil experienced by the Mississippian world be attributed in part to natural events and climatic perturbations? Was the 1453 explosion that shattered the south Pacific volcanic island of Kuwae the coup de grâce that sparked a huge wave of regional abandonments in the latter

1400s (Anderson et al. 1995; Cobb and Butler 2002; Krus and Cobb 2018; Meeks and Anderson 2013; Williams 1990)? Although there is now some question as to the exact timing of the Kuwae eruption—some would have it around five to ten years later (Bauch 2017; Sigl et al. 2013)—there are accounts ranging from Europe to China of unusual "fogs" and other phenomena indicative of a dust veil blanketing much of the globe during this time (Bauch 2017). These conditions were accompanied by pronounced precipitation and temperature oscillations, along with crop failures in the late 1400s. Even if one wishes to avoid environmental determinism, it is hard to overlook the fact that Europeans departed a continent in climatic, ecological, political, and economic flux and alighted on a different continent experiencing similar conditions.

In recognition of these natural processes, it is interesting that ethnohistorians and archaeologists alike have framed the rise and decline of the major Mississippian chiefdoms within the context of climate change (Anderson et al. 1995; DuVal 2006:26; Hahn 2004:13–16; Hall 2009:32). As they note, the Mississippian phenomenon seemed to take hold and accelerate with the onset of the Medieval Optimum period of ca. 900–1300 CE, a time of global warming and abundant precipitation. These conditions were highly favorable for increased agricultural yields and demographic expansion. This ascendance was followed by an apparent contraction of the major towns around 1300 CE, when global cooling and major climatic oscillations associated with the Little Ice Age disrupted societies worldwide.

Despite the recognition that the trajectory of Mississippian polities and climatic patterns were somehow intertwined, Dennis Blanton (2004) maintains that both historians and archaeologists tend to relegate climate to the background with the arrival of Europeans in eastern North America. With some exceptions (e.g., Cronon 1983; Silver 1990), the same could be said of ecological variables, at least in ethnohistorical research on the politics of southeastern colonialism. These tend to fade behind slaving, warfare, and geopolitical maneuvering. Archaeological research in the Southeast, with its strong grounding in environmental approaches, has seen more of an empirical focus on what might be termed the political and historical ecology of the colonial era. In this chapter, I will explore some of these trends as they played out in a trajectory beginning with the maize-based economies of Mississippian chiefdoms, followed by a shift in subsistence systems that accompanied the rising investment of Native

Americans in the deerskin trade, and culminating in the rise of the ideology and practices of the market economy as expressed in the privatization of property.

Mississippian Antecedents of Colonial Political and Historical Ecology

Mississippian political ecology was predicated to a considerable degree on the productivity of agriculture. Chiefly leaders relied on a variety of means to achieve and maintain power, including the manipulation of symbols and ritual, the support of kinship networks, and military prowess. The ability to command and redistribute tribute in the form of maize seems to stand out as a particularly important component of their political arsenal (Anderson 1994b; Milner 2006; Muller 1997). Moreover, the rise of agriculture supported higher population densities, a necessary component of the labor underpinnings of power. This, combined with a sophisticated subsistence system based on a complex mix of other domesticated plants and wild plant and animals, provided the ecological and demographic scaffolding that upheld the expansive structure of towns, villages, and hamlets constituting Mississippian polities throughout the Southeast.

The Mississippian broad-spectrum diet that revolved around maize was a long time in the making. There is an increasingly well-documented history of the use of native cultigens (prized for starchy and oily seeds) in the Midwest and Midsouth, beginning in the latter part of the first millennium BCE. (Fritz 1990; Gremillion 2002; B. Smith 1989). Members of the so-called Eastern Agricultural Complex such as goosefoot (*Chenopodium berlandieri*), sumpweed (*Iva annua*), and sunflower (*Helianthus annuus*) all show morphological changes consistent with human manipulation and domestication. Plants like knotweed (*Polygonum erectum*), little barley (*Hordeum pusillum*), and maygrass (*Phalaris caroliniana*) were encouraged. The neotropical domesticate maize appeared in the first centuries CE in the Eastern Woodlands. But recent evidence seems to suggest that it was a very minor player in the subsistence system (Simon 2017).

Beginning around 1000 CE, maize began to assume increasing prominence in Native American diets in eastern North America (Simon and Parker 2006; Wagner 1994). The domesticated bean (*Phaseolus vulgaris*, probably deriving from the American Southwest and spreading rapidly into eastern North America in the 1200s CE [Hart et al. 2002; Monaghan et al. 2014]) along with squash formed an essential triad with maize throughout eastern North America in the centuries prior to Columbus's landing. There is a correlation between the rise of social complexity and the reliance on tropical cultigens associated with the Mississippian period, but the lines of causality between these variables are hazy. Nevertheless, archaeologists have readily recognized that maize cultivation to a considerable extent made larger population densities and social hierarchy possible.

Given the increasing prominence of agriculture after 1000 CE, one of the more obvious landscape correlations in the Mississippian period is that between large settlements and the rich flood plain soils of major drainages. In the Southeast, there is hardly a river of any consequence that does not boast one or more sizable Mississippian mound centers, in addition to numerous smaller villages and hamlets. This is hardly just an idle observation. For the huge and well-drained expanse represented by the Mississippian culture area, we are talking about literally hundreds of rivers, many of them hundreds of kilometers long and home to multiple major Mississippian occupations along their entire length. This ecological multiplier effect means that by the time Europeans arrived in the Southeast, hundreds of mound centers had arisen—and in many cases fallen—and thousands of smaller settlements were dispersed across the region.

A number of important ecological-focused studies in the 1960s and 1970s demonstrated that many major Mississippian sites typically were located on elevated landforms within flood plains with rich, arable soils (Chmurney 1973; Smith 1978a; Ward 1965). William Woods's (1987) overview of protohistoric European descriptions of Native American settlement practices throughout eastern North America demonstrates that many settlements at that time were widely dispersed, in order to take advantage of the scattered high points in alluvial settings. These locations, such as remnant levees and swale ridges, provided both protection from flooding and access to well-drained, fertile soils. Woods (1987:281–285) further posited that Mississippian groups practiced a combination of cultivating large outfields in the productive bottomlands and tending mixed-crop plots near settlements, although Jon Muller (1997:255) believes it more likely that these fields were continua rather than discrete. In any event, dependence on only a few plant species is an ecologically risky strategy. What helped to buffer Mississippian communities from unpredictable droughts and floods was the tremendous biomass of wild plant and animal life associated with the meander zones. The rivers themselves, backwater sloughs, swamps, extensive flood plain forests, and oxbow lakes all contain a variety of large and small mammals, fishes, reptiles, shellfish, and plants bearing nuts, berries, and seeds (Smith 1978b). Many of the major water courses are also part of migratory flyways that are seasonally traveled by economically important birds.

Despite this abundance, the productive potential (and carrying capacity) of a flood plain region can be misleading when viewed through modern eyes. As George Milner (1993) has pointed out, large tracts of the bountiful land along the Mississippi River in southwestern Illinois were likely inundated for prolonged periods before the advent of modern flood control measures. He describes Mississippian communities in the region as "settlements amidst swamps," and suggests that they mapped onto raised "habitable spots" rather than having free rein to settle randomly in an open, arable expanse. Even with these and other environmental constraints, though, population growth during the Mississippian period led to the consolidation of some truly impressive towns. Cahokia, by far the largest and probably the best known, may have had a population of between 5,000 and 10,000 individuals at its peak in the 1100s and 1200s CE (some would argue even higher) (Holley 1999). The surrounding American Bottom region was home to a number of other substantial mound centers and hundreds of smaller settlements. Other sizable towns, such as Moundville in Alabama and Etowah in Georgia, may have numbered between 1,000 and 3,000 people (e.g., King 2003; Steponaitis 1998). While the largest Mississippian settlements may have been overshadowed by contemporary urban centers in Mesoamerica, on the average they were still a significant leap in size over anything that had preceded them in eastern North America. Maize agriculture and productive flood plains were fundamental to this growth.

Not surprisingly, the expansion of towns and outlying settlement systems was accompanied by significant anthropogenic impacts to the environment. Massive borrow pits were excavated to provide soil for the ubiquitous earthworks that seemed to be such an important symbol of Mississippian identity. Entire hillsides were pockmarked with quarries excavated to extract chert to meet the demand for stone hoes (Cobb 2000; Parish 2013). In the American Bottom of Illinois, during the thirteenth century CE, the increasing use of upland tree species for fuelwood and for the construction of houses is indicative of the overexploitation of bottom land forest along the Mississippi River (Lopinot and Woods 1993).

The deforestation of the American Bottom may have affected both hydrology and human settlement. Indirect evidence of a rising water table is suggested by a shift of settlements from an aggregated plan on flood plain ridges to a linear one that focused on higher points on the same ridges (Milner 2006:126). Mississippian peoples did not live lightly on the landscape.

It should be emphasized that many significant Mississippian sites and settlement systems occurred outside of major flood plain environs. There are many examples: In the Middle Cumberland region of Tennessee, there seems to have been a shift in settlement toward small upland drainages later in the Mississippian sequence (Smith 1992:26); during the fifteenth to sixteenth centuries CE, populations in the Upper Tombigbee Valley appear to have abandoned the river flood plain for prairie ridge tops (Clark 2017; J. Johnson 1996); there is a migration into the rugged Shawnee Hills of southern Illinois during the thirteen century CE (Cobb and Butler 2002); and there was a major population expansion along the uplands of the Oconee drainage in northern Georgia in the 1500s (Kowalewski and Hatch 1991). These settlement flows and adaptations to a wide diversity of settings are a testament to the flexibility of the Mississippian subsistence system—a strength that would prove critical to the survival of Indigenous peoples after the arrival of Europeans.

Societies in the pre-European contact era had also made sophisticated adaptations to coastal settings. Many of the first peoples encountered by Spaniards, English, and French on the shores of the Southeast had a deep history of littoral adaptations with little to no reliance on domesticated plants. This often involved the intensive exploitation of shellfish in addition to the widely varied fish and bird species from the marshes and ocean, not to mention a wide array of plant resources. The Calusas represented a highly complex chiefly polity encompassing much of southwest Florida that developed in the absence of maize cultivation (Marquardt 2014; Widmer 1988). Not only did they engage in mound building, they also expanded the size of the island that held the capital of Mound Key and constructed canals on the same landform (Thompson et al. 2016). For the Guales and Timucuas on the coast of Georgia and Florida, there has been considerable debate as to whether these groups had adopted maize or took on plant cultivation under instigation from Spanish colonials (cf. Larson 1980; Saunders 2002; Thomas 2008). Whether these groups originally were or were not strongly reliant on maize, it is clear that they were also complex foragers who quickly intensified maize cultivation with missionization.

Social Responses to Climate Change

The landscape of Mississippian subsistence systems was resilient but not static. As seen in the preceding examples, southeastern peoples were fully capable of transplanting their lifeways to a number of settings. Moreover, many groups reworked their agricultural strategies through time. One of the more important trends in plant food use seems to be a steady decline in the reliance on the Eastern Agricultural Complex with a corresponding rise in importance of maize (Fritz 1990; Simon and Parker 2006). It is less clear if significant changes were occurring in animal exploitation. There are some hints that large mammals like bear, bison, and elk may be more common in later Mississippian assemblages in some parts of the Southeast (Breitburg 1998; Johnson et al. 2008). I rely on the verbs "seems" and "may" with regard to these developments because variation in sampling and analytical protocols is still a major challenge to comparative zooarchaeological and paleobotanical research. Still, there seem to be some notable alterations in the use of plants and animals after the 1200s to 1300s CE, at least in some localities around the Southeast.

It is quite possible that these changes can be attributed to significant climatic shifts. Admittedly, it can be difficult to specify how and why cultures may react variably to climate change. There is, nonetheless, a correlation between the rise of the Little Ice Age and transformations among Mississippian societies around 1300 CE, when they experienced major declines in mound building and a rise in intergroup conflict (Anderson 1994:136–137; Krus 2016; Milner et al. 2013; Worne 2017). It is estimated that mean temperatures in North America dropped on the average below half a degree centigrade during the Little Ice Age (Mann et al. 2014). The early 1600s and early 1800s appear to have been particularly cold spells during the Little Ice Age. It must be kept in mind, though, that temperatures gyrated considerably through time and space (Bradley and Jones 1993; Mann et al. 2014). Challenges to humans during the period of cooling that lasted from the 1300s to the 1800s appear to stem more from climatic volatility, especially in rainfall, than to simple temperature downturns. The Southeast experienced these extremes beginning in the 1200s and 1300s CE, when a series of severe and repeated droughts struck the region (Bird et al. 2017; Cook et al. 2007; Cook et al. 2014).

Declining maize yields as a result of these rain shortfalls may have directly undermined Mississippian chiefly authority reliant on tribute (Anderson et al. 1995; Meeks and Anderson 2013). Just as importantly, the climatic changes may have been responsible for instigating some of the more substantial population movements ever experienced in the Southeast prior to the 1500s. In essence, the arrival of Europeans accelerated processes of displacement and emplacement by other means that had already been underway for centuries.

In a series of landmark papers, Stephen Williams (1983, 1990) articulated the "Vacant Quarter Hypothesis," the idea that 50,000 square miles of the eastern North American mid-continent were largely abandoned by Mississippian peoples around 1450 to 1550 CE (figure 6.1). Because the region he outlined was filled with sizable towns and polities before the posited exodus, widespread acceptance of the Vacant Quarter was not immediate. The scale of population movement proposed by Williams for sedentary groups was simply unprecedented in the archaeology of the region. The notion of the Vacant Quarter also implied collapse; some of the most substantial towns and polities in the Mississippian Southeast and lower Midwest were encompassed by the boundaries of the vacated region. These include Cahokia and surrounding towns in the American Bottom, a number of major towns along the Ohio River such as Kincaid, and the Middle Cumberland region in Tennessee, which seems to have been the home of a very dense population before its relatively abrupt abandonment (Benson et al. 2009; Cobb and Butler 2002; Krus and Cobb 2018; Meeks and Anderson 2013).

Although Williams entertained a multi-causal model for the abandonment, climate change was one variable in his thinking (Williams 1990:175–176). With recent strides in climatological knowledge, archaeologists are now on much firmer ground in attributing severe, multi-decadal droughts during the Little Ice Age a significant, if not singular, causal role in the Vacant Quarter phenomenon (figure 6.2). As I observed at the start of the chapter, we also cannot ignore the eruption of a massive volcano in the mid-1400s. This may have been a major "forcing" event since volcanic activity is widely considered a major contributor to acute climatic and environmental oscillations within an already volatile cooling period

Figure 6.1. Vacant Quarter and other abandoned regions.

(Gao et al. 2006; Miller et al. 2012; Robock 2000). Brian Butler and I (2002) have argued that the radiocarbon date sequences for the Lower Ohio Valley support a mid-fifteenth century abandonment for that region, suspiciously around the same time as the eruption. Meeks and Anderson (2013) have conducted an impressively comprehensive analysis of the radiocarbon dates for five regions in the Vacant Quarter. Their conclusion is that region-wide abandonment, including the Lower Ohio drainage, seems to have been a synchronic event occurring somewhat earlier, around 1420 CE. Not to bog down these discrepancies in mathematical details, but Anthony Krus and I (Krus and Cobb 2018) have countered that a Bayesian statistical approach to analyzing radiometric dates more robustly supports an abandonment of the Middle Cumberland region—

Figure 6.2. Region of severe droughts (shaded area) ca. 1450 CE (based on model from http://drought.memphis.edu/NADA/SingleYearRecon.aspx).

one of the regions in the Meeks and Anderson study sample—in the last half of the 1400s CE.

We now know that the Vacant Quarter was not a singularity (see figure 6.1). Williams (2001) later argued that the Lower Yazoo drainage of Mississippi was abandoned in the same time frame. A similar pattern seems to hold for the Savannah River Valley when populations deserted the last of the major mound centers in the late 1400s (Anderson 1994b). Given the extensive range of population evacuations from some of the richest arable lands in the Southeast, it is difficult to discount the idea that Mississippian communities were reacting to widespread climate change and the immediate social consequences—like warfare—of ecological unpredictability.

Systematic, sophisticated chronological analyses of the timing of Vacant Quarter and contemporary abandonments are still in their relative infancy. At this time it is perhaps safest to say that climate played a significant role, if not the only one, in the population shuffle of the fifteenth century. These dispersals may have laid much of the groundwork for the social strategies of addressing displacement and displacement that southeastern populations drew on with the turmoil introduced by Europeans in the subsequent century. Tascalusa (Alabama) is a prime example of the rapid changes that were occurring in the Southeast at the same time that the Reconquista was drawing to a close in Iberia. This was one of the more significant chiefdoms encountered by the Soto expedition. Notably, the chief who greeted the Spaniards in 1540 was the leader of a polity that had been in existence for only about a century. It had coalesced around 1450 CE—again, that red-letter date—in the Alabama River Valley as a nexus of three polities that had migrated from the west, south, and east (Regnier 2014).

Climate change was a force that favored neither colonial nor Native American. The same conditions to which southeastern Native communities were adapting proved to be major hurdles to the colonization of eastern North America. The English "forgotten colony" of Roanoke (Virginia) encountered extremely harsh climatic conditions from 1587 to 1589 before it was mysteriously abandoned (Blanton 2004), while the Spanish settlement of Santa Elena (South Carolina) was evacuated in 1587 following a protracted stretch of forbidding climate and terrible crop yields (Anderson et al. 1995). Climate was particularly punishing during the "forgotten century" of the 1600s, when European incursions in the Southeast had receded. Historian Samuel White (2017) has shown that climate change as much as geopolitical entanglements may have played a central role in dampening the colonial aspirations of France, England, and Spain in North America during that period. To be sure, all of the colonizing powers had major distractions in their own backyards during the seventeenth century. England was divided by a protracted civil war, France was embroiled in the highly destructive Thirty Years War, and Spain was party to the same war while at the same time attempting to stave off (unsuccessfully) the Dutch Revolt of its Low Country possessions. Meanwhile, on the western side of the Atlantic Ocean, there were three major and one minor volcanic eruptions in Mexico and South America between 1586 and 1600 (Blanton 2004:15; White 2017:76–77). This volcanic forcing, along with other climatological factors, seems to have spurred an even further decline in global temperatures such that the first decade of the 1600s was the coldest in two millennia. White (2017) convincingly argues that the challenging and highly unpredictable conditions of the era proved a major barrier to early colonizing efforts in New Mexico, southeastern Canada and New England, and along the Atlantic seaboard. Communities like Jamestown (Virginia) did manage to hang on, but with considerable loss of life and resources. Other efforts, like Roanoke, St. Croix (Maine), and Popham (Maine), collapsed. St. Augustine, established before these efforts in 1565, managed to manage through an array of political and environmental challenges. However, it did have the advantage of a support system, even if unpredictable, emanating from nearby Mexico and Cuba.

The first colonizing efforts in the Southeast during the 1500s and 1600s took place in a capricious social, political, economic, and environmental atmosphere that had been underway for some time. Mississippian polities were actively waxing and waning and waxing again, the climate was notoriously unpredictable, and the physical landscape was a dynamic mix of anthropogenic and natural processes. European efforts at establishing colonies did not skew a sociopolitical and ecological equilibrium. Rather, Native Americans drew on venerable landscape traditions to continue fashioning their cultural and natural surroundings as they had been doing for thousands of years.

Colonial Era Historical and Political Ecology

As the environmental historian William Cronon (1983:12) famously remarked, the Euro-American westward movement did not face a virgin landscape so much as a widowed one. The dramatic demographic decline of Native Americans led many newcomers to believe that they were entering the wilderness primeval rather than a landscape that had been sculpted by human hands for over 12,000 years. Compared to the Edenic views of Native Americans and their environment that once prevailed, we now have many lines of evidence for anthropogenic changes to the landscape extending back for many millennia, even well before Mississippian times. While only a desultory construction of earthworks continued after the 1300s CE, Native Americans of the colonial era engaged in many other landscape modification practices. Many of these related to subsistence. Deliberate fires are one of the oldest known ways to alter the landscape and enhance the yield of ecological resources. Scorched landscapes may provide several economically important outcomes including, but not limited to, the maintenance of open habitats for agriculture, the encouragement of edible early successional plants, and the fostering of edge environments that attract deer and other animals (Hammett 1992; Wagner 2003). Pollen and charcoal sequences demonstrate that anthropogenic fires were systematically set for many millennia prior to the arrival of Europeans (Cridlebaugh 1984; Delcourt and Delcourt 1998). Ecologists and archaeologists have used witness-tree data from General Land Office records dating to early in the federal area to reconstruct forest composition for many areas of eastern North America, and these studies suggest that culturally prescribed burning was a common practice that continued into the colonial era (Foster et al. 2004; Nelson 1997).

As a result of this activity, large portions of the forest cover in the Southeast comprised a relatively open wooded landscape. We have a sense of the long-term history of clearing from the following observation made by Thomas Nairne (1988 [1708]:57–58) in 1708: "the Country, being pleasant open forests of oak chestnuts and hickory so intermixed with savannas as if it were a made landscape . . . on the tops of these knolls live the Chickasaws, their houses a Gunn or pistole shot asunder, with their improved ground peach and plum trees about them."

Until communal Indigenous lands began to fragment into individual farms in the late eighteenth and early nineteenth centuries, many of the economic landscape practices of Native Americans proved remarkably resilient and resistant to the introduction of plants, animals, and related husbandry practices from the Eastern Hemisphere (Deagan 2008; Gremillion 2002; Pavao-Zuckerman 2007). As the Europeans promptly learned, given the productivity of Indigenous farming, gathering, fishing, and hunting there was little need for wholesale borrowing by Native Americans of Old World plants and animals. In the early years of colonial settlement, the borrowing was just as likely to go the opposite direction, as Europeans struggled to transplant their familiar plants and animals to unfamiliar landscapes within challenging climates (Deagan 2008; Pavao-Zuckerman 2007; Reitz 1990; Waselkov 1997). Spanish explorers frequently described the rich abundance of the maize fields of the southeastern chiefdoms. Indeed, the well-known sixteenth-century expeditions of Hernando de Soto, Juan Pardo, and others were absolutely reliant on the stores of maize and other foods from the towns they encountered to sustain them on their journeys. Chronicles of the Soto passage through the Southeast are sprinkled with comments like the "many maize fields" of Chiaha (eastern Tennessee) (Elvas in Robertson 1993:88), or that the lands of Chicasa (eastern Mississippi) were "fertile and abounding in maize" (Elvas in Robertson 1993:105). Biedma (in Worth 1993b:230) reports that even in a "little village" they found the equivalent of 5,000 pounds of maize. Some on this expedition, having humbler aspirations of riches than Soto, urged him to settle in what is now South Carolina around the chiefdom of Cofitachequi because "it was an excellent region . . . it is a good land and suitable for making profits"—advice that was ignored because "the governor's purpose was to seek another treasure like that of Atabalipa, the lord of Peru" rather than to establish a modest country estate (Elvas in Robertson 1993:84).

Given the well-entrenched traditions of successful farming and complementary hunting-gathering-fishing practices throughout the Southeast, there was a certain ecological imperative underlying the numerous population relocations of the seventeenth and eighteenth centuries. In other words, when people moved, they often relocated to localities that replicated natural surroundings with which they were familiar. This pattern is especially apparent in the south Appalachian region, home to the various Creek descendants of Mississippian populations. In northern Georgia, many Indigenous settlements continued the Mississippian-period emphasis on inhabiting ecotone locations that provided easy access to a wide array of natural resources (Smith 1992:7). Creek towns in particular favored alluvial settings near the Fall Line where the Appalachian Piedmont grades into the Coastal Plain physiographic regions. (Ethridge 2003:36–37; Paulett 2012:51). The Fall Line is characterized by a high biodiversity, including shoals that are a rich source of shellfish, cane breaks, a variety of forest types, and bottomland swamps and sloughs (Delcourt and Delcourt 2004:65; Shankman and Hart 2007). Because of the allure to human settlement, this zone was further characterized by important transportation junctures (Ethridge 2003:36–37; Jenkins 2009:189, 218; Smith 1992:7–8). Even the eastward exodus of peoples from the Lower Chattahoochee Valley in the 1690s (described in chapter 4) maintained this principle, as most of the towns relocated to the falls of the Ocmulgee and Oconee Rivers (Smith 1989:29–30).

The affinity for the Fall Line was not restricted to the Creeks. As groups began moving into the Savannah drainage during the seventeenth and eighteenth centuries, the Piedmont/Coastal Plain transition received the heaviest settlement of peoples. Not only was this a rich and diverse floodplain area; major trade routes into the interior from the coast ran through this location. As near as can be determined, the Westo town was established in this zone on the river in 1659, followed by the Shawnee settlement soon after (DePratter 2003). The plural trade settlement of Savano Town took root at the Fall Line in the late 1600s and Fort Moore was established by the colony of South Carolina at or by Savano Town at the start of the Yamasee War in 1715.

In a parallel fashion but in a different setting, the Chickasaws maintained the landscape settings of their ancestors—this despite being buffeted constantly by the French and their Indian allies. Sometime in the mid-1400s CE, Mississippian communities seem to have abandoned the Upper Tombigbee Valley and surrounding drainages of eastern Mississippi and aggregated on the ridgetops of the adjoining Blackland Prairie. This movement was likely a southerly extension of the Vacant Quarter phenomenon (Johnson 1996:247). After effecting an adaptation to the prairie setting, these and related populations repeatedly changed locations in subsequent centuries. But they invariably remained on the prairie uplands despite the proximity of the rich bottomlands of the Tombigbee Valley (Cegielski and Lieb 2011).

There are cases, however, where groups successfully moved to surrogate settings. These were places that while not necessarily exactly mimicking home landscapes, still provided sufficient overlap so as to sustain ingrained food procurement strategies. Indian groups at the time of French contact in the Mobile-Tensaw delta usually had villages on high bluffs with their agricultural fields in the rich bottomlands below. The village locations were eventually displaced by colonial plantations. The Indians then moved their villages to small tributary streams and cleared new fields in the surrounding vicinity (Waselkov 1997). As with other Indigenous practices during the colonial era, flexibility was the order of the day.

While communities in resource-rich ecotones and other locations drew on a broad spectrum of wild plants and animals, maize remained a mainstay of the diet. Not only do we have consistent references to maize fields from colonial explorers, traders, and agents, the archaeological record confirms its ubiquity. Beans and squash, the other two key components of the three-sisters complex, also are found on colonial-era Indian sites. Although these taxa are far less common than maize in archaeological contexts, their occurrence is impacted by issues of differential preservation. Taphonomic processes make it challenging to assess the relative importance of individual plants overall during the colonial area. But a number of important paleobotanical studies have been able to elicit some important patterns and trends.

Kristen Gremillion (1995) conducted one of the first chronological comparative paleobotanical studies of the colonial era in the Southeast. Her study localities were quite diverse, including the Graham-White site in Virginia (mid- to late 1600s), the Fredericks site in North Carolina (1680–1710), and the Fusihatchee site in Alabama (a later component dating to the 1700s). Nevertheless, the settlements were similar in that maize and mast, especially hickory, were particularly abundant. Plants associated with the Eastern Agricultural Complex were sparse. Maria Theresa Bonhage-Freund's (2007) synthesis of paleobotanical remains from four Lower Creek settlements provided a more regionally comprehensive perspective on Indigenous plant exploitation, although it lacks the same time depth as Gremillion's because her sites were limited to the latter half of the eighteenth and first part of the nineteenth centuries. This study revealed a "highly mixed and integrated economy" (Bonhage-Freund 2007:190) with some variation between the towns. Nonetheless, in broad outline we see the same patterns in Gremillion's study: a dominance of maize among domesticated plants and an abundance of nuts, while cultivated plants native to eastern North America, such as maygrass, were uncommon. Hickory was particularly favored, as it was in Gremillion's study sample. This nut is common in pre-European contact and post-European contact botanical assemblages throughout the Southeast, likely due its high energetic return relative to other nuts and wild plant foods (Gremillion 1998).

Providing yet another spatial-temporal perspective on plant use, Kandace Hollenbach (2017) evaluated three different time periods all from the same locus, the Riverfront site on the Savannah River in South Carolina. This site contained Mississippian (1000 to 1450), Contact (1600 to 1660), and Colonial (post-1680) components, the latter likely representing Shawnee (and/or Yuchi) settlements referred to in chapter 4 in the discussion on the Savannah frontier. As with the previous two studies, Hollenbach found that maize and mast were most abundant, and that the Eastern Agricultural Complex cultigens that occurred in the Mississippian and Contact features were absent in the colonial-period features.

It should be emphasized that a wide variety of other plants were identified in all of these studies. Many of these were non-subsistence taxa, related to medicinal, ritual, and other uses. Interestingly, during the colonial period examples of plants associated with the Eastern Agricultural Complex often do not show the change in seed morphology (typically increased size over wild varieties) associated with domesticated plants (Bonhage-Freund 2007). This seems to confirm that these were plants that were no longer being intensively tended, and in fact were just wild specimens. Gremillion (1995:6) could make only "a weak case" for the cultivation of the indigenous grains. In other words, maygrass, pigweed, goosefoot, and so on seem to have still been recognized as useful food plants, but they were mainly encouraged rather than actively cultivated. Their use may have become more of a hedge or back-up to shortfalls in staples (Bonhage-Freund 2007:166; Gremillion 1995:7).

The intertwined rise of maize and decline of North American domesticates and cultigens, like so many trends we have seen, seem to have their genesis in the Mississippian period. Although there is considerable regional variability and considerable variability across the Southeast in the adoption and use of various comestible plants, as noted previously, maize began to significantly supplant the Eastern Agricultural Complex by around 1200 to 1300 CE (Fritz 1990; Simon and Parker 2006). At some sites dating to the fifteenth century, maize and mast already constituted the primary bulk of recovered botanical remains (e.g., Crites 1984; Parker 2016). The end of the Eastern Agricultural Complex in colonial times followed a relatively long decline with roots in the Mississippian period.

With a few notable exceptions, such as peaches, cowpeas, and watermelons, Old World plants seem to have made slow inroads into Native American menus (Deagan 2008; Gremillion 1995). Peach pits are recorded as early as about 1670 CE at the Upper Creek Woods Island site (Waselkov and Smith 2000:247), and by the late 1700s, peach orchards seem to be commonplace throughout eastern North America. Peaches and other early imports could have been easily incorporated into the dietary repertoire without any significant change in the yearly round of cropping practices, in large part because they required little tending. The adoption of most other Old World plants lagged well behind these early successful transplants. Bonhage-Freund (2007) found that European grains were common at two of the four Creek sites in her study. But the late eighteenth-century context of this material corresponds with rapid shifts toward Euro-American subsistence practices throughout the Southeast, as discussed below. The larger portrait she evoked of the Creek subsistence landscape was of a "highly mixed and integrated economy"; this was composed of a complex field management system, with fallow old fields providing rich successional plants, as well as browse for game and livestock. This continued a tradition of outfields as communal plots and infields around habitations to provide foods for immediate consumption or to tide over families until major crops had matured (Bonhage-Freund 2007:190–191; Waselkov 1997).

Native Americans in the Southeast likewise were selective in their adoption of new animals. Horses were eagerly sought when available, but the pasturage and fencing practices necessary to keep herds of pigs and cattle were inimical to ingrained traditions of open built environments, hunting territories, and communal farming lands. The mid- to late eighteenth century seems to represent a turning point in the successful incursion of European-style farming and livestock rearing practices (Pavao-Zuckerman 2007; Waselkov 1997).

Lisa O'Steen's (2007) zooarchaeological analysis of five Lower Creek towns complements the paleobotanical study by Bonhage-Freund (2007) of the same mid-eighteenth to early nineteenth-century sites. Again, there is some significant variation between sites. But overall, the data show that by the 1750s domesticated Old World animals were making significant inroads into Indigenous animal exploitation practices. Averaging the minimum number of individuals and estimated biomass across all of her sites, O'Steen (2007:238) found that domesticated mammals, cattle and pig, in addition to chickens, constituted 53% of the diet. For the wild resources that made up the other 47%, white-tailed deer were particularly important—continuing a long-held tradition in eastern North America—but a wide variety of other taxa were also represented. These included birds, amphibians, fish, and shellfish.

Barnet Pavao-Zuckerman's (2007) faunal analysis of the multi-component Upper Creek site of Fusihatchee suggests a somewhat later commitment to livestock, likely around the late 1700s. This chronology does not so much conflict with O'Steen's as demonstrate the likely time-transgressive nature of the shift in adoption of cattle and hogs, even within the same area. Indian agent Benjamin Hawkins was closely attuned to what he viewed as distressing variability in the presence of fencing and livestock among the Creeks, one of his key material barometers of civilization. He highlighted communities like the Upper Creek village of Tussekiah, where 40 men and their families had fenced all of their fields (Hawkins 1916:71), and he speaks approvingly of the Chickasaws who "have established and fenced within two years nearly two hundred [farms]" (Hawkins 1916:393). Hawkins was just as quick to disparage the many communities that were not following these examples, such as the "indolence" of residents of Hitchiti who lacked fences.

The widely held model of subsistence continuity in the Southeast generally refers to the relative lack of impact of European plant foods and related practices until the mid- to late 1700s. Pavao-Zuckerman (2007) notes that a number of variables entered into the equation of differential adoption of livestock. For families still committed to the deerskin trade, the scheduling of deer hunting did not allow for the simultaneous tending of cattle and smallstock. Belief systems came into play as well. Some Creeks blamed disease outbreaks on beef consumption, while others were concerned that eating beef and pork led to a general feeling of dullness (Pavao-Zuckerman 2007:27).

There are recent studies indicating that some Native American peoples may have shifted emphases within their traditional inventory of plant foods in the colonial era. Many communities in the Appalachians and Piedmont (including Cherokees and adjoining groups) appear to have adopted a risk-averse strategy involving a reliance on a greater variety of native wild plant foods and a diminished dependence on maize (Melton 2018; VanDerwarker et al. 2013). This trend may reflect in part a loss in the population levels necessary to maintain large fields of maize. In addition, women may have been opting for plant foods that required less processing (VanDerwarker et al. 2013:80). Female concerns with labor allocation may have become particularly acute because of a shift in the early eighteenth-century economy that, in contrast to subsistence, was dramatically transforming Native American landscapes: the growing reliance on the deerskin trade.

The Deerskin Trade

For the colonies of Virginia and South Carolina, deerskins and enslaved Indians were twin drivers of wealth in the decades leading up to the Yamasee War. Slaves of course were instrumental to the operations of plantations. Although these large estates did provide products for the luxury market (e.g., indigo for blue dye), the market for deerskins was particularly susceptible to the whims of consumption and taste on the opposite side of the Atlantic Ocean. Deer hides were widely used in Europe for gloves, breeches, and other articles of clothing, but demand could change rapidly based on fashions of the day. Notably, the popularity of the "Carolina hat" in England, a broad-brimmed hat made from deer leather, led to one of the major upsurges in the deerskin trade in the early 1700s (Braund 1993:88; Ramsey 2008:64).

With the withdrawal of so many groups from the Carolina perimeter during the Yamasee War and the heavy harvesting of peoples that had already occurred by 1715, the Indian slave trade effectively ceased with the end of hostilities. As a consequence, the pressure on deer populations rapidly mounted as peace returned and colonials and Indians alike sought to resume accustomed levels of trade and consumption. This pressure only continued to rise as new southeastern colonies and territories—Georgia, Alabama, Mississippi—formed in the decades after the war. This trade was so lucrative that it became a pillar in the political economies of both Native Americans and colonials and a major contributor to the growing entanglement between southeastern societies and the Atlantic World.

On the European side, individual traders, as well as trading houses, were able to amass considerable fortunes in the deerskin trade. Merchants and plantation owners relied on the trade as an additional source of revenue and a way to expand their enterprises (Braund 1993; Paulett 2012). Taxes and jobs related to the deerskin trade supported the colonial infrastructure. On the Native American side, groups contoured deer hunting to their own shifting world of consumerism. When William Bartram visited Creek country in the late 1700s, he was moved to observe that "they wage eternal war against deer and bear, to procure food and clothing, and other necessaries and conveniences; which is indeed carried to an unreasonable and perhaps criminal excess, since the white people have dazzled their senses with foreign superfluities" (Bartram 1793:212). The growing reliance on slaves and then hides in Native American exchange systems was one of the more important transitions in their political economies in the colonial era. According to Robin Beck (2013:17–18), the growing reliance on portable things (and people) over agricultural surplus represented a fundamental shift in the transformation of Mississippian-period power relations. This trend is widely reflected in the archaeological record. There is a major uptick in the occurrence of goods of European origin on Native American sites in the late 1600s and 1700s, as well as evidence of differential access that points to growing economic disparity within Native American communities (e.g., Rodning 2002; Schroedl 2000; Waselkov and Smith 2000).

The export records for deerskins are testament to the demand in Europe and the hunting skills of Native Americans. Prior to the Yamasee War, between 22,000 and 121,000 hides a year passed through Charles Town (Crane 2004 [1929]:328). Virginia on the average exported significantly fewer, although the numbers still frequently ranged between an impressive 10,000 to 30,000 yearly. Although the numbers declined dramatically when hostilities broke out in 1715, they quickly resumed their pre-war levels as peace returned. By the mid-1720s and thereafter, Charles Town's exports were consistently running at over 70,000 hides per annum (Crane 2004 [1929]:33). Deerskins were not the only traded animal product in the Southeast, just the most rewarding (Lapham 2005; Nassaney 2015; Stine 1990). Thomas Nairne (1988 [1708]:47) observed that the Chickasaws sold 1,200 beaver skins a year before the lucrative trade in humans supplanted that of other animals. But animals like beaver that were sought for fur instead of hides tended to have more luxuriant growth in more northerly climes and were more avidly sought in the Great Lakes region and Canada.

Accounts of the large volume of deerskins moving through the mid-Atlantic and Southeast are mirrored in the faunal record of Native American sites in the Southeast. There is a leap in the abundance of deer as early as the 1630s, taking another dramatic surge in the eighteenth century (Lapham 2005; Pavao-Zuckerman 2007). The changing demographics of deer selection can be seen in the relative representation of bone elements. Compared to the Mississippian period, mature males became a preferred target in the colonial era (Lapham 2005). The rising prominence of hide processing is reflected in the artifact and feature record as well. Stone scrapers, used for working hides, are common on many sites in the colonial era (e.g., Brain 1988:398; Johnson 1997). Smudge pits—hollows in the ground filled with corn cobs that are burned to create a dense smog useful for removing the fur from hides—are also commonplace on historic Native American sites.

The expanding deerskin trade greatly influenced Indigenous social organization. From late Mississippian to colonial periods, archaeological and ethnohistorical accounts demonstrate that traditional Native American household architecture throughout the Southeast was often composed of a substantial winter structure (often semi-subterranean) and a lightly framed summer house (Hally 2002). Indians began to abandon this dyad in the 1700s in favor of a single ground-level building (Hally 2002; Worth 2000:284). One popular hypothesis to account for this shift is that the substantial, labor-intensive type of structure suitable for colder temperatures became obsolete as many families deserted the village to hunt deer in the fall and winter (Waselkov 1994:195). Creeks, at least, tended to hunt during those seasons to avoid conflict with planting and harvesting and to take advantage of the deer's seasonally thicker coats and more abundant meat (Braund 1993:62). This practice may not have been universal throughout the Southeast, however, since Lapham's (2005:87) study of the mortality profiles of deer from archaeological sites in Virginia suggests they may have been hunted year-round. Either way, many villages were partially abandoned as individual families departed for hunting grounds. Although it is known that these families were traveling in small, mobile camps, we have very little detail about the lived landscapes of deerskin procurement and trade in locations away from the major villages (Paulett 2012:5). It is evident, though, that the deerskin trade introduced another element of displacement into Indian communities. Not only were they prone to dislocation if their territory became a shatter zone, they were also routinely fragmenting and aggregating in their pursuit of deer.

Repeated splintering in deference to the scheduling of the deer hunt had profound consequences for gendered dimensions of labor (Braund 1993:67–68; Hatley 1989). The movement of small family work parties into hunting grounds in the fall disrupted the long-held bonds of female cooperative work structured along matrilineal and matrilocal lines. Moreover, generally speaking, females were tasked with preparing the hides for the market. This was an arduous job. As the deerskin trade became central to many economies, females faced increased demands on their labor with few people to share the burden.

The ways in which deer were hunted had a significant impact on the physical landscape. Deliberate fires were commonly used as deer drives in the Eastern Woodlands. The Chickasaws were described as creating fire rings six to eight kilometers in circumference that were used to corral deer in the center (Nairne 1988 [1708]:52), and Indians in the Carolinas drove deer into constrained necks of land with similar large-scale fires (Lawson 1967 [1709]:215–216). These may have been age-old practices.

But pollen diagram samples from the Southeast exhibit an increase in fire-resistant tree species in the 1700s along with a decrease in non-resistant species; in the same time frame, there is a noticeable increase of charcoal abundance in soil samples (Foster and Cohen 2007). Managed fires, along with the introduction of firearms, eventually took a toll on both deer and human populations. Deer herds in the Piedmont were notably declining as early as the 1720s, and there are accounts of related food shortages from loss of game (Silver 1990:92–94). Aside from the overharvesting of deer, there were likely many other indirect ecological impacts that can only be crudely assessed. Paulett (2012:130) estimates that there were probably two to three thousand pack horses a year serving Cherokee, Creek, and Chickasaw settlements at the height of the hide trade.

The consequences of the deerskin trade were uneven across the Southeast since not all Native American groups chose to participate equally. Nor were all European colonies equally involved. For example, the Quapaws in the Lower Arkansas Valley may have adopted cosmopolitan consumption habits, but their rich subsistence economy and distance from Europeans in the interior provided less of an incentive to intensively hunt deer except to trade for highly coveted items like firearms (DuVal 2006:76–83). The English dominance of the deerskin trade can overshadow the roles of the French and Spanish colonies and their Indian allies. Spanish Florida was engaged in the exchange of deerskins by the early 1600s when English colonials were only a negligible presence in North America, and the colony remained steadily involved in this trade throughout the century (Waselkov 1989b). The Apalachees in particular were dedicated to trading for deerskins with their northerly middleman neighbors, the Apalachicolas. But the rise of the English-instigated Indian slave trade in the late 1600s essentially priced the Apalachees out of the business. Apalachicolas found capturing humans so lucrative that they would only accept horses, guns, or silver—the inflationary currency of the slave trade—in exchange for deerskins (Waselkov 1989b:120).

French Louisiana avidly sought to engage the deerskin trade by establishing interior outposts and storehouses, including one in 1714 in Natchez territory and another in 1716 on the Red River in Caddo country (Usner 1998:59). The French benefited from the temporary collapse of the English-dominated trade during the Yamasee War. With the deaths or ouster of English traders from the Upper Creek villages, Indians began to port deerskins south to Mobile. Fort Toulouse was constructed in 1717 among the Upper Creeks at the invitation of the Alabamas and Tallapoosas (Waselkov and Smith 2000:249), becoming another important way station. Deerskins were so important to the Louisiana economy that even settlers relied upon them as a unit of barter to buy imported goods (Usner 1998:63). The demise of the French role in this network was due more to political rather than economic factors, since the loss of Louisiana was one of the costs of the Seven Years War.

European geopolitical landscapes also were altered by the deerskin trade. Among the English colonies, competition to gain favored access to Indian peoples dedicated to hunting deer led to considerable geographic and temporal variation in the movement of deerskins, as well as the fortunes of individuals and towns. The founding of Georgia by James Oglethorpe in 1732 signaled a major transformation in the multipronged approach toward the transportation of deerskins to Charles Town. Like the other Atlantic Seaboard colonies in their early phases, Georgia's core consisted of a major town near the ocean—Savannah, established in 1733—surrounded by plantations and farmsteads. Oglethorpe early on realized that successful trade with Indians in the interior would be necessary for the economic success of his struggling colony (Paulett 2012). To his good fortune, a splinter group from the Lower Creek towns known as the Yamacraws had already settled the lower Savannah River bluffs a few years before the arrival of the new colonists (Swanton 1922:108–109). Oglethorpe's cordial relations with this group facilitated his communications and trade endeavors with the major Creek towns in the interior.

In a bold move to insert Georgia into the thick of the deerskin trade, Oglethorpe established a fort on the Fall Line zone near the Savannah River in 1735, about 190 kilometers from Savannah. Augusta, the community that grew up around this fort, straddled the major overland route from Charles Town to Creek and Chickasaw country. Its location to the immediate west of the trade outposts of Fort Moore and Savano Town (now New Windsor) had the effect of wresting from South Carolina a crucial hinge point in the movement of deerskins toward the coast. It also served as a staging area for moving deerskins from pack trains onto boats going down the Savannah River to the ports of Savannah and Charles Town. Augusta was a town built specifically for this trade, and its rapid rise to prominence transformed it into a hub for the routinized transport of deerskins from Indian territories to the coast from the 1730s to the 1770s (Paulett 2012:79).

In 1763, the direction of the deerskin trade made another pirouette, this time from the Atlantic Seaboard to Pensacola, Florida. After Florida had been ceded to Great Britain following the Seven Years War, it provided the English for the first time a colony with a direct trade outlet to the Gulf of Mexico. Another outcome of the war was that rules on the licensing of traders were relaxed. This had the effect of opening up the territory north and west of Augusta to European settlers—which quickly became a flashpoint for conflict since Creeks considered this their territory (Paulett 2012:42). This may have led to the account of an Indian town on the Oconee River in north Georgia being burned in 1767 (Cashin 1986:50).

The deerskin trade provided a major conduit between southeastern Native Americans and their growing economic articulation with the Atlantic World. As global economies became more tightly bound through improvements in travel logistics and the early stirrings of large-scale manufacturing in the 1700s, Indigenous consumers found themselves participating in the growing Consumer Revolution that provided the impetus for the Industrial Revolution to come. With deerskins serving as a pivotal currency, kettles, scissors, cloth, alcohol, firearms, and an enormous variety of other commodities circulated with ever-increasing abundance and distance within the Southeast. The effective economic landscape of Native Americans now extended to the Caribbean, Africa, and Europe.

At the same time, the deerskin trade introduced a jarring note of socioeconomic entropy into the lived landscapes of Native Americans. As it became inscribed as a way of life across much of the Southeast, the social and economic well-being of Native American communities became increasingly subject to manipulations of credit and debt, mounting dependence on goods produced elsewhere, undermining of matrilocal and matrilineal ties, overharvesting of deer, unpredictable fluctuations in demand, and the reorientation of trade routes due to unforeseen regional and global conflicts. As the eighteenth century wore on, Native Americans increasingly faced the same conundrum encountered by modern nation-states largely dependent on export commodities to fuel the economy. As either the supply of, or demand for, those basic goods fluctuates, the repercussions are felt throughout all aspects of society. The centrality of the deerskin trade held many Native American lives in thrall to a Henry Wadsworth Longfellow paradigm: when the deerskin trade was good, life was very good indeed, but when the deerskin trade was bad, life was horrid.

Disciplining the Landscape

The horrid aspects of the vicissitudes of the deerskin trade became especially acute following the Revolutionary War. Several outcomes, large and small, worked in concert to undermine an economic system that was already faltering because of the decline of deer populations: many of the individual traders were Loyalists and lost their property even if they were lucky enough to escape with their lives; the Treaty of Paris banned commercial trade between Great Britain and the United States, severing the primary logistical link for the transport of deerskins to Europe; and the lines of credit from English banks that buttressed the trade were likewise broken (Braund 1993:169–170; Ethridge 2003:11). Adding to this misery, the war itself took a heavy toll on the stability of Native American settlements and economies. To reinvigorate the trade in deerskins (and other items), in 1795 the United States established a factory system (trade outposts under governmental oversight) that inserted the nation into the regulation of trade with Indians (Ethridge 2003:11; Nassaney 2015; Usner 1998:75–77). Even this move, however, could not reverse the laws of supply and demand. So Native Americans turned increasingly to private farms, with considerable encouragement from the United States. Meanwhile, all of the organized Native American groups were steadily forced to make large cessions of traditional territories to states and the federal government. The combined loss of lands and movement to family farms represented one of the more profound changes in their landscape histories.

But here I am getting ahead of myself. The actions of the United States merely accelerated a long-term trend toward the market economy that had begun decades earlier throughout the Atlantic World. Capitalism and the Industrial Revolution came to maturity in the nineteenth century based on a vast terrain of interlocked micro political–economic histories. In other words, the global market economy was not a monolithic phenomenon that was draconically imposed by Great Britian and other European powers on their possessions. The emerging tenets of neoliberalism may have been carried to various corners of the globe by European administrators and entrepreneurs, but these principles were continually reworked locally in political, economic, and social transactions between colonizers and Indigenous peoples. As I proposed in the first chapter, what arose was not capitalism but capitalisms.

The central role that local peoples played in the early evolution of capitalisms worldwide is illustrated by the engagements between Native Americans and South Carolina over the deer trade. As we have already seen, following the founding of Carolina in 1670, Charles Town quickly rose to prominence as a major export center for Native American slaves and deerskins. This ascension involved external and internal sources of tension. First, there was the rising ire of Native Americans against a colonial administration that reluctantly redressed their grievances against the violence and financial chicanery of English traders—the fuse that lit the Yamasee War. Second, the colonial administration and independent traders rapidly became embroiled in a long-term feud over the control of the lucrative wealth to be gained from the deerskin trade.

This intracolonial feud was expressed in the now-familiar antagonisms over the benefits of a laissez-faire versus a Keynesian managed economy (Cobb and DePratter 2016). Independent traders resented the licensing system and regulations that they believed fettered their practices and profits. Colonial administrators, concerned about continuous Indian complaints about traders' abuses and further hoping to siphon some of the wealth in deerskins, made several unsuccessful efforts to centralize that trade in the early decades of the colony. The disastrous Yamasee War gave Charles Town the excuse to enact a public monopoly over the deerskin trade in 1718. Management through the landscape was central to this policy.

During the onset and immediate aftermath of the conflict, South Carolina built several modest installations along an arc of what was perceived to be the general bounds of the colony (figure 6.3) (Cobb and Sapp 2015; Ivers 1970; Stewart and Cobb 2018). Fort Palachacolas, Fort Moore, Fort Congaree, and other outposts were typically placed at towns that had recently been deserted by Native Americans as they retreated further into the interior to avoid the conflict. These were locations that were particularly convenient for the Carolinians since the abandoned towns and agricultural fields comprised pre-cleared landscapes at strategic junctures of major drainages and well-traveled roads. The Carolina forts were nominally outfitted as military outposts, but they were also explicitly designed as trade factors with Native Americans—harbingers of the factors that the United States would establish in the following century. With the Yamasee War threatening to bankrupt South Carolina, officials worked diligently to regain the friendship of many of the peoples who had recently turned

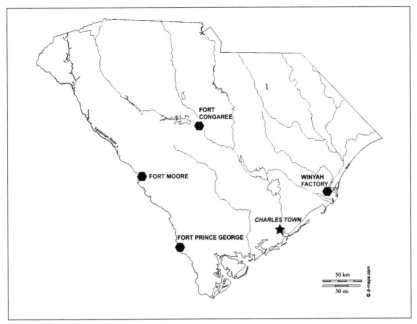

Figure 6.3. Major frontier installations in Carolina built during and immediately after the Yamasee War (adapted from d-maps.com/carte. php?num_car=19845&lang=en>).

on the colony. In pragmatic recognition of economic expediency, the officers assigned to command the forts were assigned the dual tasks of protecting the colony and providing a way station for the conduit of hides to Charles Town.

With the memory of the recent war in mind, the forts stood as both beacon and barrier: Native Americans could port deerskins in large numbers to the factors in exchange for a rich variety of goods brought from Charles Town, but without advancing any closer to the Low Country or the city itself. As a consequence, the forts also became strategic outposts for Native American habitations. Investigations at locations surrounding Fort Palachacolas and Fort Congaree have revealed concentrations of eighteenth-century Indigenous pottery accompanied by evidence for trade muskets (thin-gauge butt plates, 0.54 caliber musket balls), gunflints, bottle glass, European ceramics, and other signatures of settlements that had grown up around the forts (Cobb and DePratter 2016; Stewart and Cobb 2018). Whether they were temporary, seasonal habitations related to the deerskin trade or more permanent occupations is unclear. But it does seem that with the increased mobility of many Native American communities resulting from the growing emphasis on seasonally taking deer, Native Americans had in a sense appropriated European frontier forts and incorporated them into a logistical system of movement reminiscent of Binford's (1980) classic hunting and gathering model (Cobb 2019).

Excavations at Fort Moore underscore the dialectical spatial relationship between Native Americans and Carolina colonials (figure 6.4). This work revealed a small trade building attached to the entrance of the installation (Pohlemus 1971). As outlined by colonial policy, these were areas where hides could be exchanged for commodities without allowing Native Americans into the fort proper. However, there were also smudge pits inside the perimeters of the fort. If these were used for hide processing, a task normally allocated to Native American women, it would suggest that the segregationist policies emanating from colonial offices were ignored on the frontier (Cobb and Sapp 2014:223). The discovery of the grave of a Native American adult and child within the confines of the fort further emphasizes the social and physical porosity of the fort's defenses.

The Carolina public monopoly was short lived. Although it originally enjoyed support from merchants and planters, it was rescinded in 1722 under a continuing barrage of criticism from within the colony from traders and prominent individuals anxious to reestablish lucrative trading relationships in the interior (Stewart 2013). But the conflict over the role of the factors was as much ideological as purely economic. Many Enlightenment thinkers (as well as self-interested traders) believed that the state should not interfere with what were perceived as natural laws of economic behavior. The campaign to deregulate the deerskin trade encapsulated Bernard Mandeville's (1924 [1705]) maxim from the *Fable of the Bees* over a decade earlier that "self love works for the common good," presaging the writings of Adam Smith. Practically speaking, the end of the monopoly may have boosted the economy of South Carolina. Yet this action once again made Native Americans reliant on the deerskin trade vulnerable to the economic predations of individual colonial traders.

With the steep decline in the deerskin trade later in the century, land became the primary commodity held by Indians that whetted the appetite of a rapidly growing nation-state. As Vine Deloria (1969), among many other Native American activists, has bitterly observed, the political landscape of broken treaties and forced land cessions led to the appropriation

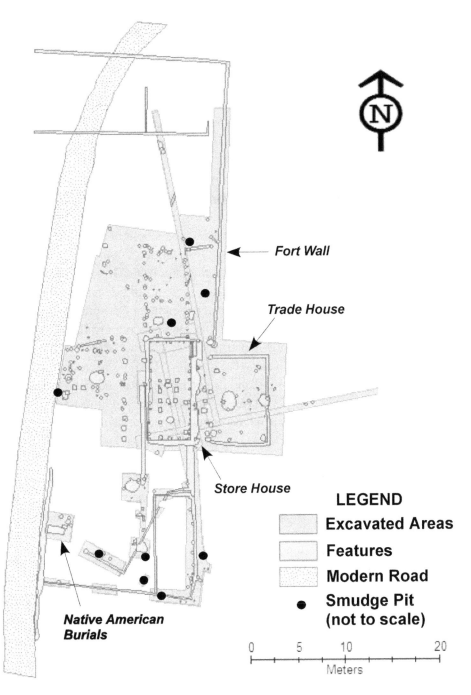

Figure 6.4. Ft. Moore as revealed through archaeological investigations (courtesy of the South Carolina Institute of Archaeology and Anthropology).

of millions of acres of Indian territory by state and federal governments throughout what would become the United States. This process was already well underway in the Southeast by the time the articles of the American constitution had been drafted. Following the Seven Years War, in 1763 the Creeks formally ceded a significant portion of their hunting grounds to the colony of Georgia (Hahn 2004:2). A decade later, the Creeks and Cherokees gave up 2.5 million acres of common hunting grounds in the complex New Purchase Treaty of 1773 (Juricek 2015), and the Cherokees deeded large tracts to colonial governments prior to the Revolutionary War. These and similar agreements elsewhere in the Southeast were met with anger by many Native peoples, particularly along intergenerational lines as a younger age group felt betrayed by the actions of the elders who had signed the cessions (Hahn 2004:48, 175; Schroedl 2000:227).

By virtue of these actions throughout the latter 1700s, Great Britain and the United States had introduced a new export to Indian territory that would have profound implications for the structure of the pre-Removal landscape: the emerging ideology of the market economy. The large-scale land grabs are typically construed by scholars as one outcome of res nullius and manifest destiny—the prevailing idea of the era that Native Americans were not using land to its full potential and thus should be willing to share it with—or lose it to—those who could most capably parse it into private plots for intensive cultivation and livestock rearing (Gosden 2004:27–28).

An alternative route to an "efficient" use of the landscape was to introduce Native Americans to the philosophy of the invisible hand of the economy so that they themselves would adopt Western practices. For Europeans and Euro-Americans of the late eighteenth and early nineteenth centuries, this path fell under the rubric of "civilizing" the Indians. For the avatars of the newly emerging market economy among the southeastern tribes, traders like James Adair and Indian agents like Benjamin Hawkins, a so-called improved landscape with fenced fields and orderly rows of crops was the sine qua non of civilization. Speaking approvingly of one Chickasaw landowner, Bernard Romans observed that he had a plantation with cattle worked by "negroe" slaves: "the savages . . . must soon generally give into this way of life for their own preservation, or else remove further from us" (Romans 1999 [1775]:128). This worldview moved to the forefront of colonial and later United States Indian policy from the eighteenth to nineteenth centuries.

By the time of George Washington's administration in the 1790s, the large amount of southern territory still remaining in Indian hands presented a pressing major political and economic headache. The Creek Nation and the state of Georgia in particular were in a chronic state of antagonism as the Creeks struggled to ward off demands for their substantial lands (Saunt 1999). Washington's secretary of war Henry Knox was charged with developing a civilization policy for Native Americans that might placate all sides (Riggs 2017:3). Although Knox envisioned "Missionaries of excellent moral character" as playing a key role in this policy, Benjamin Hawkins took the lead in promoting assimilation when he was appointed agent to the southern Indians in 1796. As Ethridge (2003:15–16) has pointed out, it is problematic to pass judgment on Hawkins' motives and biases from a twenty-first century perspective. On the one hand, he was guided by Enlightenment ideals of progress as shaped toward American expansionism; yet on the other, he was a staunch advocate for Native Americans and their well-being. Hawkins did try to play a strong role in prompting the Creeks in particular to adopt Western practices in a number of domains.

The success of Hawkins's civilization efforts are difficult to gauge because significant shifts toward privatization and nuclear-family farms were already well underway by the time he took office (Ethridge 2003; Saunt 1999). A pre-European landscape dominated by mound centers and nucleated towns ceded to one dominated by *talwas*, which in turn was replaced by the dissemination of individual homesteads and occasional Indian-owned trading posts and plantations. The net result of these trends was an Indigenous landscape after the Revolutionary War that was decreasingly communal and increasingly compartmentalized. Because of land loss and inducements to alter traditional lifestyles, extensive hunting territories and broad agricultural fields had been reworked into individual farms. "An economic survey of the Chickasaw Nation in 1827 revealed that the typical full-blood household contained five members and owned two horses, two cows, five hogs, and a small flock of poultry. The old family compound—a round winter house, a rectangular summer house, and smaller service structures—had been replaced by the familiar log cabin" (Gibson 1971:129–130). It is difficult to assign a precise chronology to this process except to say that it accelerated dramatically and spread rapidly at the close of the eighteenth century (Johnson 2000:108; Waselkov 1997:187–190; Waselkov and Smith 2000:244). In line with these changes,

Saunt (1999:172–175) describes the first fences as appearing among the Creeks in the 1760s and being commonplace by the turn of the century. Cameron Wesson's (2008) innovative longitudinal archaeological study of Creek households demonstrates the cultural depth of these changes. He argues that there were marked shifts in the ideologies of everyday practices corresponding with the larger political and economic transformations in the Southeast. There was, for instance, an apparent widening in the access to prestige goods through time in households, perhaps a function of the decline of ascribed status and the rise of status achieved through the competitiveness of the deerskin trade and other trading venues. Further, there was a general decrease in domestic space through time that seems to relate to the rising importance of the nuclear family, as well as the spread of relatively independent homesteads. By the 1830s, the latter were manifested in hewn-log cabins typical of European farm houses. Similar transitions can be seen in the archaeology of the Cherokee (e.g., Schroedl 1986).

The concern with privatization and privacy extended to individual possessions. Parallel to the trend in fencing, historical descriptions of the era indicate that the use of padlocks increased dramatically in the late 1700s (Saunt 1999:175–176). This pattern is reflected archaeologically, as padlocks begin to appear with more frequency on sites dating to the same time period (Waselkov 1997). This stands in stark contrast to the view of locks only a few decades earlier, when there are accounts of Indians physically attacking the doors and locks of the houses of European traders in their communities because they symbolized a violation of the norms of hospitality and fair exchange practices (Paulett 2012:167). It is interesting that several padlocks were included with an infant burial at Fort Moore, which likely would have dated to earlier in the century (Cobb and Sapp 2014). This pattern of use may reflect the common trajectory of sacred to profane seen in many other categories of objects of European origin.

Archaeological and ethnohistorical investigations of Indigenous domestic buildings dating to the early nineteenth century converge with historical descriptions of their similarity to European houses, while also showing some points of contrast (Riggs 1999; Waselkov and Smith 2000:255). The archetypical horizontal-log architecture popularly associated with American pioneers was widely adopted, oftentimes accompanied by a basement or root cellar. Brett Riggs' (1999) work on Cherokee households has resulted in the one multiple-site, systematic regional study of this era. He found the sites to be small, on the order of 200–1,000 m^2, adjoining rich tracts of arable land, and near perennial water sources. Interestingly, the small site-size combined with the modest abundance of artifacts led Riggs (1999:514) to propose that the Cherokees may have maintained a pattern of shifting, swidden agriculture. The material culture on these homesteads reflects a strong infusion of Euro-American objects into both domestic and work activities. The Cherokee Christy Cabin site yielded the remains of Native vessels that Riggs posits were pans and jars used for the preparing and serving of traditional foods like hominy and sour corn mush. In a way, these domestic buildings were a kind of simulacrum of the assimilation process in the Southeast. By surface appearances, they may have looked like a traditional Western style homestead, but they continued to embody selected Indigenous practices and predilections.

The diligent research of Rufus Ward, an avocational historian from Columbus, Mississippi, recently brought to my attention the fascinating account of a missionary from the Mayhew Mission to the Choctaws, who was invited to dine with Moshulitubbee, one of the chiefs ("king" in his words), in 1822:

> The king's house has three apartments. In front is a piazza about 10 feet by 25. The piazza is floored with plank. After accomplishing some business with the king we walked out to view his fields, flocks and herds. He gave orders to one of his sons and some laborers to kill an ox. We then waked [*sic*] into the piazza and passed an hour in miscellaneous conversation. The king remarked that a big council had been recently holden at his house, and no whiskey was drank on the occasion. The interpreter at length informed us that supper was ready. On entering the room I was not a little surprised to see a table set in so much order. A neat linen was spread over the table, and on it was some of the fatted ox, well cooked. Also sweet potatoes, corn bread, imported tea, and wild honey. The only thing that was Choctaw was a large native bowl of tomfullah [a form of corn mush], with two spoons made of the horns of a buffalo. (*The Dispatch*, August 13, 2018)

The account is just as fascinating for what it does not tell us as what it does. Was the meal in a sense a performance, where Moshulitubbee was attempting to make his guest feel at home by providing a familiar dining environment, material culture and all? Did Moshulitubbee dine like this on a regular basis by virtue of his status, whereas lower-income Choctaw households and practices retained more traditional features? Why would a traditional corn mush and serving bowl be the one representative Native American dish at the meal? Barring more exhaustive and comparative archaeological research on pre-Removal households, we really have no firm grasp of the penetration of Western practices and beliefs at this point in time.

Here we come full circle back to the theme of chapter 3 and the material and ideal concordance of the landscape. The rise of the free market economy is inextricably bound to transformations in landscape traditions and ideologies. The individual ownership of property and associated practices, such as fencing and enclosure of the land, correspond with the rising importance of privacy and the segmentation of extended families (M. Johnson 1996). These beliefs and practices are a stark contrast to the deep histories of social organization in the Southeast. But it is not clear to what extent, and how variably, Native Americans were "buying in" to this worldview, making pragmatic adjustments to rapidly changing political and economic conditions, or some combination of the two. From the point of view of the United States government, however, the southeastern landscape had become a testing ground for a battle over the hearts and minds of Indigenous peoples that would be played out again in the Vietnam War two centuries later: when facing difficulties gaining territory, try to convince the locals to become more like you.

A major push in this direction, again under the aegis of assimilation, occurred in 1819 when the US government passed the Civilization Fund Act (Prucha 2000). This law differed from earlier government plans to impose assimilation on Native American communities by resuscitating Henry Knox's ideas on missionization and calling on churches to partner formally in these efforts. In return, the government provided religious denominations an annuity to assist in the construction and maintenance of schools to provide Native American children with Western educations. This edict was the legal expression of a growing philosophy in nineteenth-century Europe and North America that viewed secular and moral economies as corollaries: material bounty was a manifestation of Christian faithfulness and personal industriousness (Comaroff and Comaroff 1991; Maxwell 1998; Neylan 2000; Pickering 2004). The Civilization Fund Act led to a proliferation of missions from a variety of denominations within the territories of all of the major Native American peoples.

Figure 6.5. Brafferton building and Indian school at the College of William and Mary (courtesy of commons.wikimedia.org/wiki/User:Smash_the_Iron_Cage; License: creativecommons.org/licenses/by-sa/4.0/deed.en).

One can see earlier stirrings in this direction with the activities of the Society for the Propagation of the Gospel in the Southeast (Wright 1981). This arm of the Anglican Church was established in the late 1600s with the twin goals of evangelizing and civilizing non-Western peoples. Its adherents were unsuccessful at developing missions in Indian lands, but they did manage to create a few Indian schools. These were institutions within colonial settlements that attempted to train Indigenous children in so-called industrial arts: Western-style farming, blacksmithing, sewing, and so on.

A well-known example of this effort is the Brafferton Indian School within the College of William and Mary in Virginia. It has been pointed out that the school building, a grand Georgian mansion built in 1723 and still standing today, is in itself an artifact (Moretti-Langholtz and Woodard 2017) (figure 6.5). The mansion style embodies the argument made famous by James Deetz (1977, 1996; see also Leone 1988) that in the Anglo colonial sphere, the material practices surrounding the Georgian world-view in the 1700s laid the foundation for the precepts of modernity and capitalism: a concern with management and order, a valorization of the individual, and the rise of private property. Many historical archaeologists have since demonstrated that the Georgian mind-set was indeed a powerful ideology, but it was far from uniform; it was variably received (and rejected) and reworked by Euro-American, European, African American, and Indigenous cultures (Leone 2005; Matthews 2010). Excavations at the Brafferton school carried out in 2011 and 2012 underscore this point. These recovered several examples of glass wine bottles and stemware that had been knapped into cutting implements by children apparently intent on sustaining tradition in a milieu meant to erase it (Moretti-Langholtz and Woodard 2017).

Although the success of efforts like the Brafferton school was equivocal, the passage of the 1819 Civilization Fund Act sparked a revival in the outreach of Protestant missionaries to southeastern Indians (Hiemstra 1959; Thompson 1934; Tinker 1993). The missionaries followed in the footsteps of their predecessors by building missions with schools that combined education, proselytization, and practical endeavors in farming and cottage industries (Spring 2000; Tinker 1993). The new missions differed from those in colonial times in that they were placed within Native American territories at the express invitation of the various nations (Charity Hall, described in chapter 3, is one such example). As a result, the colonial- and federal-era schools represented landscape inversions of one another. The earlier Indian schools like Brafferton were outside of traditional homelands and the transported children were more easily isolated from their traditions. In contrast, the Indian schools built as a consequence of the Civilization Fund Act were enveloped within Native territories. Accordingly, missionaries found it more difficult to shield their wards from the influences of their families and cultures, although not from lack of trying. The Caney Creek mission to the Chickasaws was built 64 kilometers away from the nearest Native town because of the concern over continuing "heathenish influences" on the children (Gibson 1971:112).

Very little archaeological study has been conducted at these fascinating spiritual workshops of capitalism. Brett Riggs (2017) has investigated the Valley Towns Baptist Mission among the Cherokees in North Carolina, which was in operation from 1821 to 1836. His documentary research shows that the complex was fairly extensive. In addition to the school house, it included many accoutrements of vocational training such as a blacksmith's shop, a sawmill, and a gristmill. The archaeological materials are not too surprising in terms of what is present, such as numerous sherds from European and American ceramics and architectural remains in the form of nails and window glass. But the artifact assemblage is particularly intriguing in terms of what is absent. Given missionary prohibitions on inappropriate behaviors, no smoking-related artifacts, remains of alcohol containers, or components of weapons were found. Equally interesting was the recovery of a small number of Catawba pottery sherds, which Riggs hypothesizes may reflect the use of traditional processing containers by Native American cooks who worked at the mission.

For the sake of balance, it should be emphasized that there were a considerable number of Euro-Americans in the Southeast that the government thought also required the guiding hand of civilization (Saunt 1999:165–167). These individuals eschewed the traditional farmstead, relying heavily on hunting, some livestock tending, and even raiding Euro-American frontier settlements. The difference between these rural Euro-Americans and Native Americans, at least in the eyes of the reformers, was that the former were viewed as evolutionary backsliders, whereas Native Americans were considered as leaning inherently toward this kind of life. The use of the derogatory term "white Indian" (Saunt 1999:165) emphasizes this point by reversing the normal emphasis of adjective and noun. Instead of an Indian become white, the white subject has been tainted by the primitive qualities of the Indian way of living in the landscape.

The transition to a market-based economy among Native Americans was often spearheaded by those of mixed ancestry, or Métis, individuals who had a foot in both Indian and Western worlds (Ethridge 2003; Saunt 1999; Waselkov 1997). They were reared in culturally plural households, had Indigenous kinship ties, and were typically fluent in two or more languages. At the same time, they were conversant in the marketing practices of the Atlantic World. Some of these persons were the offspring of Native American females and European or Euro-American males who were traders. The result was a cultural broker who often was linked through matrilineal ties to powerful clans and through their fathers to important trading houses like Panton, Leslie and Company. Others had mixed-blood parentage on both sides but still maintained a cultural fluency in both Native American and Western traditions. This new generation emerging in the latter half of the eighteenth century represented early adopters of notions of private property and new approaches toward farming and ranching. Alexander McGillivray among the Creeks, James Vann among the Cherokees, Levi Colbert among the Chickasaws, and others like them were able to leverage their relationships and knowledge to amass considerable wealth and political power among their Native peoples (Ethridge 2003:11–12; Saunt 1999:42). Such individuals were often resented by traditionalists, and their increasing prominence introduced a racialized edge to the newly emerging privatized landscapes in Indian territory (Schroedl 2000). This schism created even sharper divides when these cultural brokers began acquiring black slaves to work their plantations and enterprises (Braund 1991; Krauthamer 2013; Perdue 1987).

Capitalism had now introduced another transformation in the history of social inequality among southeastern Indians. Mississippian chiefs who mobilized power through agricultural produce and other forms of tribute gave way to enterprising individuals taking advantage of the Indian slave and deerskin trades. They, in turn, were replaced by entrepreneurs leveraging the rising availability of private land and other resources once owned communally. Certainly, other axes of power along gender and kinship lines continued to be important throughout all of these transitions, but the political economy of southeastern landscapes continued to experience dramatic changes in concert with shifts in the larger Atlantic World.

As seen with nineteenth-century farmsteads, these changes did not entail wholesale borrowings of Western ways. Hybrid practices continued to draw from the old and the new and inserted a distinctive Native American agency into the landscape of privatization. In an interesting repeat of history, this era saw the reemergence of what might be viewed as vacant ceremonial centers. As opposed to a settlement that is simply abandoned, in Mississippian-period archaeology this term implies loci that likely had only a small caretaker population and may have served as a religious gathering place for outlying populations on a periodic basis (e.g., Boudreaux 2013; Kassabaum 2018; Rafferty 1995). Some towns seem to have been deliberately built as vacant ceremonial centers, whereas others evolved into this kind of status. Moundville (Alabama), for example, once a thriving Mississippian town, was transformed into a necropolis sometime in the 1300s CE (Blitz 2010). Its residents apparently dispersed to outlying areas and only used the center to bury their dead and conduct accompanying rituals.

Native Americans resurrected this practice with the rise of the market economy, albeit in a somewhat altered form. Across Creek, Cherokee, Chickasaw, and other lands, important villages with their council houses and related political and ceremonial functions remained nominally intact even as their residents radiated out to surrounding farms (Schroedl 2000). By the early 1800s, the Cherokees were beginning to consider the "town, not as a place, but as a group of people sharing the same ceremonial and council center" (Persico 1979:106). Dr. Rush Nutt (Jennings 1947) traveled through Chickasaw territory in 1805 and recorded the following in his journal:

> [Pontatock] contains ninety three men, 99 women, & 67 Children agreeable to the numbers given in last august, when receiving their annual Stipend. Altho the above number is stated as belonging to the village or settlement of Pontatock, not more than 8 families remain in or near the village, they have settled 50 or more miles round promisicuously through their country. . . . In the year 1797 the whole nation was contained (or nearly so) in these old towns, but by the advice of the agent & other officers of the government, they have settled out, made comfortable cabins, enclosed their fields by a worm fence, & enjoy the benefits of their labour, & stock, and are measurably clothed by their own industry.

The evolution of core villages to vacant ceremonial centers was an important manifestation of the fact that Native Americans would make compromises with American-style capitalism, but those concessions would still be phrased through Indigenous practices and beliefs. New landscapes of hybrid households and de-centered towns were a powerful materialization of the autonomy that would be retained by Native Americans. But there were significant social consequences to these developments. The separation of everyday living space from the sacred loci associated with major towns may have been another significant break in the history of leadership tied to otherworldly knowledge (Wesson 2008:138). Even the sheer challenge of getting people from dispersed farmsteads to congregate at a regional center weakened the power of town councils and traditional venues of public deliberation (Persico 1979:106). Nevertheless, these new landscapes and their inhabitants were still significantly different from their Euro-American neighbors. As a result, they constituted a metonym of otherness that would continue to fuel the anti-Native American antagonism of the citizens and institutions of the United States.

Conclusion

Native American political ecologies were greatly shaped in response to the power of nature. As powerful as those forces were, Native Americans were not held hostage to them. Mississippian societies did not collapse from climatic or environmental change, but they did undergo significant transformations and relocations as they adapted to changing conditions. The Little Ice Age and volcanic eruptions continued to intervene in human activities as colonial powers attempted to make their own imprint on southeastern landscapes. As Europeans became an ever-greater presence in the region, Indigenous subsistence practices still proved remarkably resilient and resistant to change. By the 1700s, the combined weight of market forces and encroaching Atlantic Seaboard and Gulf Coast colonies were leading Native Americans to choose socioeconomic strategies like the deerskin trade that subverted venerable institutions of authority and tradition. As privatization and enclosure were adopted in Indigenous territories, Native American and Euro-American political economies began to reflect their greatest historical convergence. Nevertheless, Native Americans continued to assiduously pursue autonomy in the midst of these transformations. This strategy continued to mold unique landscape biographies, but it also was met with an attitude of fear and bigotry by the federal government and individual states that would have catastrophic consequences.

Apocalypse Now and Then?

A certain air of finality descended upon Indigenous landscapes in the Southeast on May 28, 1830. On that day, United States President Andrew Jackson signed the Indian Removal Act, setting the stage to transform the contested landscape of the region into a landscape of clearance. This law mandated that tribes east of the Mississippi River move to unsettled lands west of the river. Those unsettled lands effectively became the territory of Oklahoma. By the end of the decade, tens of thousands of Native Americans from throughout eastern North America had relocated, many forcibly, from lands occupied by their ancestors for millennia. It should be emphasized that there were exceptions to the Removal Act. The various Haudenosaunee groups in New York retained modest reservations, as just one notable example. In the Southeast, through complicated histories after the 1830s, groups like the Catawbas, the Seminoles, and the Eastern Band of Cherokees managed to emerge in control of some of their core lands. But the federal government did achieve its aims of opening up huge swaths of land to speculators, industrialists, homesteaders, plantation owners, and states anxious to expand their boundaries.

With historical hindsight, the Indigenous landscape narratives of the colonial Southeast can take on somewhat of a teleological and disheartening cast. Even given the considerable agency of Native American peoples, colonialism etched a topography with deep cultural, emotional, social, physical, and demographic scars that can seem somewhat inevitable given the larger course of industrialization, the proliferation of private farms and large estates, the growth of nation-states, and globalization. Over the last 500 years, southeastern Native Americans share a landscape history of dispossession with Native peoples in Australia, New Zealand, Hawaii, Africa, and elsewhere in the Americas. We have to be wary, however, of presuming that colonialism instigated a complete disruption with the past or that Removal effectively ended engagements with the southeastern landscape for those who departed. This attitude does seem to be common in archaeological and ethnohistorical discourse, at least with regard to the transformation from Mississippian to colonial Indigenous societies. As just a few examples:

- "Such a broad temporal parameter [1540–1730 CE] is necessary to cover the complete collapse of the Mississippian world and the full reorganization of the geopolitical landscape that followed" (Ethridge 2009:9).
- "The [Arkansas] Valley changed so dramatically in the following decades that its earlier history is wrapped in haze" (DuVal 2006:61).
- "How do we begin accounting for why and how the Mississippian world was destroyed and its surviving peoples absorbed into the Modern World?" (Hudson 2002:xxii).
- "By the late fifteenth and early sixteenth centuries, these chiefdoms had collapsed" (Saunt 1999:18–19).

The irony here is that all of the individuals just cited have an eminent scholarly history of strong advocacy of a long-term perspective in order to trace Indigenous continuities as well as discontinuities following the arrival of Europeans. They have been key figures in decolonizing modern research on Native American lifeways. So in an empirical sense, these quotations are somewhat of a red herring. Why, then, would we see these kinds of descriptions of such absolute, seismic transformation in the Native American Southeast in the period immediately after the arrival of Europeans? And, it should be pointed out, this is not just a parochial question. Steven Wernke (2007b) shows that in South America, for example, a master narrative of colonial conquest has sublimated the pre-European contact history of various forms of colonization, inequality, and power relations—a history that significantly shaped subsequent colonial histories. Why is before and after 1492 so often portrayed as a study in such stark contrasts rather than persistence in the face of colonial interventions? And why does the appearance of Europeans and the immediate aftermath tend to overshadow the many other significant transformations in southeastern landscapes that occurred with the rise of mercantile and capitalist systems?

Samuel Rose (2017:23) argues that much of the research that privileges an Indigenous vantage point on the post-European contact era falls into a paradoxical trap of the sort embodied in the preceding quotations: "Even within a single work an author can occupy both positions saying that indigenous peoples were profoundly and detrimentally impacted by colonialism, while arguing that indigenous peoples have persisted intact to this day." Part of the challenge is the question of scale. As Ethridge (2009:37) notes, if one undertakes the Charles Hudson approach, then at the level of structural history, it is easier to trace out long-term, general trends that may become increasingly vague as we move to individual case studies. As the coda to this study, I will examine the question of collapse or transformative change in more detail based on the thesis that rather than one transformative event surrounding the arrival of Europeans, there were multiple, interlinked threshold points that altered the land-scape histories of the Southeast.

Revisiting Before and After

In an earlier publication (Cobb 2005), I offered the opinion that we have to adopt a critical stance on the nature of before and after Columbus research in the Americas. It is deceptively easy to proffer stereotypical generalizations about static Indigenous histories that only gained real traction with the appearance of Europeans. Shannon Dawdy (2010) has elegantly subsumed this point under a larger critique of how our research can be influenced by the tenets of an ideology of the inevitable churn of modernity, by which the past is putatively erased by the obliterating force of the present (see also Matthews 2002). As she puts it, modernity fosters a temporal ideology of "we have never been the same again" (Dawdy 2010:763). Scholarship subscribing to this point of view is often attracted to the notion of dramatic ruptures and the assumption of a complete structural reorganization of all that follows: the Protestant Reformation, the French Revolution, the Enlightenment, and, naturally, the arrival of Christopher Columbus in the Western Hemisphere. We can see this perspective with regard to the discovery of the Americas in the popular books *The Columbian Exchange* by Alfred Crosby (1972), the 1492 bookends *1491* and *1493* by Charles Mann (2005, 2012), and Jared Diamond's (2005) *Collapse*.

Given the events and processes I have portrayed in the preceding chapters, it would be disingenuous to argue for a relatively smooth unfolding in the landscape histories of Native societies from the pre-European contact to post-European contact eras. Nevertheless, the idea that the Mississippian world collapsed or was destroyed would seem to push for an extreme in the other direction. This perspective reflects the dystopian perspective common in studies of collapse that has come under criticism by a number of archaeologists in the Southeast (Beck 2013; King 2006; Wesson 2008:xiii–xvi) and elsewhere (Fowles 2015; McAnany and Yoffee 2009). As these reassessments emphasize, collapse too frequently becomes an unexamined trope of change being largely instigated from the outside—whether that be the forces of colonialism or the climate—and significant reorganization may be misunderstood as systemic failure. The drama of collapse also discourages comparative research: how can one relate a before and an after if these phases are conceptualized as so qualitatively different as to be incomparable (Dawdy 2010:765–766; Wesson 2008:xv)? This, of course, is the opposite goal to that foregrounded by Charles Hudson and others who have pursued detailed inquiries of the Mississippian period to post-Mississippian-period trajectory.

In addition to critically examining how southeastern landscapes were transformed from the sixteenth century onward, we need a correspondingly close scrutiny of the centuries immediately preceding the arrival of Europeans. For at least some areas of the Southeast, many of the major shifts that are seen as emblematic of chiefdom collapse from the interventions of Europeans actually preceded the sixteenth century. A case in point is the Chickasaws. As briefly alluded to in the previous chapter, at least some of their ancestral groups seem to have followed an archetypical Mississippian lifestyle in the Tombigbee River Valley of eastern Mississippi. Then, in the 1400s CE, they abandoned their bottomland mound centers and gravitated westward to the Black Prairie, where it is possible they joined smaller Mississippian communities already occupying that physiographic region. At the same time, both the settlement pattern and the political structure appear to have become more decentralized. In the words of Jay Johnson (2000:89–90): "If the Chickasaws at the time of contact were not completely a tribe, they were certainly something less than the full-fledged chiefdoms of the Mississippian period. And the archaeological data clearly indicate that this reorientation of settlement and social organization preceded the entrance of Europeans into the Southeast."

Given this evidence for chiefly "devolution," terms like collapse or disaster imply an erasure of pre-European-contact political complexity that can be exaggerated. Further, in and of themselves, such concepts do not provide much nuanced insight into the various levers that prompted dramatic change in the landscapes of the Southeast—except to say that change was dramatic. Lastly, by their recurrent application primarily to the demise of Mississippian chiefdoms, these expressions draw attention away from some of the profound inflection points in subsequent Indigenous histories; they emphasize rupture as a singularity rather than a plurality. Roberto Barrios (2017) observes that anthropology has a long history of addressing catastrophes, disasters, and crises. He points out that terminology does matter. We need to be more critical in our use of such words since they can be freighted with meaning that can turn our attention away from the historical nuance required to understand how so-called catastrophes may be differentially experienced and interpreted and how they may differ in their roles in social change. I hope that what this book has demonstrated is that what we really see in the Southeast are multiple, historically braided landscape transformations through time rather than a single, synchronic one.

In sum, Native American landscape histories were so complicated in their responses to imperial designs that the notion of collapse ultimately becomes a reductionist portrayal of the significant changes that did occur in the 1500s and later. I think it fair to say that Native communities in the colonial Southeast did devote considerable time and effort to warding off the implosion of their communities. But they were also outward looking and creative in their interactions with one another and with other peoples. The transformation of colonial southeastern landscapes was co-authored by many peoples originating from many lands. This collaboration—sometimes forced, sometimes voluntary, sometimes opportunistic—also intersected with the histories of Euro-American and African American landscapes in terms of the larger evolution of modernity and the Atlantic World.

A History of Pivot Points

From the perspective of southeastern landscape histories, there was not just one (Mississippian collapse) or two (Mississippian collapse and Removal) major developments that dramatically altered the physical, social, and cultural lay of the land. Instead, there were at least four pivot points that were experienced unevenly across the region: 1) early colonial landscape clearances and polity contractions linked to epidemic disease and the decline of traditional chiefly power; 2) colonialism from about 1675 to 1750 where landscapes were altered by the deerskin and Indian slave trades, continued warring, advanced coalescence, and the rise of power linked to portable wealth; 3) late colonialism to early federalism marked by the rise of private property, the market economy, and social inequality based on capital and monetary wealth; and 4) landscapes of clearance initiated by the Removal Act and followed by very complex local and regional histories of continuity, planned disappearance, social amnesia, and diasporic relations.

These stages do not represent some sort of evolutionary continuum. To borrow Jorge Luis Borges' well-known titular metaphor, southeastern landscapes were a garden of forking paths, some white, some red, some both, that Native Americans traveled with one another, Europeans, Africans, and other peoples. Cherokees, Creeks, Choctaws, and their neighbors made their own landscape histories along the way, but always in terms of an engagement with an expanding Atlantic World. In a sense, all of these four major transformations could be considered ruptures of some sort. But how profound were they, how was each rupture differentially expressed among different peoples, and how did the history of one rupture potentially segue to another?

In contrast to the more dystopian perspectives on the Mississippian to colonial transition, a number of southeastern ethnohistorians and archaeologists have argued that the similarities between the two eras—especially in terms of political economy and complexity—may be stronger than suspected. While it may be that loyalty to towns and kinship organizations had replaced that to larger political entities of the Mississippian period (Saunt 1999:19), we really have no idea what the primary allegiances were throughout the presumably highly variable chiefdoms of the pre-European contact era. Jon Muller's (1997) overview of Mississippian political economy has led him to argue that we may have overemphasized the ubiquity of advanced Mississippian political complexity (i.e., fealty or obeisance to highly powerful individuals), and Patricia Galloway (1995:111–116) has come to a similar conclusion. This kind of complexity bias may impose stark, artificial contrasts between the Columbian before and after that would certainly accentuate the perception of a massive social breach.

In contrast to the idea that post-Mississippian societies were the result of a broad-spectrum downturn, several archaeologists have argued that Creek social formations in the 1700s exhibited many signs of reconstituted social hierarchy that are consonant with our conceptions of Mississippian complexity (King 2006; Knight 1994; Rodning 2002:158). There are hints that some Lower Chattahoochee towns—notably Coweta and Apalachicola—had several subordinate towns in the late 1600s, leading Steven Hahn (2004:38–39) to observe that perhaps "the Mississippian collapse was incomplete." The trajectory of Cherokee coalescence seems to have gone a similar route (Rodning 2002; Schroedl 2000). They may have had roots in hierarchical chiefdoms prior to the arrival of Europeans, but by the early 1700s had a strongly egalitarian and heterarchical ethos. This, in turn, may have transformed into more distinct lines of inequality through disparities in wealth made available by trade with Europeans.

Adam King (2006:182) makes what I believe is a critical point about the evolution of Creek society. If we view complexity as a multi-threaded process, then not all aspects of Native American society underwent similar degrees of scalar change after the 1400s CE. It would be hard to argue against a demographic collapse in many areas after the first wave of Spanish expeditions and into the 1600s. But political authority varied considerably synchronically as well as diachronically. Complexity is not the same thing as social inequality; the latter is just a component of the former and does not necessarily change in lockstep with all other potential variables of complexity (Paynter 1989). Rather than collapse, the argument—at least in the political sphere—could be made that many areas of the Southeast from the early to late colonial periods simply witnessed a variation on continued oscillations between simple and complex chiefdoms posited by David Anderson (1994b) or dispersed and concentrated forms of chiefly authority by John Blitz (1999) for the Mississippian period. Political authority just may have been manifested in a very different way after Europeans had shifted the landscape of power, but it did not dissipate. The more things change . . .

Because of this shifting political terrain, Robin Beck (2013:195–197) is an advocate of the term chieftancy rather than chiefdom for some of the hierarchical expressions of the later colonial era. He believes, as do others, that Mississippian political-economic power derived in large part from the ability of chiefs to command surplus from agricultural tribute and other means (see chapter 6). With the rise of colonial trade networks and corresponding contraction of the size of polities in the seventeenth century, leaders came to rely more on their ability to control the movement of commodities, especially deerskins and slaves, and the amassing of European objects in return. In making this argument, Beck draws on the distinction between staple finance and wealth finance (sensu D'Altroy and Earle 1985), whereby in chiefdoms, leaders are able to extract surplus labor and tribute from the control of comestibles and basic goods (staple finance), whereas in chieftancies, leaders derive their power from monopolizing the circulation of portable valuables (wealth finance), which may range from sacred objects to primitive forms of currency.

This line of research suggests that social and demographic transitions occurring among Native American societies during the 1600s and 1700s did not necessarily impose a ceiling on the rise of chiefly leaders; they just created new circumstances by which power could be exercised. The increasing importance of various forms of wealth finance over staple finance (but not a complete replacement) in the colonial Southeast was not simply a different route toward power and inequality. This was a saltation toward an unprecedented secularization and commodification of things and land. During the Mississippian period, portable objects of the sort associated with wealth finance, as well as agricultural surplus, were also important in the aggrandizement of individuals. Yet copper plates, shell gorgets, spatulate celts, and other so-called prestige goods were somewhat scarce, symbolically charged items. They were inalienable objects that were endowed with sacred histories and powers (sensu Weiner 1992). That so many of the first European objects in the Southeast became burial furniture suggests that they, too, attained a similar standing (Hally and Smith 2010).

With the slave and deerskin trades, Native Americans had found ways to procure European goods in greater and greater volume. Bartering and standardized rates of exchange replaced the importance of gifting and kinship obligations in the transfer of goods (McDowell 1955:269) (table 7.1). Items like iron axes and chisels that were symbols of prestige in the 1500s had become utilitarian, alienable goods largely stripped of cultural meaning by the 1700s. Joshua Piker (2004:148) frames this as a shift from a religious economy—in which humans attempt to connect to a world

Table 7.1. Example of monopoly exchange rates established at South Carolina factors

Trade Good	No. of Skins	Trade Good	No. of Skins
A gun	16	A Ditto, not laced	12
A Pound of Powder	1	A Yard of Plains or Half Thicks	2
Four pounds bullets or shot	1	A laced Hat	3
A pound red Lead	2	A plain Hat	2
Fifty flints	1	A white Duffield Blanket	8
Two knives	1	A blew or red Ditto, two yards	7
One Pound Beads	3	A course Linnen, two yards	3
Twenty-four Pipes	1	A Gallon Rum	4
A broad Hoe	3	A Pound Vermillion, [and] two Pounds red Lead, mixed	20
A Yard double striped yard-wide cloth	3	A Yard course flowered Calicoe	4
A Half Thicks or Plains Coat	1	Three yards broad scarlet Caddice gartering laced	14

Note: Spelling maintained from original document.

endowed with supernatural powers and gifts—to a nonreligious political economy of standardized commodities. The race to acquire people and deer in exchange for things of European origin completely rearranged the demographic and geopolitical composition of the Southeast. "In this new landscape, trading paths and hunting grounds were far more important for sustaining chiefly power than surplus from maize fields" (Beck 2013:197 [see also Wesson 2008]). To this set of locational variables might be added the importance of being situated as an intermediary between colonies and Native peoples in the interior.

The Indigenous histories established under these circumstances were unique in many respects, but they were also part of a worldwide, shared history of political-economic transformation that continues today. Transnational migration and diasporic flows are important components of flexible accumulation in the modern era of globalization, that is, the peculiarly nimble forms of wealth concentration characterized by massive flows of capital and labor (Clifford 1994:311). Surely the material cosmo-politanism increasingly practiced by southeastern Native Americans dur-ing the eighteenth century, founded on regional migration and diasporic flows, was an important precursor in the evolution of that process. That cosmopolitanism was made possible by the fact that goods from far away were no longer subject to the highly erratic availability, and subsequent scarcity, of exotic items and raw materials typical of small-scale economic systems. The articulation of Native American landscapes with the Atlantic World made a profusion of imports possible.

At this point, I must confess that I have presented the argument about the ability of Mississippian chiefs to command tribute in the form of maize (also discussed in the previous chapter) more or less at face value. But this widespread assumption among archaeologists about the link between Mississippian power and staple finance leaves us with some important un-answered questions. It is widely documented in ethnographic studies and in historical syntheses that leaders in kin-ordered societies rarely if ever have a direct control over the means of production; they are much more likely to attain power by finessing the circulation of prestige items (e.g., Oberg 1973; Paynter 1989:381; Tuden 1979; Wolf 1982:95). What control they do have over comestibles oftentimes involves elaborate social nego-tiations and well-understood social limits on their demands. Dean Saitta (1994) has made this argument with regard to Cahokia, where leaders did seem to have had differential access to exotic goods. Saitta believes that the archaeological record is suggestive of attempts by these individuals to further consolidate authoritarian tributary control over basic resources and enhance their power, but these efforts appear to have failed.

There seem to be two sources of data for the Mississippian staple fi-nance argument. One comes from climatic data, where there is an appar-ent correlation between intervals of plentiful rainfall and the thriving of polities and, conversely, periods of drought and chiefdom instability (An-derson 1994b; Meeks and Anderson 2013). However, this correlation does not really inform us about the mechanisms of chiefly power; it merely shows that polities thrived when climatic conditions permitted. A second source of support for the chiefly mobilization of maize in the Southeast stems from the Spanish narratives attesting to the ability of chiefs to pro-vide foodstuffs for the constant and enormous demands of the expedi-tions of the 1500s. To be sure, there are numerous references to leaders being owed tribute by vassals or else provisioning the Spaniards. At the town of Toalli, the principal men had "many large barbacoas [raised storage structures] in which they gather together the tribute paid them by their Indians which consists of maize and deerskins and native blankets" (Elvas in Robertson 1993:75). This is but one of a number of accounts of chiefs appearing with gifts of fish, blankets, skins, and maize for Spanish forays into the interior (e.g., Elvas in Robertson 1993:112–113; 118, 120).

Missing from these accounts are any descriptions of how the chiefs actually acquired these goods. While a chief may have been a funnel to the Spaniards, it is still unclear how foodstuffs were amassed and what kind of social predicaments this created. As is so often the case, one has to wonder whether Europeans were projecting onto local leaders powers that were held by their own monarchs. Could a chief simply demand that all households hand over their stores? Or did a chief largely rely on his or her own extensive network of family ties to provide the bulk of the expedition needs, only leaning on other families as demands required? After the Europeans left, was a chief left with a clean slate due to their power to demand food and supplies, or had he or she assumed a complex mixture of obligations as a result of their intermediary role with the demanding visitors? It was also commonplace for expeditions to be supplied with burden carriers and "women as slaves" (e.g., Elvas in Robertson 1993:94). Could chiefs simply mandate this kind of service without any social repercussions from their own people? In some cases, at least, Soto's men had to imprison leaders or other individuals in order to coerce communities into providing bearers and women to the Spaniards (Galloway 1995:114).

I am not arguing against the idea that some powerful Mississippian leaders may have transcended traditional social sanctions on the accrual of surplus and labor. However, this ability may have been far more challenging than we are wont to believe, and it certainly must have varied from polity to polity and individual to individual. The ethnographic and archaeological literature on feasting is a useful illustration of the lesson that stockpiling goods of any sort in non-state societies often relied on a complex web of debt obligations. Debt is a subject deserving of far more attention in the story of the major transformations experienced by southeastern communities in the colonial era, for reasons that follow.

Feasting is widely viewed as an activity that has both commensal and exploitative dimensions (Dietler and Hayden 2001; Hayden 2014). Events where foodstuffs and valuables are distributed to various sorts of participants can serve as a bonding experience and social adhesive. At the same time, the hosts of these events strategically disburse goods to foster debt obligations. Recipients of this largesse can anticipate that at a future date, a significant favor or gift of equal or even greater value will be expected. The holder of this social credit oftentimes remains in an advantageous position of moral authority. Rather than the sterile paper shuffle at a bank that accompanies a loan application, the gift creates a complex network of ties sustained by a notion of delayed return—a liminal period of social entanglement when the debtor is beholden to the gifter. Elites did not escape this web of obligations. Because of their often precarious hold over the means of production, chiefly leaders typically had to enter into protracted negotiations and agreements—often taking months and even years—to accumulate the foodstuffs and preciosities that would be consumed and gifted at a feasting event. They, too, found themselves in debt until the feast event could be used to discharge their social and material dues.

Archaeological research suggests that feasting was widespread in Mississippian communities (Blitz 1993; Cobb and Stephenson 2017; Hudson 1976; Pauketat et al. 2002; VanDerwarker 1999; Wallis and Blessing 2015). Some of these occasions appear to have been widely attended commensal events focusing on food consumption and conviviality. Others seem to have been restricted to elite segments of society, where the repast was complemented by the use or transfer of exotic raw materials, objects, valued animal elements (such as swan wings), and psychoactive plants like tobacco and *Datura*. If we presume that Mississippian communities participated in feasting in structurally similar ways as elsewhere in the world, we also have to infer that an intricate balance of debt obligations surrounded these events. I would thus argue that any kind of gathering of large quantities of goods in Mississippian communities, in feasting or any other context, likely involved the elaborate social mesh of indebtedness.

The commodification of debt with the arrival of Europeans stripped away many of the social niceties of credit and debt. Although Native Americans anticipated gifts from colonial leaders as part and parcel of political and economic alliance building, these exchanges were far different than the debts accrued through the exchange of slaves and deerskins. The upward spiral of Indigenous consumption during the colonial era was supported to a significant degree by traders providing goods for the promise of future delivery, with a strict accounting of numbers owed and when due. This inserted a notion of standardized bookkeeping into the discharge of debt that was as foreign to Native American worldviews as it was ruthlessly enforced by colonial traders and administrators. By virtue of their proximity to Carolina, the Yamasees in particular regularly suffered from "beatings, kidnappings, and robberies" from colonials intent on squaring their balance sheets (Oatis 2004:115–116). The mounting volume of deerskin debt in the eighteenth century is no less than staggering. By 1711, the Ochese Creeks in northern Georgia owed 100,000 deerskins to Carolina, or about 250 per Ochese hunter (Hahn 2004:76–77). Prior to the Yamasee War, the Yamasees were indebted to English creditors 10,000 pounds sterling (Oatis 2004:115), or the equivalent of $2,000,000 today.

Eventually, the ratio of the abundance of trade goods entering Native American lands and the number of people and deerskins moving out could not be sustained. By the second quarter of the eighteenth century, there were few remaining Native American groups not already allied with European colonies who could be enslaved. By the third quarter of the eighteenth century, the deer populations were faltering even as Native Americans were making increasingly larger concessions of their hunting territories to rapidly expanding colonies (and later, states). A spiral of debt continued to consume land, resources, and people. The entire landscape of the Southeast was now engaged in a historical drama that had been rehearsed many times locally. The Yamasees were one of the first in the queue in the early 1700s when encroachment on their lands and degradation of their forested areas in South Carolina prompted a steep decline in deer populations, accompanied by the corresponding upsurge in debt that led them to fear for their freedom (Oatis 2004:117).

The end of Indian slaving and the later eclipse of the deerskin trade did not halt the pas de deux of consumption and debt. Southeastern Indians remained dedicated to trading deerskins and other items to American factors into the early 1800s. However, with the federal government now involved in overseeing the calculation of credit, immediate cessions of land replaced delayed payments in skins as the currency of debt discharge. No less than the office of the presidency was enjoined in this effort as Thomas Jefferson in 1802 envisioned the now-familiar philosophical carrot and accounting stick:

The Indians being once closed in between strong settled countries on the Mississippi and Atlantic, will, for want of game, be forced to agriculture, will find that small portions of land, well improved, will be worth more to them than extensive forests unemployed, and will continually be parting with portions of them for money to buy stock, utensils, and necessaries for their farms and families. (Bergh 1907:373)

Jefferson was so confident of the predictability of this cycle that he recommended establishing factors among the Chickasaws—notorious for their reluctance to give up land—because "encouraging these and especially their leading men, to run in debt for these [trade goods] beyond their individual means of paying; and whenever in that situation, they will always cede lands to rid themselves of debt" (Bergh 1907:374). This became a widespread strategy in the first decade of the nineteenth century, as the federal government and the large trading companies that oversaw the factors worked hand-in-hand to deprive Native Americans of vast amounts of acreage (Usner 1998:77–79).

The Indigenous peoples of the Southeast were not unique in their trajectory. In his magnum opus on the history of debt, David Graeber (2011:332) forwards his thesis that

the story of the origins of capitalism, then, is not the story of the gradual destruction of traditional communities by the impersonal power of the market. It is, rather, the story of how an economy of credit was converted into an economy of interest; of the gradual transformation of moral networks by the intrusion of the impersonal—and often vindictive—power of the state.

Saunt (1999:46–47) suggests that the accelerated loss of hunting territory in the late 1700s and late 1800s, attributable in no small part to the manipulation of debt, must have prompted an existential identity crisis among Native Americans. This is perhaps both true and false. It is true insofar as southeastern Native Americans are construed as a generic ontology of people who were steadily deprived of a way of life linked to exploiting large tracts of land (for gathering and fishing, it might be added, as well as hunting). However, the idea of an identity "crisis" is problematic in the context of the complicated histories of coalescence and hybrid practices that Indians pursued both before and after the arrival of Europeans. Identity formation among Mississippian peoples and their ancestors always seems to have been malleable and in flux (e.g., Bardolph 2014; Meyers 2017; Waselkov and Smith 2017; Wilson 2010).

The introduction of European practices and material culture to the Southeast simply expanded the size of the palette from which identity was constructed, a process that was not unique in the annals of colonialism. In his work on "the political economy of elegance," Jonathan Friedman (1994) has documented how some cultures in the French Congo region of the 1950s began to compete in emulating Parisian dress styles, in effect adopting European fashion as a form of self-definition. In this case, he argues that notions of identity became tightly intertwined in the appropriation of otherness and melding it with local tradition. Is this any different than the course many Native Americans had embarked upon when they first began incorporating materials from Spanish expeditions and shipwrecks into their clothing and burial practices in the 1500s? Even by the 1800s, groups like the Cherokees continued to integrate Euro-American material culture into old patterns. "They transformed silk shawls into turbans, wooden kegs into dance drums, and straight pins into conjurers' *kanuga* [a ritual flesh-scratching implement]" (Riggs 1999:32). It is evident that Native Americans assumed an increasingly cosmopolitan stance—already flexible to begin with—of what would be defined as traditional identity even in the face of massive land losses (see Loren 2008, 2010).

These commodities from afar ensured a sense of security, stability, and identity by provisioning Native peoples with "essential" guns, "necessary" metal tools and manufactured cloth, and the "luxury" of ornamental items like glass beads and brass tinkler cones (Braund 1993:121–126). In other words, Native American groups intensified established practices like deer hunting and warfare and contoured them to the growing world of consumerism and things that engulfed not only Indigenous societies, but literally every corner of the Atlantic World. But while drawing on objects near and far may have lent an aura of cosmopolitanism to southeastern groups, local or regional autonomy remained a central objective. Notwithstanding the new world of goods entering the Southeast, one cannot help but be reminded of the axiom put forth by Marshall Sahlins (1993:17): "The first commercial impulse of the people is not to become just like us, but more like themselves." This impulse to stay more like themselves while weaving silver gorgets (England), porcelain (China), slaves (Africa), and log cabins (United States/Scandinavia) into their everyday lives led to

Native American landscape histories that were defined by "demographic circulation, intercommunity connection, and the physical colonization of new territories" (Jordan 2013:30).

I still agree with Saunt's assessment that Native Americans' relationship with the landscape had changed dramatically with the rise of the market economy, whether or not that involved an existential crisis. In fact, the loss of hunting (and gathering and fishing) territories and the rise of private farms and estates once again had swung the pendulum between the primacy of staple finance and wealth finance. As deerskins and other goods collected from the diminishing forests steadily lost their premium, agricultural produce and livestock became a major mainstay of wealth and status. Although much of the Indigenous Southeast was sprouting modest farmsteads, some individuals presided over plantations with slaves that had all of the trappings of properties owned by wealthy whites. James Vann, who was half Cherokee, constructed a mansion on his sizable estate in 1804 as one of these elites (De Baillou 1963). This building bears all of the hallmarks of the Georgian symmetry and order that give rise to the Federalist style (figure 7.1). Limited excavations in the yard yielded "fine, 19th century china and glass" among other categories of artifacts (De Baillou 1957).

And here is a key point: even with the loss of huge stretches of land to the United States, the decline of the deerskin trade, and the rise of individual farmsteads, most Native Americans, wealthy or not, were able to successfully navigate these changes. Like the bordering Euro-American territory, theirs became productive agrarian landscapes. In his 1826 *An Address to the Whites*, a treatise on the progress of his people toward civilization, the well-known Cherokee leader Elias Boudinott (1826:8) observed that there were

> 22,000 cattle; 7,600 horses; 46,000 swine; 2,500 sheep; 762 looms; 2,488 spinning wheels; 172 wagons; 2,943 ploughs; 10 saw mills; 31 gristmills; 62 blacksmith shops; 8 cotton machines; 18 schools; 18 ferries; and a number of public roads. In one district there were, last winter, upwards of 1,000 volumes of good books; and 11 different periodical papers both religious and political, which were taken and read. On the public roads there are many decent Inns, and few houses for convenience, &c., would disgrace any country.

Figure 7.1. James Vann house in northern Georgia (courtesy of commons.wikimedia. org/wiki/User:Thomson200).

One gets the sense that Cherokee economic landscapes were thriving with their adaptations to contemporary American definitions of success. Recognition of this fact by the American government and its citizens, and the attendant reality that Native Americans were not going to relocate of their own volition, seems to have been much of the impetus for Removal.

The landscape of the market economy represented a rupture with the mercantile system of slaves and deerskins that was just as profound as the dissolution and rearrangement of Mississippian chiefdoms in the 1600s. This shift was felt at multiple scales. Politically, widespread angst over the continuing loss of lands was a major factor in the creation of overarching Native American governments among the Creeks and Cherokees (e.g., Persico 1979). The Cherokees, for example, under their central government, imposed regulations on the sales of land and improvements (Perdue 1979:114–116). The town still may have been a seat of everyday authority, but land loss and concerns over Indigenous citizens selling their property and moving west were forcing collaborative action at a regional scale.

Still, widespread, concerted action was difficult to sustain because of the continuing dialectical pull between the primacy of the parochial and the wider need for self-preservation among the various Indian nations. As one of a number of failed examples, at the turn of the nineteenth century, the Upper Creek leader Mad Dog attempted to unite the Upper Creeks, Lower Creeks, and Seminoles as a necessary bulwark against American encroachments in the late 1700s (Peach 2018). This was a person who had all the right stuff. He rose to prominence as a successful warrior, and through his ability to morph into a mad dog "he mastered the proper cosmic powers to earn his laurels as a war leader, ritual specialist, and diplomat" (Peach 2018:105). His attempts to assume intertribal leadership and create a unified Creek political landscape only spurred the predictable pushback from local leaders. In the following decades, wealthy landowners emerged as a new form of leadership replacing the warrior-priests. "The Republican government of the Cherokee Nation rested largely in the hands of slaveholders; over half the signers of the Constitution of 1827 owned bondsmen" (Perdue 1979:115). This new class had somewhat more success in centralizing power in a regional authority.

The centrality of the *talwa* to the political-economic landscape was further endangered by the rise of individual farms and the diminishment of communality. The bounded parcels of Native smallholdings and large estates across the Southeast embodied the maturation of geographies of management: the reorganization of space under capitalism expressly for political and economic purposes. As witnessed in all places where capitalism was gathering force, dynamic cultural landscapes were redefined as commodified, abstract polygons demarcated by walls and fences at the same time that social relations tied to specific places were undermined (Given 2004; Johnson 1996; Trouillot 2002).

Michel Foucault (1977:141–153) famously argued that this era also witnessed a major transformation in the articulation of body and object. With the rise of modernity and the development of market economies, demands on the human body became a "coercive link with the apparatus of production." In that process, humans were increasingly disciplined in their work habits not just through enclosure and standardization in the built environment and landscape, but even within the household itself. Archaeologists have demonstrated that this social segmentation and compartmentalization was mediated through the use of mass-produced objects in the home, goods that were increasingly removed from their source of production and correspondingly denatured of social meaning (Johnson 1996:182–188; Shackel 1993). These goods were also correlated with the regimentation of corporeal household behaviors, ranging from dining to hygiene practices.

As provocative as Foucault's model is, it has most force when applied as a flexible template rather than as a structural history. If we are to privilege a notion of capitalisms as opposed to capitalism, then we really need far more detailed and combined ethnohistorical and archaeological investigations of the individual Protestant missions, Indigenous homesteads, lucrative trading posts, and wealthy plantations that dotted southeastern lands in the pre-Removal era—not just as specific sites, but also as tethered nodes that comprised a larger landscape of Indigenous free-market economies. From what we do know, these places were distinctive from their Euro-American parallels, and they varied from one another as well. As we saw in Brett Riggs' studies of pre-Removal Cherokee households and a Baptist mission to the Cherokees (chapter 6), important aspects of Indigenous lifeways weathered the tribulations of the market economy. They likely shaped it as well.

To step back a bit in time, the idea that there are multiple capitalisms also corresponds with the views of many that there were multiple Enlightenments (Himmelfarb 2004; Porter 2000; Porter and Teich 1981). In this light, it is noteworthy that when Spain gained the western half of Louisiana at the close of the Seven Years War, the influx of bureaucrats attempted to instill notions of landscape management based on Enlightenment ideals under the Bourbon Reform that emphasized increased government intervention in the economy (DuVal 2006:120; Lynch 1989); not the laissez-faire Anglo-centric principles that I have leaned on so heavily in the latter part of this study. In fact, the kind of dynamic symmetry that we associate with the Georgian world view first seems to have gained traction in France (Heath 2016). What kind of variable material expressions of these multiple Enlightenments might we see in the archaeological record of the eighteenth-century Southeast, as Native Americans engaged with Europeans undergoing their own distinct trajectories in world view?

This kind of broader perspective will be necessary in future research to gain a deeper understanding of the heterogeneity of southeastern landscape histories. It is particularly important to critically evaluate how many of the thresholds associated with the rise of the market economy, and that are typically associated with Great Britain, were also taking place elsewhere under somewhat different guises. The institutionalization of wage labor under the British Industrial Revolution was a cornerstone of the evolution of capitalism, but other European nations and Indigenous peoples were simultaneously shaping variations on this theme in the mercantile era of the 1600s. We can see this played out in various ways in relation to Spanish Florida, where labor arrangements with the mission Indians under the *repartimiento* presaged the wage-labor system of market exchange (Worth 1998:190–195). Native American laborers received the equivalent of one real per workday in trade goods, which over a six-month commitment could realize "perhaps a few pounds of glass beads, a dozen yards or so of Spanish cloth, and several iron hand tools" (Worth 1998:193). Importantly, a laborer's chief was entitled to distribute (or withhold) these wages-in-kind, making the dissemination of pay a function of asymmetrical power relations rather than a guaranteed return on one's work.

In a fascinating account, Dr. Francis Le Jau described those Apalachees who were forcibly moved to Carolina by Governor Moore in 1704 as continuing to ring a bell to regulate their daily routine (Wright 1981:191). This custom, carried over from their recent history on Franciscan missions, showed that not all Indians necessarily objected to the structured segmentation of their work day—as opposed to the destruction of bells seen in earlier revolts in the mission system (chapter 3). This is not the sort of time discipline that E. P. Thompson (1967) equated with the rise of industrial capitalism. But it is certainly in the modern lineage of the regimented workplace, albeit with a particular Native American and Iberian twist.

Longitudinal archaeological research on the ways in which southeastern Indians engaged the variable and evolving European views of landscape from the Renaissance through the post-Enlightenment is still embryonic. This work will need to attend to the idiosyncratic histories of local landscapes and at the same time acknowledge the larger sweep of world events and processes. Hopefully this dual approach will help illuminate how Native Americans spanned the gap between their own subjective experiences and the classificatory ambitions and political-economic demands of colonizers (see, for example, Given [2004:69–92] and Stoler [2002] for examples of the circumvention of colonial classificatory schemes by local peoples).

Removal, too, is a part of the landscape history of Native Americans. This appalling event, or series of events, is not a part of my landscape overview. A few comments are in order, however. A blunt assessment of Removal is that it was the culmination of a process of structured genocide embedded within a long-term practice of settlement displacement on the part of colonial and federal regimes. This tragedy is, of course, well documented. But it is also important to balance the scale with attention to how Native American agency crafted yet a new series of landscape histories surrounding the 1830s exodus.

One important illustration of this history is the "settlement Indians" of South Carolina. They are analogous to the *petites nations* Indians described in chapter 5, the small communities who lived alongside or in close proximity to French colonial settlements in Louisiana. Among such groups were the Itwans, described in the Carolina census in chapter 4 (table 4.1) as "Mixed with ye English Settlements." Carl Steen's (2012) study of the Carolina settlement Indians emphasizes that they occupied an ambiguous cultural and physical place in the colony. As he describes it, South Carolina had very geographically expansive and unrealistic views of Native Americans under their control. But there were a modest number of outlying settlements from Charles Town that were integrated into the Carolina political landscape and that persisted until after the Revolutionary War. Theirs was a liminal world, where they attempted to sustain their identities but also fell under the domain of the state's laws, requiring, for example, title to their homelands and foregoing many of their traditional practices. Pressures to assimilate were heightened by chronic conflicts South Carolina had with Native Americans to the west of the colony, creating a need for settlement Indians to distinguish themselves as peaceful and accommodating neighbors. Over the long term, strategies of fitting in diminished the differences between their lifeways and those of Euro-Americans to the point of near invisibility—at least from the Western perspective. This cultural alignment allowed for exemption from Removal. However, a modern outcome of this history of cultural redaction is a difficulty in achieving federal recognition because of the irony that survival entailed the relinquishment of traditional modes of dress, living, and language. Although we take it for granted that most of today's American society has changed tremendously in the last 200 years, the modern descendants of the settlement Indians have been punished for not looking and speaking like their forebears. This paradox has been widely experienced by Native Americans in North America (e.g., Cook 2017; Liebmann 2008). South Carolina, to its credit, has an expansive list of state-recognized tribes who have pursued histories of structured disappearance, although this is not true for all states.

A landscape study of Removal could take many directions. First, there is the question of how Native American groups both displaced and emplaced themselves in yet a new setting. Second, one must consider how the groups who remained in the Southeast, like the Carolina settlement Indians, continued to develop new forms of landscape histories, ranging from formal reservations to resistance to strategic disappearance. Added to this mix would be the important issue of diaspora and sustained ties between Indigenous cultures, such as the Oklahoma Cherokees and Eastern Band of Cherokees, split between two locations. Suffice it to say that the modern terrain of reservation casinos and oil wells, diasporic returns to the Southeast, contestations over identity, and struggles related to heritage and the archaeological record are a logical outgrowth of these landscape histories.

∗   ∗   ∗

The arc of Native American lived landscapes from the Mississippian to the early federal eras is an important example of "sustained colonialism" (sensu Lightfoot and Gonzalez 2018). Various Indigenous peoples faced unceasing and unpredictable waves of colonial encroachments from different directions and were constantly engaged in developing new innovations as evolving circumstances dictated. As an empirical generalization, one can probably say that shatter zones consistently fractured the landscapes of the colonial Southeast. Even with the uneasy stabilization that began to prevail by the mid-1700s, conflict was a frequent, devastating visitor. Adding to the turmoil was the constant presence of disease. Lastly, the evolution of the Atlantic World increasingly tethered Native American lifeways to the political, economic, and ideological strains of, first, mercantilism, and then, capitalism.

Still, the enormous transformations witnessed in the Indigenous landscapes in the Southeast were a mix of creative responses and adjustments, rather than a protracted history of fighting a cultural rearguard action. There is considerable and fascinating comparative work to be done by historical archaeologists on the variation in Native American landscape ideologies and practices and how they articulated with equally diverse

European landscape ideologies and practices. By relying on their traditional yardstick of deep history, archaeologists can provide new insights into how Native Americans navigated and contributed to the unfolding of multiple Renaissances, Enlightenments, and Capitalisms while at the same time creating landscapes that were distinctly their own.

References

Abler, Thomas S.
1991   Beavers and Muskets: Iroquois Military Fortunes in the Face of European
            Colonization. In *War in the Tribal Zone: Expanding States and Indigenous
            Warfare*, edited by R. B. Ferguson and N. L. Whitehead, pp. 151–174. School
            of American Research Press, Santa Fe.
Adair, James
2005 [1775] *The History of the American Indians*. The University of Alabama Press,
            Tuscaloosa.
Adelman, Jeremy, and Stephen Aron
1999   From Borderlands to Borders: Empires, Nation-States, and the Peoples
            in Between in North American History. *American Historical Review*
            104(3):814–841.
Albers, Patricia C.
2002   Marxism and Historical Materialism in American Indian History. In
            Clearing a Path: Theorizing the Past in Native American Studies, edited by
            N. Shoemaker, pp. 107–136. Routledge, New York.
Alt, Susan M.
2001   Cahokian Change and the Authority of Tradition. In *The Archaeology of
            Traditions: Agency and History Before and After Columbus*, edited by T. K.
            Pauketat, pp. 141–156. University Press of Florida, Gainesville.
2006   The Power of Diversity: Settlement in the Cahokian Uplands. In *Leader-
            ship and Polity in Mississippian Society*, edited by B. M. Butler and P. D.
            Welch, pp. 289–308. Occasional Paper No. 33. Center for Archaeological
            Investigations, Southern Illinois University Carbondale.
Alvarez, Robert R., Jr.
1995   The Mexican-US Border: The Makings of an Anthropology of Border-
            lands. *Annual Review of Anthropology* 24:447–470.
Anderson, David G.
1994a   Factional Competition and the Political Evolution of Mississippian Chief-
            doms in the Southeastern United States. In *Factional Competition in the
            New World*, edited by E. M. Brumfiel and J. W. Fox, pp. 61–76. Cambridge
            University Press, Cambridge, United Kingdom.

1994b   *The Savannah River Chiefdoms: Political Change in the Late Prehistoric Southeast.* University of Alabama Press, Tuscaloosa.

1999   Examining Chiefdoms in the Southeast: An Application of Multiscalar Analysis. In *Great Towns and Regional Polities in the Prehistoric American Southwest and Southeast*, edited by J. E. Neitzel, pp. 215–241. Amerind Foundation/University of New Mexico Press, Albuquerque.

Anderson, David G., David W. Stahle, and Malcolm K. Cleaveland

1995   Paleoclimate and the Potential Food Reserves of Mississippian Societies: A Case Study from the Savannah River Valley. *American Antiquity* 60(2):258–286.

Anderson, David G., and Kenneth E. Sassaman

2012   *Recent Developments in Southeastern Archaeology: From Colonization to Complexity.* The SAA Press, Washington, DC.

Anthony, David W.

1997   Prehistoric Migration as Social Process. In *Migrations and Invasions in Archaeological Explanation*, edited by J. Chapman and H. Hamerow, pp. 21–32. Archaeopress, Oxford.

Appadurai, Arjun

1991   Global Ethnoscapes: Notes and Queries for a Transnational Anthropology. In *Recapturing Anthropology: Working in the Present*, edited by R. G. Fox, pp. 191–210. School of American Research Press, Santa Fe.

1995   The Production of Locality. In *Counterworks: Managing the Diversity of Knowledge*, edited by R. Fardon, pp. 204–225. Routledge, New York.

Armitrage, David

2009   Three Concepts of History. In *The British Atlantic World, 1500–1800*, edited by D. Armitrage and M. J. Braddick, pp. 13–29. 2nd ed. Palgrave Macmillan, New York.

Arnade, Charles W.

1959   *The Siege of St. Augustine in 1702.* University of Florida Press, Gainesville.

1962   The English Invasion of Spanish Florida, 1700–1706. *The Florida Historical Quarterly* 41(1):29–37.

Ashley, Keith

2018   Yamasee Migrations into the Mocama and Timucua Mission Provinces of Florida, 1667–1683: An Archaeological Perspective. In *The Yamasee Indians: From Florida to South Carolina*, edited by D. I. Bossy, pp. 55–79. University of Nebraska Press, Lincoln.

Ashmore, Wendy, A. and Bernard Knapp (editors)

1999   *Archaeologies of Landscape.* Blackwell, Malden, Massachusetts.

Atkinson, James R.

2004   *Splendid Land, Splendid People: The Chickasaw Indians to Removal.* The University of Alabama Press, Tuscaloosa.

Bardolph, Dana N.

2014   Evaluating Cahokian Contact and Mississippian Identity Politics in the

Late Prehistoric Central Illinois River Valley. *American Antiquity* 79(1):69–89.

Barnes, Jodi A. (editor)
2011   *The Materiality of Freedom: Archaeologies of Postemancipation Life.* University of South Carolina Press, Columbia.

Barr, Daniel B. (editor)
2006   *The Boundaries Between Us: Natives and Newcomers along the Frontiers of the Old Northwest Territory, 1750–1850.* Kent State University Press, Kent, Ohio.

Barrios, Roberto
2017   What Does Catastrophe Reveal for Whom? The Anthropology of Crises and Disasters at the Onset of the Anthropocene. *Annual Review of Anthropology* 46:151–166.

Barth, Fredrik
1969   *Ethnic Groups and Boundaries: The Social Organization of Cultural Difference.* Allen & Unwin, London.

Bartram, William
1793   *Travels through North and South Carolina, Georgia, East and West Florida, the Cherokee Country, the Extensive Territories of the Muscogulges or Creek Confederacy, and the Country of the Chactaws.* J. Moore, W. Jones, R. McAllister, and J. Rice, Dublin, Ireland.

Basso, Keith H.
1996   *Wisdom Sits in Places: Landscape and Language Among the Western Apache.* University of New Mexico Press, Albuquerque.

Bates, James Frederick
1982   An Analysis of the Aboriginal Ceramic Artifacts from Chota-Tanasee, an Eighteenth Century Overhill Cherokee Town. Master's thesis, Department of Anthropology, University of Tennessee, Knoxville.

Bauch, Martin
2017   The Day the Sun Turned Blue: A Volcanic Eruption in the Early 1460s and Its Possible Climatic Impact—A Natural Disaster Perceived Globally in the Late Middle Ages? In *Historical Disaster Experiences: Towards a Comparative and Transcultural History of Disasters*, edited by G. J. Schenk, pp. 108–138. Springer, Cham, Switzerland.

Beck, Robin
2013   *Chiefdoms, Collapse, and Coalescence in the Early American South.* Cambridge University Press, Cambridge, United Kingdom.

Bender, Barbara
1993   *Landscape Politics and Perspectives.* Berg, Oxford.

Benjamin, Thomas
2009   *The Atlantic World: Europeans, Africans, Indians and Their Shared History, 1400–1900.* Cambridge University Press, Cambridge, United Kingdom.

Benson, Larry V., Timothy R. Pauketat, and Edward R. Cook
2009   Cahokia's Boom and Bust in the Context of Climate Change. *American Antiquity* 74(3):467–483.

Berg, Maxine
2004   In Pursuit of Luxury: Global History and British Consumer Goods in the Eighteenth Century. *Past & Present* 182:85–142.

Bergh, Albert Ellery (editor)
1907   *The Writings of Thomas Jefferson*, Vol. 17. The Thomas Jefferson Memorial Association of the United States, Washington, DC.

Berleant, Arnold
1997   *Living in the Landscape: Toward an Aesthetics of Environment*. University of Kansas, Lawrence.

Bernardini, Wesley
2005   *Hopi Oral Tradition and the Archaeology of Identity*. University of Arizona Press, Tucson.

Berryman, Hugh E.
1984   The Averbuch Skeletal Series: A Study of Biological and Social Stress at a Late Mississippian Period Site from Middle Tennessee. In *Averbuch: A Late Mississippian Manifestation in the Nashville Basin*, edited by W. E. Klippel and W. M. Bass. National Park Service, Atlanta.

Besom, Thomas
2013   *Inka Human Sacrifice and Mountain Worship: Strategies for Empire Unification*. University of New Mexico Press, Albuquerque.

Bickham, Troy O.
2005   *Savages Within the Empire: Representations of American Indians in Eighteenth-Century Britain*. Clarendon Press, Oxford.

Binford, Lewis R.
1980   Willow Smoke and Dogs' Tails: Hunter-Gatherer Settlement Systems and Archaeological Site Formation. *American Antiquity* 45(1):4–20.

Bird, Broxton W., Jeremy J. Wilson, William P. Gilhooly III, Byron A. Steinman, and Lucas Stamps
2017   Midcontinental Native American Population Dynamics and Late Holocene Hydroclimate Extremes. *Scientific Reports* 7, doi:10.1038/srep41628.

Blanton, Dennis B.
2004   The Climate Factor in Late Prehistoric and Post-Contact Human Affairs. In *Indian and European Contact in Context: The Mid-Atlantic Region*, edited by D. B. Blanton and J. A. King, pp. 6–21. University Press of Florida, Gainesville.

Blim, Michael
2000   Capitalisms in Late Modernity. *Annual Review of Anthropology* 29:25–38.

Blitz, John H.
1993   Big Pots for Big Shots: Feasting and Storage in a Mississippian Community. *American Antiquity* 58(1):80–96.

1999   Mississippian Chiefdoms and the Fission–Fusion Process. *American Antiquity* 64:577–592.
2010   New Perspectives in Mississippian Archaeology. *Journal of Archaeological Research* 18(1):1–39.
Blitz, John H., and Karl G. Lorenz
2002   The Early Mississippian Frontier in the Lower Chattahoochee–Apalachicola River Valley. *Southeastern Archaeology* 21(2):117–135.
Bonhage-Freund, Mary Theresa
2007   Botanical Remains. In *Archaeology of the Lower Muskogee Creek Indians, 1715–1836*, edited by H. Thomas Foster II, pp. 136–193. The University of Alabama Press, Tuscaloosa.
Borić, Dušan
2002   'Deep Time' Metaphor: Mnemonic and Apotropaic Practices at Lepenski Vir. *Journal of Social Archaeology* 3(1):46–74.
Bossy, Denise I.
2018   Introduction: Recovering Yamasee History. In *The Yamasee Indians: From Florida to South Carolina*, edited by D. I. Bossy, pp. 1–24. University of Nebraska Press, Lincoln.
Boudinott, Elias
1826   *An Address to the Whites*. William F. Geddes, Philadelphia.
Boudreaux, Edmond A., III
2013   Community and Ritual Within the Mississippian Center at Town Creek. *American Antiquity* 78(3):483–501.
Bowne, Eric E.
2005   *The Westo Indians: Slave Traders of the Early Colonial South*. The University of Alabama Press, Tuscaloosa.
Boyce, Douglas W.
1987   "As the Wind Scatters the Smoke": The Tuscaroras in the Eighteenth Century. In *Beyond the Covenant Chain: The Iroquois and Their Neighbors in Indian North America, 1600–1800*, edited by D. K. Richter and J. H. Merrell, pp. 151–163. Syracuse University Press, Syracuse, New York.
Boyer, Willet A., III
2005   *Nuestra Señora del Rosario de La Punta*: Lifeways of an Eighteenth-Century Colonial Spanish Refugee Mission Community, St. Augustine, Florida. PhD dissertation, Department of Anthropology, University of Florida, Gainesville.
Bradley, Raymond S., and Philip D. Jones
1993   "Little Ice Age" Summer Temperature Variations: Their Nature and Relevance to Recent Global Warming Trends. *The Holocene* 3(4):367–376.
Bradley, Richard
2000   *An Archaeology of Natural Places*. Routledge, New York.
Brain, Jeffrey P.
1988   *Tunica Archaeology*. Papers of the Peabody Museum of Archaeology and Ethnology Vol. 78. Harvard University, Cambridge, Massachusetts.

Braund, Kathryn E. Holland
1991   The Creek Indians, Blacks, and Slavery. *The Journal of Southern History*
            54(4):601–636.
1993   *Deerskins & Duffels: Creek Indian Trade with Anglo-America, 1685–1815.*
            University of Nebraska Press, Lincoln.
Breen, T. H.
2004   *The Marketplace of Revolution: How Consumer Politics Shaped American*
            Independence. Oxford University Press, Oxford.
Breitburg, Emanuel
1998   Faunal Remains. In *Gordontown: Salvage Archaeology at a Mississippian*
            Town in Davidson County, Tennessee, edited by M. C. Moore and E. Breit-
            burg, pp. 147–168. Tennessee Division of Archaeology, Nashville.
Bridges, Patricia S., Keith P. Jacobi, and Mary Lucas Powell
2000   Warfare-Related Trauma in the Late Prehistory of Alabama. In *Bioarchae-*
            ological Studies of Life in the Age of Agriculture: A View from the Southeast,
            edited by P. M. Lambert, pp. 35–63. The University of Alabama Press, Tus-
            caloosa.
Brieschke, Walter L., and Frank Rackerby
1973   The "Stone Forts" of Illinois. *Outdoor Illinois* 12(2):19–26.
Brighton, Stephen A.
2009   *Historical Archaeology of the Irish Diaspora: A Transnational Approach.*
            The University of Tennessee Press, Knoxville.
Brown, Ian W.
1982   An Archaeological Study of Culture Contact and Change in the Natchez
            Bluffs Region. In *La Salle and His Legacy: Frenchmen and Indians in the*
            Lower Mississippi Valley, edited by P. K. Galloway, pp. 176–193. University
            Press of Mississippi, Jackson.
Brown, Ian W., and Vincas P. Steponaitis
2017   The Grand Village of the Natchez Indians was Indeed Grand: A Recon-
            sideration of the Fatherland Site Landscape. In *Forging Southeastern Iden-*
            tities: Social Archaeology, Ethnohistory, and Folklore of the Mississippian
            to Early Historic South, edited by G. A. Waselkov and M. T. Smith, pp.
            182–204. The University of Alabama Press, Tuscaloosa.
Brown, James
2007   Sequencing the Braden Style within Mississippian Period Art and Iconog-
            raphy. In *Ancient Objects and Sacred Realms: Interpretations of Mississip-*
            pian Iconography, edited by F. K. Reilly III and J. F. Garber, pp. 213–245.
            University of Austin Press, Austin.
Brown, James A., Richard A. Kerber, and Howard D. Winters
1990   Trade and the Evolution of Exchange Relations at the Beginning of the
            Mississippian Period. In *The Mississippian Emergence,* edited by B. D.
            Smith, pp. 251–280. Smithsonian Institution Press, Washington, DC.
Brown, James A., and Robert K. Vierra
1983   What Happened in the Middle Archaic?: Introduction to an Ecological

Approach to Koster Site Archaeology. In *Archaic Hunters and Gatherers in the American Midwest*, edited by J. L. Phillips and J. A. Brown, pp. 165–195. Academic Press, New York.

Bruno, David, and Julian Thomas (editors)
2008 *Handbook of Landscape Archaeology*. Left Coast Press, Walnut Creek, California.

Bushnell, Amy Turner
1990 The Sacramental Imperative: Catholic Ritual and Indian Sedentism in the Provinces of Florida. In *Columbian Consequences: 2. Archaeological and Historical Perspectives on the Spanish Borderlands East*, edited by D. H. Thomas, pp. 475–490. Smithsonian Institution Press, Washington, DC.
1994 *Situada and Sabana: Spain's Support System for the Presidio and Mission Provinces of Florida*. American Museum of Natural History Anthropological Papers No. 74. University of Georgia Press, Athens.

Butler, Brian M., and Charles R. Cobb
2012 Paired Mississippian Communities. *Midcontinental Journal of Archaeology* 37(1):45–72.

Cameron, Catherine M.
2013 How People Moved Among Ancient Societies: Broadening the View. *American Anthropologist* 115(2):218–231.

Cameron, Catherine M., Paul Kelton, and Alan C. Swedlund (editors)
2015 *Beyond Germs: Native Depopulation in North America*. University of Arizona Press, Tucson.

Carson, Cary
2017 *Face Value: The Consumer Revolution and the Colonizing of America*. University of Virginia Press, Charlottesville.

Casey, Edward
2008 Place in Landscape Archaeology: A Western Philosophical Prelude. In *Handbook of Landscape Archaeology*, edited by B. David and J. Thomas, pp. 44–50. Left Coast Press, Walnut Creek, California.

Cashin, Edward J., (editor)
1986 *Colonial Augusta: "Key of the Indian Countrey."* Mercer University Press, Macon, Georgia.

Cashin, Edward J.
2009 *Guardians of the Valley: Chickasaws in Colonial South Carolina and Georgia*. University of South Carolina Press, Columbia.

Cayton, Andrew R. L., and Fredericka A. Teute (editors)
1998 *Contrast Points: American Frontiers from the Mohaw Valley to the Mississippi, 1750–1830*. University of North Carolina Press, Chapel Hill.

Cegielski, Wendy
2010 A GIS-Based Analysis of Chickasaw Settlement in Northeast Mississippi: 1650–1840. Master's thesis, Department of Sociology and Anthropology, University of Mississippi, Oxford.

Cegielski, Wendy, and Brad R. Lieb
2011   Hina' Falaa, "The Long Path": An Analysis of Chickasaw Settlement Using GIS in Northeast Mississippi, 1650–1840. *Native South* 4:24–54.

Chmurney, William Wayne
1973   The Ecology of the Middle Mississippian Occupation of the American Bottom. PhD dissertation, Department of Anthropology, University of Illinois, Urbana-Champaign.

Clark, Emily
2017   An Analysis of Contact-Era Settlements in Clay, Lowndes, and Oktibbeha Counties in Northeast Mississippi. Master's thesis, Department of Anthropology, University of Mississippi, Oxford.

Clifford, James
1994   Diasporas. *Cultural Anthropology* 9(3):302–338.
1997   *Routes: Travel and Translation in the Late Twentieth Century*. Harvard University Press, Cambridge, Massachusetts.

Cobb, Charles R.
2000   *From Quarry to Cornfield: The Political Economy of Mississippian Hoe Production*. The University of Alabama Press, Tuscaloosa.
2003   Mississippian Chiefdoms: How Complex? *Annual Review of Anthropology* 32:63–84.
2005   Archeology and the "Savage Slot": Displacement and Emplacement in the Premodern World. *American Anthropologist* 104(4):563–574.
2008   From Frontier to Border Along the Iroquois Southern Door. *Archaeologies* 4(1):110–128.
2014   What I Believe: A Memoir of Processualism to Neohistorical Anthropology. *Southeastern Archaeology* 33(2):214–225.
2015   Mississippian Microhistories and Sub-Mound Moments. In *The Archaeology of Events: Cultural Change and Continuity in the Pre-Columbian Southeast*, edited by Z. I. Gilmore and J. M. O'Donoughue, pp. 196–219. The University of Alabama Press, Tuscaloosa.
2019   Flat Ontologies, Cosmopolitanism, and Space at Carolina Forts. *Historical Archaeology*, doi.org/10.1007/s41636-019-00160-4.

Cobb, Charles R., and Brian M. Butler
2002   The Vacant Quarter Revisited: Late Mississippian Abandonment of the Lower Ohio Valley. *American Antiquity* 67:625–641.
2017   Mississippian Plazas, Performances, and Portable Histories. *Journal of Archaeological Method and Theory* 24(3):676–702.

Cobb, Charles R., and Chester B. DePratter
2012   Multi-sited Research on Colonowares and the Paradox of Globalization. *American Anthropologist* 114(3):446–461.
2016   Carolina's Southern Frontier: Edge of a New World Order. In *Archaeology in South Carolina: Exploring the Hidden Heritage of the Palmetto State*, edited by A. King, pp. 43–61. University of South Carolina Press, Columbia.

Cobb, Charles R., and Patrick H. Garrow
1996   Woodstock Culture and the Question of Mississippian Emergence. *American Antiquity* 61:1–16.

Cobb, Charles R., and Stephanie M. Sapp
2014   Imperial Anxiety and the Dissolution of Colonial Space and Practice at Fort Moore, South Carolina. In *Rethinking Colonial Pasts through Archaeology*, edited by N. Ferris, R. Harrison, and M. Wilcox, pp. 212–231. Oxford University Press, Oxford.

Cobb, Charles R., Steven B. Smith, James B. Legg, Brad R. Lieb, and Chester B. Depratter
2017   Ackia and Ogoula Tchetoka: Defining Two Battlefields of the 1736 French and Chickasaw War in Southeastern North America. *Journal of Field Archaeology* 42(5):423–436.

Cobb, Charles R., and Keith D. Stephenson
2017   Cosmic Debt and Relational Consumption. In *Foreign Objects: Rethinking Indigenous Consumption in American Archaeology*, edited by C. N. Cipolla, pp. 143–161. University of Arizona Press, Tucson.

Coleman, Kenneth, and Milton Ready (editors)
1982   *The Colonial Records of the State of Georgia*, Vol. 20. University of Georgia Press, Athens.

Comaroff, Jean, and John L. Comaroff
1991   *Of Revelation and Revolution: 1. Christianity, Colonialism, and Consciousness in South Africa*. University of Chicago Press, Chicago.

Cook, Benjamin I., Jason E. Smerdon, Richard Seager, and Edward R. Cook
2014   Pan-continental Droughts in North America over the Last Millennium. *Journal of Climate* 27:383–397.

Cook, Edward R., Richard Seager, Mark A. Cane, and David W. Stahle
2007   North American Drought: Reconstructions, Causes, and Consequences. *Earth Science Reviews* 81:93–134.

Cook, Robert A.
2017   *Continuity and Change in the Native American Village: Multicultural Origins and Descendants of the Fort Ancient Culture*. Cambridge University Press, Cambridge, United Kingdom.

Cooper, Frederick
2005   *Colonialism in Question: Theory, Knowledge, History*. University of California Press, Berkeley.

Cordell, Ann S.
2002   Continuity and Change in Apalachee Pottery Manufacture. *Historical Archaeology* 36(1):36–54.

Corkran, David H.
1967   *The Creek Frontier, 1540–1783*. University of Oklahoma Press, Norman.

Crane, Verner W.
1916   The Tennessee River as the Road to Carolina: The Beginnings of Exploration and Trade. *The Mississippi Valley Historical Review* 3(1):3–17.

2004 [1929]   *The Southern Frontier, 1670–1732*. The University of Alabama Press. Tuscaloosa.
Cridlebaugh, Patricia A.
1984   American Indian and Euro-American Impact upon Holocene Vegetation
in the Lower Little Tennessee River Valley, East Tennessee. PhD dissertation, Department of Anthropology, University of Tennessee, Knoxville.
Crites, Gary D.
1984   Late Mississippian Paleoethnobotany in the Nashville Basin: The Evidence
from Averbuch. In *Averbuch: A Late Mississippian Manifestation in the
Nashville Basin*, edited by W. E. Klippel and W. M. Bass, pp. 12.11–12.23.
Report submitted to the National Park Service. Department of Anthropology, University of Tennessee, Knoxville.
Cronon, William
1983   *Changes in the Land: Indians, Colonists, and the Ecology of New England*.
Hill and Wang, New York.
Crook, Morgan R., Jr.
1990   *Rae's Creek: A Multicomponent Archaeological Site at the Fall Line Along
the Savannah River*. Report submitted to the Georgia Department of
Transportation. Department of Anthropology, Georgia State University,
Atlanta.
Crosby, Alfred W., Jr.
1972   *The Columbian Exchange: Biological and Cultural Consequences of 1492*.
Greenwood Press, Westport, Connecticut.
D'Altroy, Terence D., and Timothy K. Earle
1985   Staple Finance, Wealth Finance, and Storage in the Inka Political Economy. *Current Anthropology* 26(2):187–206.
Dalan, Rinita A., George R. Holley, William I. Woods, Harold W. Watters, Jr., and John
A. Koepke
2003   *Envisioning Cahokia: A Landscape Perspective*. Northern Illinois University Press, DeKalb.
Davis, R. P. Stephen, Jr., and Brett H. Riggs
2004   An Introduction to the Catawba Project. *North Carolina Archaeology* 53:1–
41.
Davis, R. P. Stephen, Jr., Brett H. Riggs, and David J. Cranford
2015   *Archaeology at Ayers Town: An Early Federal Period Community in the Catawba Nation*. Research Report 37. Research Laboratories of Archaeology,
University of North Carolina, Chapel Hill.
Dawdy, Shannon L.
2000   Understanding Cultural Change Through the Vernacular: Creolization in
Louisiana. *Historical Archaeology* 34(3):107–123.
2010   Clockpunk Anthropology and the Ruins of Modernity. *Current Anthropology* 51(6):761–793.

De Baillou, Clemens
1957   The Chief Vann house, The Vann's Tavern and Ferry. *Early Georgia* 2(2):3–11.
1963   James Vann, A Cherokee Chief. *The Georgia Review* 17(3):271–283.
Deagan, Kathleen A.
1983   *Spanish St. Augustine: The Archaeology of a Colonial Creole Community.* Academic Press, New York.
2008   Environmental Archaeology and Historical Archaeology. In *Case Studies in Environmental Archaeology*, edited by E. Reitz, C. M. Scarry and S. J. Scudder, pp. 21–42. Springer, New York.
Deetz, James F.
1977   *In Small Things Forgotten: Archaeology and Early American Life.* Anchor Books, New York.
1996   *In Small Things Forgotten: Archaeology and Early American Life, Revised and Expanded Edition.* Anchor Books, New York.
Delcourt, Paul A., and Hazel R. Delcourt
1998   The Influence of Prehistoric Human-Set Fires on Oak-Chestnut Forests in the Southern Appalachians. *Castanea* 63(3):337–345.
2004   *Prehistoric Native Americans and Ecological Change: Human Ecosystems in Eastern North America since the Pleistocene.* Cambridge University Press, Cambridge, United Kingdom.
Deloria, Vine, Jr.
1969   *Custer Died for Your Sins: An Indian Manifesto.* Macmillan, New York.
1992   *God Is Red: A Native View of Religion.* 2nd ed. North American Press, Golden, Colorado.
DePratter, Chester B.
1989   Cofitachequi: Ethnohistorical and Archaeological Evidence. In *Studies in South Carolina Archaeology: Essays in Honor of Robert L. Stephenson*, edited by I. Albert C. Goodyear and G. T. Hanson, pp. 133–156. University of South Carolina, Columbia.
1991   *Late Prehistoric and Early Historic Chiefdoms in the Southeastern United States.* Garland, New York.
2003   The Savannah River Valley A.D. 1540 to 1715. In *The Savannah River Valley to 1865*, edited by A. Callahan, pp. 15–27. Georgia Museum of Art, University of Georgia, Athens.
2009   Irene and Altamaha Ceramics from the Charlesfort/Santa Elena Site, Parris, Island, South Carolina. In *From Santa Elena to St. Augustine: Indigenous Ceramic Variability (A.D. 1400–1700)*, edited by K. Deagan and D. H. Thomas, pp. 19–47. American Museum of Natural History, New York.
Diamond, Jared
2005   *Collapse: How Societies Choose to Fail or Succeed.* Penguin, New York.
Dickens, Roy S., Jr.
1976   *Cherokee Prehistory: The Pisgah Phase in the Appalachian Summit Region.* The University of Tennessee Press, Knoxville.

Dietler, Michael, and Brian Hayden (editors)
2001   *Feasts: Archaeological and Ethnographic Perspectives on Food, Politics, and Power.* Smithsonian Institution Press, Washington, DC.

Dobyns, Henry F.
1983   *Their Number Become Thinned: Native American Population Dynamics in Eastern North America.* University of Tennessee Press, Knoxville.

Donnan, Hastings, and Thomas M. Wilson
1999   *Borders: Frontiers of Identity, Nation and State.* Berg, Oxford.

Drooker, Penelope B., and C. Wesley Cowan
2001   Transformation of the Fort Ancient Cultures of the Central Ohio Valley. In *Societies in Eclipse: Archaeology of the Eastern Woodlands Indians, A.D. 1400–1700,* edited by D. S. Brose, C. W. Cowan and Robert C. Mainfort Jr., pp. 83–106. Smithsonian Institution Press, Washington, DC.

Dunlop, J. G.
1929   Capt. Dunlop's Voyage to the Southward. 1687. *The South Carolina Historical and Genealogical Magazine* 30(3):127–133.

DuVal, Kathleen
2006   *The Native Ground: Indians and Colonists in the Heart of the Continent.* University of Pennsylvania Press, Philadelphia.

Dye, David H.
1995   Feasting with the Enemy: Mississippian Warfare and Prestige-Goods Circulation. In *Native American Interactions: Multiscalar Analyses and Interpretations in the Eastern Woodlands,* edited by M. S. Nassaney and K. E. Sassaman, pp. 289–316. University of Tennessee Press, Knoxville.
2009   *War Paths, Peace Paths: An Archaeology of Cooperation and Conflict in Native Eastern North America.* Altamira Press, New York.

Early, Ann M.
2011   The Greatest Gathering: The Second French-Chickasaw War in the Mississippi Valley and the Potential for Archaeology. In *French Colonial Archaeology in the Southeast and Caribbean,* edited by K. G. Kelly and M. D. Hardy, pp. 81–96. University Press of Florida, Gainesville.

Edmonds, Mark
1999   *Ancestral Geographies of the Neolithic: Landscapes, Monuments and Memory.* Routledge, London.

Ehle, John
1988   *Trail of Tears: The Rise and Fall of the Cherokee Nation.* Doubleday, New York.

Eisenberg, Leslie E.
1991   Mississippian Cultural Terminations in Middle Tennessee: What the Bioarchaeological Evidence Can Tell Us. In *What Mean These Bones? Studies in Southeastern Bioarchaeology,* edited by M. L. Powell, P. S. Bridges and A. M. W. Mires, pp. 70–88. University of Alabama Press, Tuscaloosa.

Elliott, Daniel T.
1991   Lost and Found: Eighteenth-Century Towns in the Savannah River Region. *Early Georgia* 19(2):61–92.
2012   Yuchi in the Lower Savannah Valley: Historical Context and Archaeological Confirmation. In *Enigmatic Origins: On the Yuchi of the Contact Era*, edited by J. B. Jackson, pp. 73–99. University of Nebraska Press, Lincoln.
Elliott, Daniel T., and Rita F. Elliott
1997   *The Yuchi Village at Mount Pleasant*. Lamar Institute Publication Series Report Number 137. The Lamar Institute, Savannah, Georgia.
Elliott, Dolores
1977   Otsiningo, An Example of an Eighteenth Century Settlement Pattern. In *Current Perspectives in Northeastern Archeology: Essays in Honor of William A. Ritchie*, edited by R. E. Funk and C. F. Hayes, pp. 93–105. New York State Archaeological Association, Albany.
Emerson, Thomas E., and Eve Hargrave
2000   Strangers in Paradise? Recognizing Ethnic Mortuary Diversity on the Fringes of Cahokia. *Southeastern Archaeology* 19(1):1–23.
Engel, Katherine Carté
2009   *Religion and Profit: Moravians in Early America*. *University of Pennsylvania Press, Philadelphia*.
Ethridge, Robbie
2003   *Creek Country: The Creek Indians and Their World*. University of North Carolina Press, Chapel Hill.
2006   Creating the Shatter Zone: The Indian Slave Traders and the Collapse of the Southeastern Chiefdoms. In *Light on the Path: The Anthropology and History of the Southeastern Indians*, edited by T. J. Pluckhahn and R. Ethridge, pp. 207–218. The University of Alabama Press, Tuscaloosa.
2009   Introduction: Mapping the Mississippian Shatter Zone. In *Mapping the Mississippian Shatter Zone*, edited by R. Ethridge and S. M. Shuck-Hall, pp. 1–62. University of Nebraska Press, Lincoln.
2010   *From Chicaza to Chickasaw*. University of North Carolina Press, Chapel Hill.
Ethridge, Robbie, and Charles Hudson (editors)
2002   *The Transformation of the Southeastern Indians*. University Press of Mississippi, Jackson.
Ethridge, Robbie, and Sheri M. Shuck-Hall (editors)
2009   *Mapping the Mississippian Shatter Zone*. University of Nebraska Press, Lincoln.
Falkner, James
2015   *The War of the Spanish Succession, 1701–1714*. Pen & Sword Military, South Yorkshire, United Kingdom.
Fennell, Christopher C.
2007   *Crossroads & Cosmologies: Diasporas and Ethnogenesis in the New World*. University Press of Florida, Gainesville.

Ferris, Neal
2009   *The Archaeology of Native-Lived Colonialism: Challenging History in the Great Lakes.* University of Arizona Press, Tucson.
Ferris, Neal, Rodney Harrison, and Michael V. Wilcox (editors)
2014   *Rethinking Colonial Pasts Through Archaeology.* Oxford University Press, Oxford.
Fitts, Mary Elizabeth
2006   Mapping Catawba Coalescence. *North Carolina Archaeology* 55:1–59.
2017   *Fit for War: Sustenance and Order in the Mid-Eighteenth-Century Catawba Nation.* University of Florida Press, Gainesville.
Foster, H. Thomas, II
2007   *Archaeology of the Lower Muskogee Creek Indians, 1715–1836.* The University of Alabama Press, Tuscaloosa.
2016   Variable Diversity from Managed Ecosystems in Long-Term Chronosequences from the Southeastern United States. In *Viewing the Future in the Past: Historical Ecology Applications to Environmental Issues,* edited by H. T. Foster II, L. M. Paciulli, and D. J. Goldstein, pp. 163–177. University of South Carolina Press, Columbia.
2017   The Identification and Significance of Apalachicola for the Origins of the Creek Indians in the Southeastern United States *Southeastern Archaeology* 36(1):1–13.
Foster, H. Thomas, II, and Arthur D. Cohen
2007   Palynological Evidence of the Effects of the Deer Skin Trade on Eighteenth Century Forests of Southeastern North America. *American Antiquity* 72(1):35–51.
Foster, H. Thomas, II, Bryan Black, and Marc D. Abrams
2004   A Witness Tree Analysis of the Effects of Native American Indians on the pre-European Settlement Forests in East-Central Alabama. *Human Ecology* 32(1):27–47.
Foucault, Michel
1977   *Discipline and Punish: The Birth of the Prison.* Translated by A. Sheridan. Vintage, New York.
Fowles, Severin M.
2009   The Enshrined Pueblo: Villagescape and Cosmos in the Northern Rio Grande. *American Antiquity* 74(3):448–466.
2010   The Southwest School of Landscape Archaeology. *Annual Review of Anthropology* 39:453–468.
2015   Writing Collapse. In *Social Theory in Archaeology and Ancient History: The Present and Future of Counternarratives,* edited by G. Emberling, pp. 205–230. Cambridge University Press, Cambridge, United Kingdom.
Francis, J. Michael, and Kathleen M. Kole, with contribution by David Hurst Thomas
2011   *Murder and Martyrdom in Spanish Florida: Don Juan and the Guale Uprising of 1597.* Anthropological Papers 95. The American Museum of Natural History, New York.

Friedman, Jonathan
1994   *Cultural Identity and Global Process.* Sage, London.
Fritz, Gayle J.
1990   Multiple Pathways to Farming in Precontact Eastern North America. *Journal of World Prehistory* 4(4):387–435.
Gallay, Alan
2002   *The Indian Slave Trade: The Rise of the English Empire in the American South, 1670–1717.* Yale University Press, New Haven.
Gallivan, Martin D.
2005   Reconnecting the Contact Period and Late Prehistory: Household and Community Dynamics in the James River Basin. In *Contact Period Archaeology of the Chesapeake,* edited by D. B. Blanton and J. A. King, pp. 22–46. University of Florida Press, Gainesville.
2007   Powhatan's Werowocomoco: Constructing Place, Polity, and Personhood in the Chesapeake, C.E. 1200–1609. *American Anthropologist* 109(1):85–100.
2012   Native History in the Chesapeake: The Powhatan Chiefdom and Beyond. In *The Oxford Handbook of North American Archaeology,* edited by T. Pauketat, pp. 310–322. Oxford University Press, New York.
2016   *The Powhatan Landscape: An Archaeological History of the Algonquian Chesapeake.* University Press of Florida, Gainesville.
Galloway, Patricia K.
1995   *Choctaw Genesis, 1500–1700.* University of Nebraska Press, Lincoln.
1998   Debriefing Explorers: Amerindian Information in the Delisles' Mapping of the Southeast. In *Cartographic Encounters: Perspectives on Native American Mapmaking and Map Use,* edited by G. M. Lewis, pp. 223–240. The University of Chicago Press, Chicago.
Gannon, Michael V.
1989   *The Cross in the Sand.* 2nd ed. University Presses of Florida, Gainesville.
Gao, Chaochao, Alan Robock, Stephen Self, Jeffrey B. Witter, J. P. Steffensen, Henrik Brink Clausen, Marie-Louise Siggaard-Andersen, Sigfus Johnsen, Paul A. Mayewski, and Caspar Ammann
2006   The 1452 or 1453 A.D. Kuwae Eruption Signal Derived from Multiple Ice Core Records: Greatest Volcanic Sulfate Event of the Past 700 Years. *Journal of Geophysical Research: Atmospheres* 111:(D12) D12107.
Gatschet, Albert S.
1884   *A Migration Legend of the Creek Indians,* Vol. I. D. G. Brinton, Philadelphia.
Gibson, Arrell M.
1971   *The Chickasaws.* University of Oklahoma Press, Norman.
Giddens, Anthony
1990   *The Consequences of Modernity.* Stanford University Press, Stanford, California.

Given, Michael
2004   *The Archaeology of the Colonized.* Routledge, London.
Gosden, Christopher
2004   *Archaeology and Colonialism: Cultural Contact from 5000 BC to the Present.* Cambridge University Press, Cambridge, United Kingdom.
Graeber, David
2011   *Debt: The First 5,000 Years.* Melville House Publishing, Brooklyn, New York.
Green, William
1992   The Search for Altamaha: The Archaeology and Ethnohistory of an Early 18th Century Yamasee Indian Town. In *Volumes in Historical Archaeology 21,* edited by S. South. South Carolina Institute of Archaeology and Anthropology, University of South Carolina, Columbia.
Green, William, Chester DePratter, and Bobby Southerlin
2002   The Yamasee in South Carolina: Native American Adaptation and Interaction Along the Carolina Frontier. In *Another's Country: Archaeological and Historical Perspectives on Cultural Interactions in the Southern Colonies,* edited by J. W. Joseph and M. Zierden, pp. 13–29. The University of Alabama Press, Tuscaloosa.
Greene, Lance
2010   Identity in a Post-Removal Cherokee Household, 1838–50. In *American Indians and the Market Economy, 1775–1850,* edited by L. Greene and M. R. Plane, pp. 53–66. The University of Alabama Press, Tuscaloosa.
Gremillion, Kristen J.
1995   Comparative Paleo-ethnobotany of Three Native Southeastern Communities of the Historic Period. *Southeastern Archaeology* 14(1):1–16.
1998   Changing Roles of Wild and Cultivated Plant Resources Among Early Famers of Eastern Kentucky. *Southeastern Archaeology* 17(2):140–157.
2002   Human Ecology at the Edge of Prehistory. In *Between Contacts and Colonies: Archaeological Perspectives on the Protohistoric Southeast,* edited by C. B. Wesson and M. A. Rees, pp. 12–31. The University of Alabama Press, Tuscaloosa.
Gresham, Thomas H.
1990   Historic Patterns of Rock Piling and the Rock Pile Problems. *Early Georgia* 18(1–2):1–40.
Gupta, Akhail, and James Ferguson
1997   Culture, Power, Place: Ethnography at the End of an Era. In *Culture, Power, Place: Explorations in Critical Anthropology,* edited by A. Gupta and J. Ferguson, pp. 1–29. Duke University Press, Durham, North Carolina.
Hahn, Steven C.
2004   *The Invention of the Creek Nation, 1670–1763.* University of Nebraska Press, Lincoln.
2006   The Cussita Migration Legend: History, Ideology, and the Politics of Myth-making. In *Light on the Path: The Anthropology and History of the South-*

eastern Indians, edited by T. J. Pluckhahn and R. Ethridge, pp. 57–92. The University of Alabama Press, Tuscaloosa.

2012   *The Life and Times of Mary Musgrove.* University Press of Florida, Gainesville.

Hall, Amanda A.

2016   San Antonio de Pocotalaca: An Eighteenth-Century Yamasee Indian Town in St. Augustine, Florida, 1716–1752. Master's thesis, Department of History, University of North Florida, Jacksonville.

Hall, Joseph M., Jr.

2009   *Zamumo's Gifts: Indo-European Exchange in the Colonial Southeast.* University of Pennsylvania Press, Philadelphia.

Hally, David J.

1979   *Archaeological Investigation of the Little Egypt Site (9MU102) Murray County, Georgia, 1969 Season.* Laboratory of Archaeology Series, Report No. 18. University of Georgia, Athens.

1986   The Cherokee Archaeology of Georgia. In *The Conference on Cherokee Prehistory*, edited by D. G. Moore, pp. 95–121. Warren Wilson College, Swannanoa, North Carolina.

1993   The Territorial Size of Mississippian Chiefdoms. In *Archaeology of Eastern North America: Papers in Honor of Stephen Williams*, edited by J. B. Stoltman, pp. 143–168. Mississippi Department of Archives and History, Jackson.

1994   The Chiefdom of Coosa. In *The Forgotten Centuries: Indians and Europeans in the American South, 1521–1704*, edited by C. Hudson and C. C. Tesser, pp. 227–253. University of Georgia Press, Athens.

1996   Platform Mound Construction and the Instability of Mississippian Chiefdoms. In *Political Structure and Change in the Prehistoric Southeastern United States*, edited by J. F. Scarry, pp. 92–127. University of Florida Press, Gainesville.

2002   "As Caves beneath the Ground": Making Sense of Aboriginal House Form in the Protohistoric and Historic Southeast. In *Between Contacts and Colonies: Archaeological Perspectives on the Protohistoric Southeast*, edited by C. B. Wesson and M. A. Rees, pp. 90–109. The University of Alabama Press, Tuscaloosa.

2008   *King: The Social Archaeology of a Late Mississippian Town in Northwestern Georgia.* The University of Alabama Press, Tuscaloosa.

Hally, David J., and Marvin T. Smith

2010   Sixteenth-Century Mechanisms of Exchange. *Journal of Global Initiatives* 5(1):53–65.

Hamilakis, Yannis

2013   *Archaeology of the Senses: Human Experience, Memory, and Affect.* Cambridge University Press, Cambridge, United Kingdom.

Hammett, Julie E.
1992   Ethnohistory of Aboriginal Landscapes in the Southeastern United States. *Southern Indian Studies* 41:1–50.

Hann, John H.
1986   Demographic Patterns and Changes in Mid-Seventeenth Century Timucua and Apalachee. *Florida Historical Quarterly* 64(4):371–392.
1988   *Apalachee: The Land between the Rivers.* University of Florida Press, Gainesville.
1991   *Missions to the Calusa.* University Press of Florida, Gainesville.
1996   Late Seventeenth-Century Forebears of the Lower Creeks and Seminoles. *Southeastern Archaeology* 15(1):66–80.
2003   *Indians of Central and South Florida, 1513–1763.* University Press of Florida, Gainesville.

Hanson, Lee H.
1966   *The Hardin Village Site.* Studies in Anthropology, Vol. 4. University of Kentucky, Lexington.

Hare, Timothy S.
2004   Using Measures of Cost Distance in the Estimation of Polity Boundaries in the Postclassic Yuatepec Valley, Mexico. *Journal of Archaeological Science* 31(6):799–824.

Harn, Alan D.
1978   Mississippian Settlement Patterns in the Central Illinois River Valley. In *Mississippian Settlement Patterns*, edited by B. D. Smith, pp. 233–268. Academic Press, New York.

Harrison, Rodney
2004   Shared Histories and the Archaeology of the Pastoral Industry in Australia. In *After Captain Cook: The Archaeology of the Recent Indigenous Past in Australia*, edited by R. Harrison and C. Williamson, pp. 37–58. AltaMira Press, Walnut Creek, California.

Hart, John P., David L. Asch, C. Margaret Scarry, and Gary W. Crawford
2002   The Age of the Common Bean (*Phaseolus vulgaris* L.) in the Northern Eastern Woodlands of North America. *Antiquity* 76:377–383.

Hart, William B.
1998   Black "Go-Betweens" and the Mutability of "Race," Status, and Identity on New York's Pre-Revolutionary Frontier. In *Contact Points: American Frontiers from the Mohawk Valley to the Mississippi, 1750–1830*, edited by A.R.L. Cayton and F. J. Teute, pp. 88–113. University of North Carolina Press, Chapel Hill.

Hatch, James W.
1995   Lamar Period Farmsteads of the Oconee River Valley, Georgia. In *Mississippian Communities and Households*, edited by J. D. Rogers and B. D. Smith, pp. 135–155. University of Alabama Press, Tuscaloosa.

Hatley, M. Thomas
1989   The Three Lives of Keowee: Loss and Recovery in Eighteenth Century Cherokee Villages. In *Powhatan's Mantle: Indians in the Colonial Southeast*, edited by P. H. Wood, G. A. Waselkov and M. T. Hatley, pp. 223–248. University of Nebraska Press, Lincoln.

Hauptman, Laurence M.
1980   Refugee Havens: The Iroquois Villages of the Eighteenth Century. In *American Indian Environments*, edited by C. Vecsey and R. W. Venables, pp. 128–207. Syracuse University Press, Syracuse, New York.

Hawkins, Benjamin
1916   *Letters of Benjamin Hawkins 1796–1806*. Collections of the Georgia Historical Society, Vol. 9 Georgia Historical Society, Savannah.

Hayden, Brian
2014   *The Power of Feasts: From Prehistory to the Present*. Cambridge University Press, Cambridge, United Kingdom.

Headlam, Cecil (editor)
1933   America and West Indies: January 1720, 1–15. In *Calendar of State Papers Colonial, America and West Indies: 31. 1719–1720*. His Majesty's Stationery Office, London.

Heath, Barbara J.
2016   Dynamic Landscapes: The Emergence of Formal Spaces in Colonial Virginia. *Historical Archaeology* 50(1):27–44.

Heffernan, Michael
1999   Historical Geographies of the Future: Three Perspectives from France, 1750–1825. In *Geography and Enlightenment*, edited by David N. Livingstone and Charles W. J. Withers, pp. 125–164. The University of Chicago Press, Chicago.

Hemmings, Thomas, and Kathleen Deagan
1973   *Excavations on Amelia Island in Northeast Florida*. Contributions of the Florida State Museum. Florida State Museum, Gainesville.

Henderson, A. Gwynn, David Pollack, and Christopher A. Turnbow
1992   Chronology and Cultural Patterns. In *Fort Ancient Cultural Dynamics in the Middle Ohio Valley*, edited by A. G. Henderson, pp. 253–279. Prehistory Press, Madison, Wisconsin.

Hiemstra, William L.
1959   Presbyterian Missions Among Choctaw and Chickasaw Indians. *Journal of the Presbyterian Historical Society* 37(1):51–59.

Himmelfarb, Gertrude
2004   *The Roads to Modernity: The British, French, and American Enlightenments*. Vintage, New York.

Hirsch, Eric
1995   Landscape: Between Place and Space. In *The Anthropology of Landscape: Perspectives on Place and Space*, edited by E. Hirsch and M. O'Hanlon, pp. 1–30. Clarendon Press, Oxford.

Hodge, Christina
2014   *Consumerism and the Emergence of the Middle Class in Colonial America.*
            Cambridge University Press, Cambridge, United Kingdom.
Hoffman, Paul E.
1997   Did Coosa Decline Between 1541 and 1560? *Florida Anthropologist*
            50(1):25–29.
Hollenbach, Kandace D.
2017   Plant Use at a Mississippian and Contact-Period Site in the South Carolina
            Coastal Plain. In *Forging Southeastern Identities: Social Archaeology, Eth-
            nohistory, and Folklore of the Mississippian to Early Historic South*, edited
            by G. A. Waselkov and M. T. Smith, pp. 157–181. The University of Ala-
            bama Press, Tuscaloosa.
Holley, George R.
1999   Late Prehistoric Towns in the Southeast. In *Great Towns and Regional
            Polities in the Prehistoric American Southwest and Southeast*, edited by J.
            Neitzel, pp. 23–38. University of New Mexico Press, Albuquerque.
Hudson, Charles
1976   *The Southeastern Indians.* The University of Tennessee Press, Knoxville.
1990   *The Juan Pardo Expeditions: Exploration of the Carolinas and Tennessee,
            1566–1568.* The University of Alabama Press, Tuscaloosa.
2002   Introduction. In *The Transformation of the Southeastern Indians, 1540–
            1760*, edited by R. Ethridge and C. Hudson, pp. xi–xxxix. University of
            Mississippi Press, Jackson.
Hudson, Charles, Marvin T. Smith, Chester B. DePratter, and Emilia Kelley
1989   The Tristán de Luna Expedition, 1559–1561. *Southeastern Archaeology*
            8(1):31–45.
Hudson, Charles, Marvin Smith, David Hally, Richard Polhemus, and Chester DePratter
1985   Coosa: A Chiefdom in the Sixteenth-Century Southeastern United States.
            American Antiquity 50(4):723–737.
Hudson, Charles, and Carmen Chaves Tesser
1994   Introduction. In *The Forgotten Centuries: Indians and Europeans in the
            American South, 1521–1704*, edited by C. Hudson and C. C. Tesser, pp. 1–14.
            University of Georgia Press, Athens.
Hultman, Maja
2013   Soundscape Archaeology: Ringing Stone Research in Sweden. *Time and
            Mind* 7(1):3–12.
Hutchinson, Dale L., and Clark Spencer Larsen
2001   Enamel Hypopolasia and Stress in La Florida. In *Bioarchaeology of Span-
            ish Florida: The Impact of Colonialism*, edited by C. S. Larsen, pp. 181–206.
            University Press of Florida, Gainesville.
Ingold, Tim
1993   The Temporality of the Landscape. *World Archaeology* 25(2):152–174.
2000   *The Perception of the Environment: Essays on Livelihood, Dwelling and Skill.*
            Routledge, London.

Ivers, Larry E.
1970   *Colonial Forts of South Carolina*. Tricentennial Booklet Number 3. University of South Carolina Press, Columbia.

Ives, Timothy H.
2013   Remembering Stone Piles in New England. *Northeast Anthropology* 79–80:37–80.

Jefferies, Richard W.
1976   *The Tunacunnhee Site: Evidence of Hopewell Interaction in Northwest Georgia*. Anthropological Papers of the University of Georgia Number 1. The University of Georgia, Athens.

1997   Middle Archaic Bone Pins: Evidence of Mid-Holocene Regional-Scale Social Groups in the Southern Midwest. *American Antiquity* 62(3):464–487.

Jenkins, Ned J.
2009   Tracing the Origins of the Early Creeks, 1050–1700 CE. In *Mapping the Mississippian Shatter Zone: The Colonial Indian Slave Trade and Regional Instability in the American South*, edited by R. Ethridge and S. M. Shuck-Hall, pp. 188–249. University of Nebraska Press, Lincoln.

Jennings, Jesse E.
1947   Nutt's Trip to the Chickasaw Country. *Journal of Mississippi History* 9(1):34–61.

Johnson, Jay K.
1996   The Nature and Timing of the Late Prehistoric Settlement of the Black Prairie in Northeast Mississippi: A Reply to Hogue, Peacock, and Rafferty. *Southeastern Archaeology* 15(2):244–249.

1997   Stone Tools, Politics, and the Eighteenth-Century Chickasaw in Northeast Mississippi. *American Antiquity* 62(2):215–230.

2000   *The Chickasaws*. In *Indians of the Greater Southeast: Historical Archaeology and Ethnohistory*, edited by B. G. McEwan, pp. 85–121. University Press of Florida, Gainesville.

Johnson, Jay K., John W. O'Hear, Robbie Ethridge, Brad R. Lieb, Susan L. Scott, and H. Edwin Jackson
2008   Measuring Chickasaw Adaptation on the Western Frontier of the Colonial South: A Correlation of Documentary and Archaeological Data. *Southeastern Archaeology* 27(1):1–30.

Johnson, Matthew
1996   *An Archaeology of Capitalism*. Blackwell, Cambridge, Massachusetts.

2012   Phenomenological Approaches in Landscape Archaeology. *Annual Review of Anthropology* 41:269–284.

Jones, Andrew M.
2005   Lives in Fragments? Personhood and the European Neolithic. *Journal of Anthropological Archaeology* 5(2):193–224.

2007   *Memory and Material Culture*. Cambridge University Press, Cambridge, United Kingdom.

Jones, Eric E.

2010   An Analysis of the Factors Influencing Sixteenth- and Seventeenth-Century Haudenosaunee (Iroquois) Settlement Locations. *Journal of Anthropological Archaeology* 29(1):1–14.

2016   Multiscalar Settlement Ecology Study of Piedmont Village Tradition Communities In North Carolina, AD 1000–1600. *Southeastern Archaeology* 35(2):85–114.

2017   Significance and Context in GIS-Based Spatial Archaeology: A Case Study from Southeastern North America. *Journal of Archaeological Science* 84:54–62.

Jones, Siân

1997   *The Archaeology of Ethnicity: Constructing Identities in the Past and Present*. Routledge, New York.

Jordan, Kurt A.

2013   Incorporation and Colonization: Postcolumbian Iroquois Satellite Communities and Process of Indigenous Autonomy. *American Anthropologist* 115(1):29–43.

Juricek, John T.

2015   *Endgame for Empire: British-Creek Relations in Georgia and Vicinity, 1763–1776*. University Press of Florida, Gainesville.

Kassabaum, Megan

2018   Early Platforms, Early Plazas: Exploring the Precursors to Mississippian Mound-and-Plaza Centers. *Journal of Archaeological Research*, doi. org/10.1007/s1081.

Keel, Bennie C.

1976   *Cherokee Archaeology: A Study of the Appalachian Summit*. The University of Tennessee Press, Knoxville.

Kelly, John H.

1991   Cahokia and Its Role as a Gateway Center in Interregional Exchange. In *Cahokia and the Hinterlands*, edited by T. E. Emerson and R. B. Lewis, pp. 61–80. University of Illinois Press, Urbana.

Kelton, Paul

2007   *Epidemics and Enslavement: Biological Catastrophe in the Native Southeast, 1492–1715*. University of Nebraska Press, Lincoln.

Kennedy, Roger G.

1994   *Hidden Cities: The Discovery and Loss of Ancient North American Civilization*. Penguin Books, New York.

Kidder, Tristram R.

2004   Plazas as Architecture: An Example from the Raffman Site, Northeast Louisiana. *American Antiquity* 69:514–532.

King, Adam

2003   *Etowah: the Political History of a Chiefdom Capital*. The University of Alabama Press, Tuscaloosa.

2006   The Historic Period Transformation of Mississippian Societies. In *Light on the Path: The Anthropology and History of the Southeastern Indians*, edited by T. J. Pluckhahn and R. Ethridge, pp. 179–195. The University of Alabama Press, Tuscaloosa.

Knauft, Bruce M.
2002   Critically Modern: An Introduction. In *Critically Modern: Alternatives, Alterities, Anthropologies*, edited by B. M. Knauft, pp. 1–54. Indiana University Press, Bloomington.

Knight, V. James, Jr.
1981   Mississippian Ritual, PhD dissertation, Department of Anthropology, University of Florida, Gainesville.
1994   The Formation of the Creeks. In *The Forgotten Centuries: Indians and Europeans in the American South, 1521–1704*, edited by C. Hudson and C. C. Tesser, pp. 373–392. University of Georgia Press, Athens.
1998   Moundville as a Diagrammatic Ceremonial Center. In *Archaeology of the Moundville Chiefdom*, edited by V. J. Knight, Jr., and V. P. Steponaitis, pp. 44–62. Smithsonian Institution Press, Washington, DC.

Koldehoff, Brad
1989   Cahokia's Immediate Hinterland. *Illinois Archaeology: The Mississippian Occupation of Douglas Creek* 1(1):39–68.

Koldehoff, Brad, Timothy R. Pauketat, and John E. Kelly
1993   The Emerald Site and the Mississippian Occupation of the Central Silver Creek Valley. *Illinois Archaeology* 5(1–2):331–343.

Konstam, Angus
2008   *Piracy: The Complete History*. Osprey Publishing, Oxford.

Kowalewski, Stephen A.
2006   Coalescent Societies. In *Light on the Path: Anthropology and History of the Southeastern Indians*, edited by T. J. Pluckhahn and R. Ethridge, pp. 94–122. The University of Alabama Press, Tuscaloosa.

Kowalewski, Stephen A., and James W. Hatch
1991   The Sixteenth-Century Expansion of Settlement in the Upper Oconee Watershed. *Southeastern Archaeology* 10:1–17.

Krauthamer, Barbara
2013   *Black Slaves, Indian Masters: Slavery, Emancipation, and Citizenship in the Native American South*. The University of North Carolina Press, Chapel Hill.

Krus, Anthony M.
2016   The Timing of Precolumbian Militarization in the U.S. Midwest and Southeast. *American Antiquity* 81(3):375–388.

Krus, Anthony M., and Charles R. Cobb
2018   The Mississippian Fin de Siècle in the Middle Cumberland Region of Tennessee. *American Antiquity* 83(2):302–319.

Kuttruff, Carl
2010   *Fort Loudoun in Tennessee, 1756–1760: History, Archaeology, Replication,*

Exhibits, and Interpretation. Research Series No. 17. Tennessee Division of Archaeology, Nashville.

Kwass, Michael

2003   Ordering the World of Goods: Consumer Revolution and the Classification of Objects in Eighteenth-Century France. *Representations* 82(1):87–116.

Lakomäki, Sami

2014   *Gathering Together: The Shawnee People through Diaspora and Nationhood, 1600–1870.* Yale University Press, New Haven.

Lankford, George E.

1993   Red and White: Some Reflections on Southeastern Symbolism. *Southern Folklore* 50(1):53–80.

Lapham, Heather

2005   *Hunting for Hides.* The University of Alabama Press, Tuscaloosa.

Larsen, Clark Spencer, Margaret J. Schoeninger, Dale L. Hutchinson, Katherine F. Russell, and Christopher B. Ruff

1990   Beyond Demographic Collapse: Biological Adaptation and Change in Native Populations of La Florida. In *Columbian Consequences: 2. Archaeological and Historical Perspectives on the Spanish Borderlands East,* edited by D. H. Thomas, pp. 409–428. Smithsonian Institution Press, Washington, DC.

Larson, Lewis H.

1980   *Aboriginal Subsistence Technology on the Southeastern Coastal Plain during the Late Prehistoric Period.* University Presses of Florida, Gainesville.

Laudonnière, René

2001 [1587]   *Three Voyages.* Translated by C. E. Bennett. The University of Alabama Press, Tuscaloosa.

Lawson, John

1967 [1709]   *A New Voyage to Carolina.* University of North Carolina Press, Chapel Hill.

Le Page du Pratz, A.-S.

1975 [1758]   *The History of Louisiana.* Translated by J. J. G. Tregle. Louisiana State University Press, Baton Rouge.

Leacock, Eleanor

1954   *The Montagnais "Hunting Territory" and the Fur Trade.* Memoir 78. American Anthropological Association, Washington, DC.

Lekson, Stephen H., and Catherine M. Cameron

1995   The Abandonment of Chaco Canyon, the Mesa Verde Migrations, and the Reorganization of the Pueblo World. *Journal of Anthropological Archaeology* 14:184–202.

Leone, Mark P.

1988   The Georgian Order as the Order of Merchant Capitalism. In *The Recovery of Meaning: Historical Archaeology in the Eastern United States,* edited by M. P. Leone and J. Parker B. Potter, pp. 223–261. Smithsonian Institution Press, Washington, DC.

2005   *The Archaeology of Liberty in an American Capital: Excavations in Annapolis.* University of California Press, Berkeley.

Lewis, R. Barry, Charles Stout, and Cameron B. Wesson

1998   The Design of Mississippian Towns. In *Mississippian Towns and Sacred Spaces: Searching for an Architectural Grammar*, edited by R. B. Lewis and C. Stout, pp. 1–21. University of Alabama Press, Tuscaloosa.

Lieb, Brad Raymond

2008   The Natchez Indian Diaspora: Ethnohistoric Archaeology of the Eighteenth-Century Natchez Refuge Among the Chickasaws. PhD dissertation, Department of Anthropology, University of Alabama, Tuscaloosa.

Liebmann, Matthew

2008   Postcolonial Cultural Affiliation: Essentialism, Hybridity, and NAGPRA. In *Archaeology and the Postcolonial Critique*, edited by M. Liebmann and U. Z. Rizvi, pp. 73–90. AltaMira Press, Lanham, Maryland.

Liebmann, Matthew, and Uzma Z. Rizvi (editors)

2008   *Archaeology and the Postcolonial Critique.* AltaMira Press, Lanham, Maryland.

Lightfoot, Kent G., and Sara L. Gonzalez

2018   The Study of Sustained Colonialism: An Example from the Kashaya Pomo Homelands in Northern California. *American Antiquity* 83(3):427–443.

Lightfoot, Kent G., and Antoinette Martinez

1995   Frontiers and Borders in Archaeological Perspective. *Annual Review of Anthropology* 24:471–492.

Lilly, Ian

2006   Archaeology, Diaspora and Decolonization. *Journal of Social Archaeology* 6(1):28–47.

Livingood, Patrick

2015   The Many Dimensions of Hally Circles. In *Archaeological Perspectives on the Southern Appalachians: Multiscalar Approaches*, edited by R. Gougeon and M. Meyers, pp. 245–262. University of Tennessee Press, Knoxville.

Lopinot, Neal H., and William I. Woods

1993   Wood Overexploitation and the Collapse of Cahokia. In *Foraging and Farming in the Eastern Woodlands*, edited by C. M. Scarry, pp. 206–321. University Press of Florida, Gainesville.

Loren, Diana DePaolo

2008   *In Contact: Bodes and Spaces in the Sixteenth- and Seventeenth-Century Eastern Woodlands.* Altamira, Lanham, Maryland.

2010   *The Archaeology of Clothing and Bodily Adornment in Colonial America.* University Press of Florida, Gainesville.

Loucks, Lana Jill

1993   Spanish-Indian Interactions on the Florida Missions. In *Spanish Missions of La Florida*, edited by B. G. McEwan, pp. 193–216. University Press of Florida, Gainesville.

Lovell, Nadia

1998 Introduction: Belonging in Need of Emplacement. In *Locality and Belonging*, edited by N. Lovell, pp. 1–24. Routledge, London.

Low, Setha M., and Denise Lawrence-Zúñiga

2003 Locating Culture. In *The Anthropology of Space and Place: Locating Culture*, edited by S. M. Low and D. Lawrence-Zúñiga, pp. 1–48. Blackwell, Malden, Massachusetts.

Lynch, John

1989 *Bourbon Spain, 1700–1808.* Basil Blackwell, London.

Mack, Dustin J.

2018 The Chickasaws' Place World: The Mississippi River in Chickasaw History and Geography. *Native South* 11:1–28.

MacLeitch, Gail D.

2011 *Imperial Entanglements: Iroquois Change and Persistence on the Frontiers of Empire.* University of Pennsylvania Press, Philadelphia.

Mandeville, Bernard

1924 [1705] *The Fable of the Bees: Or, Private Vices, Publick Benefits.* Clarendon Press, Oxford.

Mann, Charles C.

2005 *1491: New Revelations of the Americas Before Columbus.* Vintage, New York.

2012 *1493: Uncovering the New World Columbus Created.* Vintage, New York.

Mann, Michael E., Zhihua Zhang, Scott Rutherford, Raymond S. Bradley, Malcolm K. Hughes, Drew Shindell, Caspar Ammann, Greg Faluvegi, and Fenbiao Ni

2014 Global Signatures and Dynamical Origins of the Little Ice Age and Medieval Climate Anomaly. *Science* 326(5957):1256–1260.

Mann, Rob

2005 Intruding on the Past: The Reuse of Ancient Earthen Mounds by Native Americans. *Southeastern Archaeology* 24(1):1–10.

Marcoux, Jon Bernard

2010 *Pox, Empire, Shackles, and Hides.* The University of Alabama Press, Tuscaloosa.

Marcus, George E., and Michael M. J. Fischer

1984 *Anthropology as Cultural Critique: An Experimental Moment in the Human Sciences.* University of Chicago Press, Chicago.

Marquardt, William H.

2014 Tracking the Calusa: A Retrospective. *Southeastern Archaeology* 33(1):1–24.

Marshall, P. J., and Glyn Williams

1982 *The Great Map of Mankind: British Perceptions of the World in the Age of Enlightenment.* J. M. Dent and Sons, London.

Marshall, Richard (editor)

1985 *The Emergent Mississippian: Proceedings of the Sixth Mid-South Archaeo-*

logical Conference. Cobb Institute of Archaeology, Mississippi State University, Starkville.

Martin, Ann Smart

2008   *Buying into the World of Goods: Early Consumers in Backcountry Virginia.* The John Hopkins University Press, Baltimore.

Martindale, Andrew

2009   Entanglement and Tinkering. *Journal of Social Archaeology* 9(1):59–91.

Maschner, Herbert

1996   The Politics of Settlement Choice on the Northwest Coast: Cognition, GIS, and Coastal Landscapes. In *Anthropology, Space, and Geographic Information Systems,* edited by M. Aldenderfer and H. Maschner, pp. 175–189. Oxford University Press, Oxford.

Matthews, Christopher N.

2002   *An Archaeology of History and Tradition: Moments of Danger in the Annapolis Landscape.* Kluwer Academic/Plenum, New York.

2010   *The Archaeology of American Capitalism.* University Press of Florida, Gainesville.

Maxwell, David

1998   "Delivered from the Spirit of Poverty?": Pentecostalism, Prosperity and Modernity in Zimbabwe. *Journal of Religion in Africa* 28(3):350–373.

McAnany, Patricia A., and Norman Yoffee (editors)

2009   *Questioning Collapse: Human Resilience, Ecological Vulnerability, and the Aftermath of Empire.* Cambridge University Press, Cambridge, United Kingdom.

McDonnold, Benjamin Wilburn

1899   *History of the Cumberland Presbyterian Church.* Board of Publication of Cumberland Presbyterian Church, Nashville.

McDowell, William

1955   *Journals of the Commissioners of the Indian Trade, September 20, 1710-August 29, 1718.* South Carolina Department of Archives and History, Columbia.

McKivergan, David. A., Jr.

1991   Migration and Settlement Among the Yamasee in South Carolina, Master's thesis, Department of Anthropology, University of South Carolina, Columbia.

Meeks, Scott C., and David G. Anderson

2013   Drought, Subsistence Stress, and Population Dynamics: Assessing Mississippian Abandonment of the Vacant Quarter. In *Soils, Climate, and Society: Archaeological Investigations in Ancient America,* edited by J. D. Wingard and S. E. Hayes, pp. 61–83. University Press of Colorado, Boulder.

Melton, Mallory A.

2018   Cropping in an Age of Captive Taking: Exploring Evidence for Uncertainty and Food Insecurity in the Seventeenth-Century North Carolina Piedmont. *American Antiquity* 83(2):204–223.

Merrell, James H.

1989   *The Indians' New World: Catawbas and Their Neighbors from European Contact through the Era of Removal.* University of North Carolina Press, Chapel Hill.

1999   *Into the American Woods: Negotiators on the Pennsylvania Frontier.* W. W. Norton, New York.

Meyers, Maureen

2009   From Refugees to Traders: The Transformation of the Westo Indians. In *Mapping the Mississippian Shatter Zone: The Colonial Indian Slave Trade and Regional Instability in the American South*, edited by R. Ethridge and S. M. Shuck-Hall, pp. 81–103. University of Nebraska Press, Lincoln.

2017   Social Integration at a Frontier and the Creation of Mississippian Social Identity in Southwestern Virginia. *Southeastern Archaeology* 36(2):144–155.

Mignolo, Walter

2000   The Many Faces of Cosmo-polis: Border Thinking and Critical Cosmo-politanism. *Public Culture* 12:721–748.

Milanich, Jerald T.

1978   The Western Timucua: Patterns of Acculturation and Change. In *Tacachale: Essays on the Indians of Florida and Southeastern Georgia during the Historic Period*, edited by J. Milanich and S. Proctor, pp. 59–88. University of Florida Press, Gainesville.

1999   *Laboring in the Fields of the Lord: Spanish Missions and Southeastern Indians.* Smithsonian Institution Press, Washington, DC.

Miller, Gifford H., Áslaug Geirsdóttir, Yafang Zhong, Darren J. Larsen,Bette L. Otto-Bliesner, Marika M. Holland, David A. Bailey, Kurt A. Refsnider, Scott J. Lehman, John R. Southon, Chance Anderson, Helgi Björnsson, and Thorvaldur Thordarson

2012   Abrupt Onset of the Little Ice Age Triggered by Volcanism and Sustained by Sea-Ice/Ocean Feedbacks. *Geophysical Research Letters* 39(2):1–5.

Milne, George Edward

2009   Picking Up the Pieces: Natchez Coalescence in the Shatter Zone. In *Mapping the Mississippian Shatter Zone: The Colonial Indian Slave Trade and Regional Instability in the American South*, edited by R. Ethridge and S. M. Shuck-Hall, pp. 388–417. University of Nebraska Press, Lincoln.

Milner, George R.

1993   Settlements Amidst Swamps. *Illinois Archaeology* 5:374–380.

1999   Warfare in Prehistoric and Early Historic North America. *Journal of Archaeological Research* 7(2):105–151.

2006   *The Cahokia Chiefdom: The Archaeology of a Mississippian Society.* University Press of Florida, Gainesville.

Milner, George R., Eve Anderson, and Virginia G. Smith

1991   Warfare in Late Prehistoric West-Central Illinois. *American Antiquity* 56:581–603.

Milner, George R., George Chaplin, and Emily Zavodny
2013   Conflict and Societal Change in Late Prehistoric North America. *Evolutionary Anthropology* 22(3):96–102.

Mintz, Max M.
1999   *Seeds of Empire: The American Revolutionary Conquest of the Iroquois.* New York University Press, New York.

Mintz, Sidney W.
1985   *Sweetness and Power: The Place of Sugar in Modern History.* Viking Penguin, New York.

Momaday, N. Scott
1974   Native American Attitudes to the Environment. In *Seeing with a Native Eye: Essays on Native American Religion,* edited by W. H. Capps, pp. 79–85. Harper and Row, New York.

Monaghan, G. William, Timothy M. Schilling, and Kathryn E. Parker
2014   The Age and Distribution of Domesticated Beans (*Phaseolous vulgaris*) in Eastern North America: Implications for Agricultural Practices and Group Interactions. *Midwest Archaeological Conference Occasional Papers* 1:33–52.

Mooney, James
1900   *Myths of the Cherokees.* Nineteenth Annual Report of the Burau of American Ethnology. Smithsonian Institution, Washington, DC.

Moore, Charity M., and Matthew Victor Weiss
2016   The Continuing "Stone Mound Problem": Identifying and interpreting the Ambiguous Rock Piles of the Upper Ohio Valley. *Journal of Ohio Archaeology* 4:39–72.

Moore, David G.
2002   *Catawba Valley Mississippian: Ceramics, Chronology, and Catawba Indians.* The University of Alabama Press, Tuscaloosa.

Moore, Michael C., and Kevin E. Smith
2009   *Archaeological Expeditions of the Peabody Museum in Middle Tennessee, 1877–1884.* Tennessee Department of Environment and Conservation, Division of Archaeology, Nashville.

Moretti-Langholtz, Danielle, and Buck Woodard
2017   An Evidence-Based Reinterpretation of the Brafferton Indian School. Paper presented at the 83rd Annual Meeting of the Society for American Archaeology, Washington DC.

Muller, Jon
1978   The Kincaid System: Mississippian Settlement in the Environs of a Large Site. In *Mississippian Settlement Patterns,* edited by B. D. Smith, pp. 269–292. Academic Press, New York.
1987   Salt, Chert, and Shell: Mississippian Exchange and Economy. In *Specialization, Exchange, and Complex Societies,* edited by E. M. Brumfiel and T. K. Earle, pp. 10–21. Cambridge University Press, Cambridge, United Kingdom.

1997   *Mississippian Political Economy.* Plenum Press, New York.
Myer, William E.
1928   Indian Trails of the Southeast. In *Forty-Second Annual Report of the Bu-reau of American Ethnology,* pp. 727–737. Smithsonian Institution, Washington, DC.
Nabokov, Peter
2002   *A Forest of Time: American Indian Ways of History.* Cambridge University Press, Cambridge, United Kingdom.
2006   *Where the Lightning Strikes: The Lives of American Indian Sacred Places.* Penguin Books, New York.
Nairne, Thomas
1988 [1708] *Nairne's Muskhogean Journals: The 1708 Expedition to the Mississippi River.* Edited by Alexander Moore. University Press of Mississippi, Jackson.
Nammack, Georgiana C.
1969   *Fraud, Politics, and the Dispossession of the Indians: The Iroquois Land Frontier in the Colonial Period.* University of Oklahoma Press, Norman.
Nassaney, Michael S.
2015   *The Archaeology of the North American Fur Trade.* University Press of Florida, Gainesville.
Naum, Magdalena
2010   Re-emerging Frontiers: Postcolonial Theory and Historical Archaeology of the Borderlands. *Journal of Archaeological Method and Theory* 17:101–131.
Needham, Maggie M.
2011   Cultural Pluralism, Migration and Ceramics: Reconsidering an Eighteenth Century Yuchi Settlement on the Savannah River (9EF169). Master's thesis, Department of Anthropology, University of South Carolina, Columbia.
Neitzel, Robert S.
1965   *Archaeology of the Fatherland Site: The Grand Village of the Natchez.* Anthropological Papers 51(1). American Museum of Natural History, New York.
Nelson, John C.
1997   Presettlement Vegetation Patterns along the 5th Principal Meridian, Missouri Territory, 1815. *American Midland Naturalist* 137(1):79–94.
Newsom, Lee Ann, and Barbara A. Purdy
1990   Florida Canoes: A Maritime Heritage from the Past. *The Florida Anthropologist* 43(3):164–180.
Neylan, Susan
2000   Longhouses, Schoolrooms and Worker's Cottages: Nineteenth-Century Protestant Missions to the Tsimshian and the Transformation of Class through Religion. *Journal of the Canadian Historical Association* 11(1):51–86.

Oatis, Steven J.
2004 *A Colonial Complex: South Carolina's Frontiers in the Era of the Yamasee War, 1680–1730.* University of Nebraska Press, Lincoln.

Oberg, Kalervo
1973 *The Social Economy of the Tlingit Indians.* University of Washington Press, Seattle.

O'Brien, Michael J., and Carl Kuttruff
2012 The 1974–75 Excavations at Mound Bottom, A Palisaded Mississippian Center in Cheatham County, Tennessee. *Southeastern Archaeology* 31(1):70–86.

O'Brien, Tim
1990 *The Things They Carried.* Houghton Mifflin, New York.

Oliphant, John Stuart
2001 *Peace and War on the Anglo-Cherokee Frontier, 1756–1763.* Louisiana State University Press, Baton Rouge.

Onuf, Peter S.
2000 *Jefferson's Empire: The Language of American Nationhood.* University Press of Virginia, Charlottesville.

Orser, Charles E., Jr.
1998 Archaeology of the African Diaspora. *Annual Review of Anthropology* 27:63–82.
2018 *An Archaeology of the English Atlantic World, 1600–1700.* Cambridge University Press, Cambridge, United Kingdom.

O'Steen, Lisa
2007 Animal Remains. In *Archaeology of the Lower Muskogee Creek Indians, 1715–1836,* by H. Thomas Foster II, pp. 194–255. University of Alabama Press, Tuscaloosa.

Panich, Lee M., and Tsim D. Schneider (editors)
2014 *Indigenous Landscapes and Spanish Missions: New Perspectives from Archaeology and Ethnohistory.* University of Arizona Press, Tucson.

Parish, Ryan M.
2013 Relationships between Procurement Strategies and Geological Provenience in the Dover Quarry Site Complex, Tennessee. *North American Archaeologist* 34(4):369–385.

Parker, Bradley J.
2006 Toward an Understanding of Borderland Processes. *American Antiquity* 71(1):77–100.

Parker, Kathryn
2016 *Botanical Remains from Stark Farm (200K778) in Regional Context.* Report submitted to Chickasaw Nation. Manuscript on file, Florida Museum of Natural History, Gainesville.

Pauketat, Timothy R.
2003 Resettled Farmers and the Making of a Mississippian Polity. *American Antiquity* 68(1):39–66.

2007   *Chiefdoms and Other Archaeological Delusions.* AltaMira Press, Lanham,
            Maryland.
2013   *An Archaeology of the Cosmos: Rethinking Agency and Religion in Ancient
            America.* Routledge, New York.
Pauketat, Timothy, and Susan Alt
2003   Mounds, Memory, and Contested Mississippian History. In *Archaeologies
            of Memory,* edited by R. V. Dyke and S. Alcock, pp. 151–179. Blackwell,
            Oxford.
Pauketat, Timothy, Susan M. Alt, and Jeffery D. Kruchten
2017   The Emerald Acropolis: Elevating Moon and Water in the Rise of Cahokia.
            Antiquity 91(355):207–222.
Pauketat, Timothy R., Robert F. Boszhardt, and Danielle M. Benden
2015   Trempealeau Entanglements: An Ancient Colony's Causes and Effects.
            American Antiquity 80(2):260–289.
Pauketat, Timothy R., Lucretia S. Kelly, Gayle J. Fritz, Neal H. Lopinot, Scott Elias, and
Eve Hargrave
2002   The Residues of Feasting and Public Ritual at Early Cahokia. *American
            Antiquity* 67(2):257–279.
Pauketat, Timothy R., Mark A. Rees, and Stephanie L. Pauketat
1998   *An Archaeological Survey of the Horseshoe Lake State Park, Madison Coun-
            ty, Illinois.* Reports of Investigations No. 55. Illinois State Museum, Spring-
            field.
Paulett, Robert
2012   *An Empire of Small Places: Mapping the Southeastern Anglo-Indian Trade,
            1732–1795.* The University of Georgia Press, Athens.
Pavao-Zuckerman, Barnet
2007   Deerskins and Domesticates: Creek Subsistence and Economic Strategies.
            American Antiquity 72(1):5–33.
Pavao-Zuckerman, Barnet, Tracie Mayfield, Chance Copperstone, and H. Thomas Foster
II
2018   "Horned Cattle and Pack Horses": Zooarchaeological Legacy Collections
            from the Unauthorized (and Unscreened) Spanish Fort. *Southeastern Ar-
            chaeology* 37(3):190–203.
Paynter, Robert
1989   The Archaeology of Equality and Inequality. *Annual Review of Anthropol-
            ogy* 18:369–399.
Peach, Steven J.
2018   The Failure of Political Centralization: Mad Dog, the Creek Indians, and
            the Politics of Claiming Power in the American Revolutionary Era. *Native
            South* 11:81–116.
Peacock, Evan, Philip J. Carr, Sarah E. Price, John R. Underwood, William L. Kingery,
and Michael Lilly
2010   Confirmation of an Archaic Period Mound in Southwest Mississippi.
            Southeastern Archaeology 29(2):355–368.

Perdue, Theda
1987   *Slavery and the Evolution of Cherokee Society, 1540–1866.* The University of
            Tennessee Press, Knoxville.

Persico, V. Richard, Jr.
1979   Early Nineteenth-Century Cherokee Political Organization. In *The Chero-
            kee Indian Nation: A Troubled History,* edited by D. H. King, pp. 92–109.
            The University of Tennessee Press, Knoxville.

Phillips, Philip, and James A. Brown
1978   *Pre-Columbian Shell Engravings from the Craig Mound at Spiro, Oklahoma.*
            2 vols. Peabody Museum Press, Cambridge, Massachusetts.

Pickering, Kathleen
2004   Decolonizing Time Regimes: Lakota Conceptions of Work, Economy, and
            Society. *American Anthropologist* 106(1):85–97.

Piker, Joshua
2004   *Okfuskee: A Creek Indian Town in Colonial America.* Harvard University
            Press, Cambridge, Massachusetts.

Pluckhahn, Thomas J.
2010   The Sacred and the Secular Revisited: The Essential Tensions of Early
            Village Society in the Southeastern United States. In *Becoming Villagers:
            Comparing Early Village Societies,* edited by M. S. Bandy and J. R. Fox, pp.
            100–118. The University of Arizona Press, Tucson.

Pluckhahn, Thomas J., and Robbie Ethridge (editors)
2006   *Light on the Path: The Anthropology and History of the Southeastern Indi-
            ans.* The University of Alabama Press, Tuscaloosa.

Pluckhahn, Thomas J., Robbie Ethridge, Jerald T. Milanich, and Marvin T. Smith
2006   Introduction. In *Light on the Path: The Anthropology and History of the
            Southeastern Indians,* edited by T. J. Pluckhahn and R. Ethridge, pp. 1–25.
            The University of Alabama Press, Tuscaloosa.

Pohlemus, Richard
1971   Excavations at Fort Moore: Savano Town (38AK4&5) *SCIAA Notebook*
            3(6):132–133.

Pollack, David, and A. Gwynn Henderson
1984   A Mid-Eighteenth Century Historic Indian Occupation in Greenup
            County, Kentucky. In *Current Archaeological Research in Kentucky,* edited
            by D. Pollack, pp. 188–203. Kentucky Heritage Council, Frankfort.

Pollard, Joshua, and Mark Gillings
1998   Romancing the Stones: Towards a Virtual and Elemental Avebury. *Archae-
            ological Dialogues* 5(2):143–164.

Porter, Roy
2000   *Enlightenment: Britain and the Creation of the Modern World.* Penguin,
            London.

Porter, Roy, and Mikulas Teich (editors)
1981   *The Enlightenment in National Context.* Cambridge University Press, Cam-
            bridge, United Kingdom.

Prezzano, Susan C., and Vincas P. Steponaitis
1990   *Excavations at the Boland Site, 1984–1987: A Preliminary Report*. Research Report 9. Research Laboratories of Anthropology, University of North Carolina, Chapel Hill.

Priestley, Herbert Ingram (translator and editor)
2010 [1928]   *The Luna Papers, 1559–1561*, Vols. 1 & 2. The University of Alabama Press, Tuscaloosa.

Prucha, Francis Paul
2000   *Documents of United States Indian Policy*. Library of Congress Cataloging-in-Publication, Washington, DC.

Putnam, Laura
2006   To Study the Fragments/Whole: Microhistory and the Atlantic World. *Journal of Social History* 39(3):615–630.

Rafferty, Janet
1995   *Owl Creek Mounds: Test Excavations at a Vacant Mississippian Mound Center*. Report of Investigations 7. Cobb Institute of Archaeology, Mississippi State University, Starkville.

Ramsey, William L.
2008   *The Yamasee War: A Study of Culture, Economy, and Conflict in the Colonial South*. University of Nebraska Press, Lincoln.

Rankin, Robert L.
1993   Language Affiliations of Some de Soto Place Names in Arkansas. In *Expedition of Hernando de Soto West of the Mississippi, 1541–1543: Proceedings of the De Soto Symposia, 1988 and 1990*, edited by G. A. Young and M. P. Hoffman, pp. 210–221. University of Arkansas Press, Fayetteville.

Rees, Mark
2001   A Historical Anthropology of Mississippian Political Culture. In *The Archaeology of Traditions*, edited by T. R. Pauketat, pp. 121–140. University of Florida Press, Gainesville.

Regnier, Amanda L.
2014   *Reconstructing Tascalusa's Chiefdom: Pottery Styles and the Social Composition of Late Mississippian Communities along the Alabama River*. The University of Alabama Press, Tuscaloosa.

Reitz, Elizabeth J.
1990   Zooarchaeological Evidence for Subsistence at Spanish Missions. In *Columbian Consequences: 2. Archaeological and Historical Perspectives on the Spanish Borderlands East*, edited by D. H. Thomas, pp. 543–554. Smithsonian Institution Press, Washington, DC.

Richter, Daniel K.
1992   *The Ordeal of the Longhouse: The Peoples of the Iroquois League in the Era of European Colonization*. The University of North Carolina Press, Chapel Hill.

Riggs, Brett H.
1999   Removal Period Cherokee Households in Southwestern North Carolina:

Material Perspectives on Ethnicity and Cultural Differentiation. PhD dissertation, Department of Anthropology, University of Tennessee, Knoxville.

2010 Temporal Trends in Native Ceramic Traditions of the Lower Catawba River Valley *Southeastern Archaeology* 29(1):31–43.

2012 Reconsidering Chestowee: The 1713 Raid in Regional Perspective. In *Enigmatic Origins: On the Yuchi of the Contact Era*, edited by J. B. Jackson, pp. 43–71. University of Nebraska Press, Lincoln.

2017 Archaeological Investigations at the Valley Towns Baptist Mission (31CE661). *North Carolina Archaeology* 66:1–26.

Rippeteau, Bruce

1978 The Upper Susquehanna Valley Iroquois: An Iroquoian Enigma. In *Essays in Northeastern Anthropology in Honor of Marian E. White*, edited by W. E. Engelbrecht and D. K. Grayson, pp. 123–151. Department of Anthropology, Pierce College, Rindge, New Hampshire.

Robertson, James Alexander (translator)

1993 The Account by a Gentleman from Elvas. In *The De Soto Chronicles: The Expedition of Hernando de Soto to North American in 1539–1543*, Vol. 1, edited by L. A. Clayton, V. J. Knight Jr., and E. C. Moore, pp. 19–219. The University of Alabama Press, Tuscaloosa.

Robinson, Rebecca

2018 *Voices from Bears Ears: Seeking Common Ground on Sacred Land*. University of Arizona Press, Tucson.

Robock, Alan

2000 Volcanic Eruptions and Climate. *Reviews of Geophysics* 38(2):191–219.

Rodning, Christopher B.

2002 Reconstructing the Coalescence of Cherokee Communities in Southern Appalachia. In *The Transformation of the Southern Indians, 1540–1760*, edited by R. Ethridge and C. Hudson, pp. 155–175. University Press of Mississippi, Jackson.

2009 Mounds, Myths, and Cherokee Townhouses in Southwestern North Carolina. *American Antiquity* 74(4):627–663.

2010 Architectural Symbolism and Cherokee Townhouses. *Southeastern Archaeology* 29(1):59–79.

2015 Mortuary Patterns and Community History at the Chauga Mound and Village site, Oconee County, South Carolina. *Southeastern Archaeology* 34(3):169–195.

Rodning, Christopher B., and Jayur M. Mehta

2016 Resilience and Persistent Places in the Mississippi River Delta in Louisiana. In *Beyond Collapse: Archaeological Perspectives on Resilience, Revitalization, and Reorganization in Complex Societies*, edited by R. K. Faulseit, pp. 342–379. Southern Illinois University, Center for Archaeological Investigations, Carbondale.

Romans, Bernard
1999 [1775]   *A Concise Natural History of East and West Florida.* The University of Alabama Press, Tuscaloosa.

Rönnbäck, Klas
2010   An Early Modern Consumer Revolution in the Baltic? *Scandinavian Journal of History* 35(2):177–197.

Roper, L. H.
2004   *Conceiving Carolina: Proprietors, Planters, and Plots, 1662–1729.* Palgrave MacMillan, New York.

Rose, Samuel W.
2017   Marxism, Indigenism, and the Anthropology of Native North America: Divergence and a Possible Future. *Dialectical Anthropology* 41:13–31.

Roseberry, William
1988   Political Economy. *Annual Review of Anthropology* 17:161–185.
1989   *Anthropologies and Histories: Essays in Culture, History, and Political Economy.* Rutgers University Press, New Brunswick, New Jersey.

Russo, Michael
1996   Southeastern Archaic Mounds. In *Archaeology of the Mid-Holocene Southeast*, edited by K. E. Sassaman and D. G. Anderson, pp. 259–287. University Press of Florida, Gainesville.

Sahlins, Marshall
1993   Goodby to Tristes Tropes: Ethnography in the Context of World History. *The Journal of Modern History* 65:1–25

Said, Edward W.
1978   *Orientalism.* Pantheon, New York.

Saitta, Dean J.
1994   Agency, Class, and Archaeological Interpretation. *Journal of Anthropological Archaeology* 13(3):201–227.

Salley, Alexander S. (editor)
1916   *Commissions and Instructions from the Lords Proprietors of Carolina to Public Officials of South Carolina, 1685–1715.* Historical Commission of South Carolina, Columbia.

Saunders, Joe W., Rolfe D. Mandel, C. Garth Sampson, Charles M. Allen, E. Thurman Allen, Daniel A. Bush, James K. Feathers, Kristen J. Gremillion, C. T. Hallmark, H. Edwin Jackson, Jay K. Johnson, Reca Jones, Roger T. Saucier, Gary L. Stringer, and Malcolm F. Vidrine
2005   Watson Brake: A Middle Archaic Mound Complex in Southeastern Louisiana. *American Antiquity* 70(4):631–668.

Saunders, Rebecca
1993   Architecture of the Missions Santa María and Santa Catalina de Amelia. In *The Spanish Missions of La Florida*, edited by B. G. McEwan, pp. 35–61. University Press of Florida, Gainesville.
2000   *Stability and Change in Guale Indian Pottery, A.D. 1300–1702.* The University of Alabama Press, Tuscaloosa.

2002   Seasonality, Sedentism, Subsistence, and Disease in the Protohistoric: Ar-
            chaeological versus Ethnohistoric Data along the Lower Atlantic Coast. In
            *Between Contacts and Colonies: Archaeological Perspectives on the Proto-
            historic Southeast*, edited by C. B. Wesson and M. A. Rees, pp. 32–48. The
            University of Alabama Press, Tuscaloosa.

Saunt, Claudio
1999   *A New Order of Things: Property, Power, and the Transformation of the
            Creek Indians, 1733–1816*. Cambridge University Press, Cambridge, United
            Kingdom.

Schofield, John (editor)
2014   The Archaeology of Sound and Music. *World Archaeology* 46(3):289–291.

Schroedl, Gerald F.
1986   *Overhill Cherokee Archaeology at Chota-Tanasee*. Report of Investigations,
            No. 38. Department of Anthropology, University of Tennessee, Knoxville.

1994   *A Summary of Archaeological Studies Conducted at the Chattooga Site,
            Oconee County, South Carolina, 1989–1994*. Report submitted to the U.S.
            Forest Service, Francis Marion and Sumter National Forests, Columbia,
            South Carolina.

2000   Cherokee Ethnohistory and Archaeology from 1540 to 1838. In *Indians of
            the Greater Southeast*, edited by B. G. McEwan, pp. 204–241. University
            Press of Florida, Gainesville.

Schutt, Amy C.
1999   Tribal Identity in the Moravian Missions on the Susquehanna. *Pennsylva-
            nia History* 66(3):378–398.

Seeber, Katherine Erica
2011   Mapping Oquaga: Reconstructing the Socio-Political Landscape of an 18th
            Century Oneida and Refugee Community. Master's thesis, Department of
            Anthropology, State University of New York Binghamton, Binghamton.

Shackel, Paul
1993   *Personal Discipline and Material Culture: An Archaeology of Annapolis,
            Maryland, 1695–1870*. University of Tennessee Press, Knoxville.

Shankman, David, and Justin L. Hart
2007   The Fall Line: A Physiographic-Forest Vegetation Boundary. *Geographical
            Review* 97(4):502–519.

Shapiro, Gary, and John H. Hann
1990   The Documentary Image of the Council Houses of Spanish Florida Test-
            ed by Excavations at the Mission of San Luis de Talimali. In *Columbian
            Consequences: 2. Archaeological and Historical Perspectives on the Spanish
            Borderlands East*, edited by D. H. Thomas, pp. 511–526. Smithsonian Insti-
            tution Press, Washington, DC.

Shaw, Andrew, Martin Bates, Chantal Conneller, and Clive Gamble
2016   The Archaeology of Persistent Places: The Palaeolithic Case of La Cotte de
            St Brelade, Jersey. *Antiquity* 90(354):1437–1453.

Shuck-Hall, Sheri M.

2009   Alabama and Coushatta Diaspora and Coalescence in the Mississippian Shatter Zone. In *Mapping the Mississippian Shatter Zone: The Colonial Indian Slave Trade and Regional Instability in the American South*, edited by R. Ethridge and S. Shuck-Hall, pp. 250–271. University of Nebraska Press, Lincoln.

Sigl, Michael, Joseph R. McConnell, Lawrence Layman Olivia Maselli, Ken McGwire, Daniel Pasteris, Dorthe Dahl-Jensen, Jørgen Peder Steffensen, Bo Vinther, Ross Edwards, Robert Mulvaney, and Sepp Kipfstuhl

2013   A New Bipolar Ice Core Record of Volcanism from WAIS Divide and NEEM and Implications for Climate Forcing of the Last 2000 Years. *Journal of Geophysical Research: Atmospheres* 118:1151–1169.

Silliman, Stephen

2015   A Requiem for Hybridity? The Problem with Frankensteins, Purées, and Mules. *Journal of Social Archaeology* 15(3):277–298.

Silver, Timothy

1990   *A New Face on the Countryside: Indians, Colonists, and Slaves in South Atlantic Forests, 1500–1800.* Cambridge University Press, Cambridge, United Kingdom.

Simek, Jan F., Alan Cressler, Nicholas P. Herrmann, and Sarah C. Sherwood

2013   Sacred Landscapes of the South-Eastern USA: Prehistoric Rock and Cave Art in Tennessee. *Antiquity* 87:430–446.

Simon, Mary L.

2017   Reevaluating the Evidence for Middle Woodland Maize from the Holding Site. *American Antiquity* 82(1):145–150.

Simon, Mary L., and Kathryn E. Parker

2006   Prehistoric Plant Use in the American Bottom: New Thoughts and Interpretations. *Southeastern Archaeology* 25(2):212–257.

Singleton, Theresa

1995   The Archaeology of Slavery in North America. *Annual Review of Anthropology* 24:119–140.

Slater, Philip A., Kristin M. Hedman, and Thomas E. Emerson

2014   Immigrants at the Mississippian Polity of Cahokia: Strontium Isotope Evidence for Population Movement. *Journal of Archaeological Science* 44:117–127.

Smith, Betty Anderson

1979   Distribution of Eighteenth-Century Cherokee Settlements. In *The Cherokee Indian Nation: A Troubled History*, edited by D. H. King, pp. 46–60. University of Tennessee Press, Knoxville.

Smith, Bruce D. (editor)

1978a   *Mississippian Settlement Patterns.* Academic Press, New York.

Smith, Bruce D.

1978b   Variation in Mississippian Settlement Patterns. In *Mississippian Settlement*

Patterns, edited by Bruce D. Smith, pp. 479–503. Academic Press, New York.

1984   Mississippian Expansion: Tracing the Development of an Explanatory Model. *Southeastern Archaeology* 3:13–32.

1989   Origins of Agriculture in Eastern North America. *Science* 246:1566–1571.

1990   Introduction: Research on the Origins of Mississippian Chiefdoms in Eastern North America. In *The Mississippian Emergence*, edited by B. D. Smith, pp. 1–8. Smithsonian Institution Press, Washington DC.

1995   The Analysis of Single-Household Mississippian Settlements. In *Mississippian Communities and Households*, edited by J. D. Rogers and B. D. Smith, pp. 224–249. The University of Alabama Press, Tuscaloosa.

Smith, Kevin E.

1992   The Middle Cumberland Region: Mississippian Archaeology in North Central Tennessee. PhD dissertation, Department of Anthropology, Vanderbilt University, Nashville.

Smith, Maria O.

2003   Beyond Palisades: The Nature and Frequency of Late Prehistoric Deliberate Violent Trauma in the Chickamauga Reservoir of East Tennessee. *American Journal of Physical Anthropology* 121(4):303–318.

Smith, Marvin T.

1987   *Archaeology of Aboriginal Culture Change in the Interior Southeast: Depopulation During the Early Historic Period*. University Presses of Florida, Gainesville.

1989   Aboriginal Population Movements in the Early Historic Period Interior Southeast. In *Powhatan's Mantle: Indians in the Colonial Southeast*, edited by P. H. Wood, G. Waselkov and M. T. Hatley, pp. 21–34. University of Nebraska Press, Lincoln.

1992   *Historic Period Indian Archaeology of Northern Georgia*. Laboratory of Archaeology Series Report No. 30. University of Georgia, Athens.

2000   *Coosa: The Rise and Fall of a Southeastern Mississippian Chiefdom*. University Press of Florida, Gainesville.

2002   Aboriginal Population Movements of the Postcontact Southeast. In *The Transformation of the Southeastern Indians, 1540–1760*, edited by R. Ethridge and C. Hudson, pp. 3–20. University Press of Mississippi, Jackson.

Smithers, Gregory D.

2015   *The Cherokee Diaspora: An Indigenous History of Migration, Resettlement, and Identity*. Yale University Press, New Haven.

Smyth, Edward Glenn

2016   The Natchez Diaspora: A History of Indigenous Displacement and Survival in the Atlantic World. PhD dissertation, Department of History, University of California Santa Cruz, Santa Cruz.

Spivak, Gayatri Chakravorty

1988   Can the Subaltern Speak? In *Marxism and the Interpretation of Culture*,

　　　　　　　　　edited by C. Nelson and L. Grossberg, pp. 271–313. University of Chicago
　　　　　　　　　Press, Chicago.

1990　　　　　　*The Post-Colonial Critic: Interviews, Strategies, Dialogues.* Routledge, London.

Spring, Joel

2000　　　　　　*Deculturalization and the Struggle for Equality: A Brief History of the Education of Dominated Cultures in the United States.* Routledge, New York.

Stahl, Ann B.

2002　　　　　　Colonial Entanglements and the Practices of Taste: An Alternative to Logocentric Approaches. *American Anthropologist* 104(3):827–845.

Steadman, Dawnie Wolfe

2008　　　　　　Warfare Related Trauma at Orendorf, a Middle Mississippian Site in West-Central Illinois. *American Journal of Physical Anthropology* 136(1):51–64.

Steadman, Sharon R.

2005　　　　　　Reliquaries on the Landscape: Mounds as Matrices of Human Cognition. In *Archaeologies of the Middle East: Critical Perspectives*, edited by S. Pollock and R. Bernbeck, pp. 286–307. Blackwell, Malden, Massachusetts.

Steen, Carl

2012　　　　　　An Archaeology of the Settlement Indians of the South Carolina Lowcountry. *South Carolina Antiquities* 44:19–34.

Steere, Benjamin A.

2015　　　　　　Revisiting Platform Mounds and Townhouses in the Cherokee Heartland: A Collaborative Approach. *Southeastern Archaeology* 34(3):196–219.

Stein, Gil

2002　　　　　　Colonies without Colonialism: A Trade in Diaspora Model of Fourth Millennium B.C. Mesopotamian Enclaves in Anatolia. In *The Archaeology of Colonialism*, edited by C. L. Lyons and J. K. Papadopoulos, pp. 27–64. Getty Research Institute, Los Angeles.

Steponaitis, Vincas P.

1978　　　　　　Location Theory and Complex Chiefdoms. In *Mississippian Settlement Patterns*, edited by B. D. Smith, pp. 417–453. Academic Press, New York.

1998　　　　　　Population Trends at Moundville. In *Archaeology of the Moundville Chiefdom*, edited by V. J. Knight, Jr., and V. P. Steponaitis, pp. 26–43. Smithsonian Institution Press, Washington, DC.

Stewart, James A.

2013　　　　　　Congeries in the Backcountry. Master's thesis, Department of Anthropology, University of South Carolina, Columbia.

Stewart, James A., and Charles R. Cobb

2018　　　　　　Fort Congaree: A Cosmopolitan Outpost on the Rim of Empire. *Native South* 11:29–55.

Stine, Linda F.

1990　　　　　　*Mercantilism and Piedmont Peltry: Colonial Perspectives of the Southern Fur Trade, circa 1640–1740.* Volume XIV in Historical Archaeology, the

Conference on Historic Site Archaeology. Institute of Archaeology and Anthropology, University of South Carolina, Columbia.

Stojanowski, Christopher M.

2013 *Mission Cemeteries, Mission Peoples: Historical and Evolutionary Dimensions of Intracemetery Bioarchaeology in Spanish Florida*. University Press of Florida, Gainesville.

Stoler, Ann Laura

1985 *Capitalism and Confrontation in Sumatra's Plantation Belt, 1870–1979*. The University of Michigan Press, Ann Arbor.

2002 *Carnal Knowledge and Imperial Power: Race and the Intimate in Colonial Rule* University of California Press, Berkeley.

Stubbs, John D., Jr.

1982 The Chickasaw Contact with the La Salle Expedition in 1682. In *La Salle and His Legacy: Frenchmen and Indians in the Lower Mississippi Valley*, edited by P. K. Galloway, pp. 41–48. University Press of Mississippi, Jackson.

Swanton, John R.

1922 *Early History of the Creek Indians and Their Neighbors*. Bureau of American Ethnology Bulletin 43. Smithsonian Institution, Washington, DC.

Sweeney, Alex

2003 Investigating Yamasee Identity: Archaeological Research at Pocotaligo. Master's thesis, Department of Anthropology, University of South Carolina, Columbia.

Sweeney, Alex, and Eric C. Poplin

2016 The Yamasee Indians of Early Carolina. In *Archaeology in South Carolina: Exploring the Hidden Heritage of the Palmetto State*, edited by A. King, pp. 62–81. University of South Carolina Press, Columbia.

Thomas, David Hurst

1990 The Spanish Missions of La Florida: An Overview. In *Columbian Consequences: 2. Archaeological and Historical Perspectives on the Spanish Borderlands East*, edited by D. H. Thomas, pp. 357–397. Smithsonian Institution Press, Washington, DC.

2008 *Native American Landscapes of St. Catherines Island, Georgia: 3. Synthesis and Conclusions*. Anthropological Papers No. 88. The American Museum of Natural History, New York.

2017 Materiality Matters: Colonial Transformations Spanning the Southwestern and Southeastern Borderlands. In *New Mexico and the Pimería Alta: The Colonial Period in the American Southwest*, edited by J. G. Douglass and W. Graves, pp. 379–414. University Press of Colorado, Louisville.

Thomas, Julian

2001 Archaeologies of Place and Landscape. In *Archaeological Theory Today*, edited by I. Hodder, pp. 165–186. Blackwell, Malden, Massachusetts.

2008a Landscape, Archaeology and Dwelling. In *Manual of Landscape Archaeology*, edited by D. Bruno and J. Thomas, pp. 300–306. Left Coast Press, Walnut Creek, California.

2008b   On the Ocularcentrism of Archaeology. In *Archaeology and the Politics of Vision in a Post-Modern Context*, edited by J. Thomas and V. O. Jorge, pp. 1–12. Cambridge Scholars Publishing, Newcastle-upon-Tyne, United Kingdom.

Thompson, E. P.
1967   Time, Work-Discipline, and Industrial Capitalism. *Past & Present* 38:56–97.

Thompson, Ernest Trice
1934   *Presbyterian Missions in the Southern United States.* Presbyterian Committee of Publishing, Richmond, Virginia.

Thompson, Victor D., William H. Marquardt, Alexander Cherkinsky, Amanda D. Roberts Thompson, Karen J. Walker, Lee A. Newsom, and Michael Savarese
2016   From Shell Midden to Midden-Mound: The Geoarchaeology of Mound Key, an Anthropogenic Island in Southwest Florida, USA. *Plos One*, doi.org/10.1371/journal.pone.0154611.

Thompson, Victor D., and Thomas J. Pluckhahn
2012   Monumentalization and Ritual Landscapes at Fort Center in the Lake Okeechobee Basin of South Florida. *Journal of Anthropological Archaeology* 31:49–65.

Thompson, Victor D., and James C. Waggoner, Jr. (editors)
2013   *The Archaeology and Historical Ecology of Small Scale Economies.* University Press of Florida, Gainesville.

Thornton, Russell
1990   *The Cherokees: A Population History.* University of Nebraska Press, Lincoln.

Tilley, Christopher
2004   *The Materiality of Stone: Explorations in Landscape Phenomenology.* Berg, Oxford.

Tinker, George E.
1993   *Missionary Conquest: The Gospel and Native American Cultural Genocide.* Fortress Press, Minneapolis, Minnesota.

Trigger, Bruce G.
1993   Marxism in Contemporary Western Archaeology. In *Advances in Archaeological Method and Theory,* Vol. 5, edited by M. B. Schiffer, pp. 159–200. The University of Arizona Press, Tucson.

Trouillot, Michel-Rolph
2002   North Atlantic Universals: Analytical Fictions, 1492–1945. *The South Atlantic Quarterly* 101(4):839–858.

Tuden, Arthur
1979   An Exploration of a Pre-Capitalist Mode of Production. In *New Directions in Political Economy: An Approach from Anthropology,* edited by M. B. Léons and F. Rothstein, pp. 19–32. Greenwood Press, Westport, Connecticut.

Turner, Frederick Jackson
1920 [1893]   *The Frontier in American History*. Holt, New York.
Usner, Daniel H., Jr.
1992   *Indians, Settlers, & Slaves in a Frontier Exchange Economy: The Lower Mississippi Valley Before 1783*. University of North Carolina Press, Chapel Hill.
1998   *American Indians in the Lower Mississippi Valley: Social and Economic Histories*. University of Nebraska Press, Lincoln.
Van Dyke, Ruth M., R. Kyle Bocinsky, Thomas C. Windes, and Tucker J. Robinson
2016   Great Houses, Shrines, and High Places: Intervisibility in the Chacoan World. *American Antiquity* 81(2):205–230.
VanDerwarker, Amber M.
1999   Feasting and Status at the Toqua Site. *Southeastern Archaeology* 18(1):24–34.
VanDerwarker, Amber M., Jon B. Marcoux, and Kandace D. Hollenbach
2013   Farming and Foraging at the Crossroads: The Consequences of Cherokee and European Interaction Through the Late Eighteenth Century. *American Antiquity* 78(1):68–88.
VanValkenburgh, Parker
2017   Unsettling Time: Persistence and Memory in Spanish Colonial Peru. *Journal of Archaeological Method and Theory* 24(1):117–148.
Vidal, Cécile
2009   From Incorporation to Exclusion: Indians, Europeans, and Americans in the Mississippi Valley from 1699 to 1830. In *Empires of the Imagination: Transatlantic Histories of the Louisiana Purchase*, edited by P. J. Kastor and F. Weil, pp. 62–93. University of Virginia Press, Charlottesville.
Vidoli, Giovanna M., and Heather Worne
2018   Relationships and Trauma: Lived Perspectives at Averbuch. *Tennessee Archaeology* 9(2):156–169.
Voss, Barbara L.
2015   What's New? Rethinking Ethnogenesis in the Archaeology of Colonialism. *American Antiquity* 80(4):655–670.
Wagner, Gail E.
1994   Corn and Eastern Woodland Prehistory. In *Corn and Culture in the Prehistoric New World*, edited by C. Hastorf and S. Johannessen, pp. 335–436. Westview Press, Boulder.
2003   Eastern Woodlands Anthropogenic Ecology. In *People and Plants in Ancient Eastern North America*, edited by P. E. Minnis, pp. 126–171. Smithsonian Institution, Washington, DC.
Wagner, Mark J., Mary R. McCorvie, and Charles A. Swedlund
2004   Mississippian Cosmology and Rock-Art at the Millstone Bluff Site, Illinois. In *The Rock-Art of Eastern North America: Capturing Images and Insight*, edited by C. Diaz-Granados and J. R. Duncan, pp. 42–64. The University of Alabama Press, Tuscaloosa.

Wallis, Neill J.
2008   Networks of History and Memory: Creating a Nexus of Social Identities in
            Woodland Period Mounds on the Lower St. Johns River, Florida. *Journal
            of Social Archaeology* 8(2):236–271.
2019   Powers of Place in the Predestined Middle Woodland Village. In *The Ar-
            chaeology of Villages in Eastern North America*, edited by J. Birch and V.
            Thompson, pp. 36–53. University of Florida Press, Gainesville.
Wallis, Neill J., and Meggan E. Blessing
2015   Big Feasts and Small Scale Foragers: Pit Features as Feast Events in the
            American Southeast. *Journal of Anthropological Archaeology* 39:1–18.
Ward, H. Trawick
1965   Correlation of Mississippian Sites and Soil Types. *Southeastern Archaeo-
            logical Conference Bulletin* 3:42–48.
2002   Fiction from Fact at the Townson Site in Southwestern North Carolina. In
            *The Archaeology of Native North Carolina: Papers in Honor of H. Trawick
            Ward*, edited by J. E. Eastman, C. B. Rodning and E. A. Boudreaux III,
            pp. 84–91. Special Publication 7. Southeastern Archaeological Conference,
            Biloxi, Mississippi.
Ward, Rufus
2018   Dinner at Moshulitubbee's, 1822. *The Dispatch* August 4.
Warren, Stephen, and Randolph Noe
2009   "The Greatest Travelers in America": Shawnee Survival in the Shatter
            Zone. In *Mapping the Mississippian Shatter Zone: The Colonial Indian
            Slave Trade and Regional Instability in the American South*, edited by R.
            Etheridge and S. M. Shuck-Hall, pp. 163–187. University of Nebraska Press,
            Lincoln.
Waselkov, Gregory A.
1989a   Indian Maps of the Colonial Southeast. In *Powhatan's Mantle: Indians in
            the Colonial Southeast*, edited by P. H. Wood, G. A. Waselkov, and M. T.
            Hatley, pp. 292–343. University of Nebraska Press, Lincoln.
1989b   Seventeenth-Century Trade in the Colonial Southeast. *Southeastern Ar-
            chaeology* 8(2):117–133.
1993   Historic Period Indian Responses to European Trade and the Rise of Po-
            litical Factions. In *Ethnohistory and Archaeology: Approaches to Post-con-
            tact Change in the Americas*, edited by J. D. Rogers and S. M. Wilson, pp.
            123–132. Plenum Press, New York.
1994   The Macon Trading House and Early European-Indian Contact in the
            Colonial Southeast. In *Ocmulgee Archaeology, 1936–1986*, edited by D. J.
            Hally, pp. 190–196. University of Georgia Press, Athens.
1997   Changing Strategies of Indian Field Location in the Early Historic South-
            east. In *People, Plants and Landscape: Case Studies in Paleoethnobotany*,
            edited by K. J. Gremillion, pp. 179–194. The University of Alabama Press,
            Tuscaloosa.
1998   Indian Maps of the Colonial Southeast: Archaeological Implications and

Prospects. In *Cartographic Encounters: Perspectives on Native American Mapmaking and Map Use*, edited by G. M. Lewis, pp. 205–221. The University of Chicago Press, Chicago.

Waselkov, Gregory A., and Marvin T. Smith

2000   Upper Creek Archaeology. In *Indians of the Greater Southeast: Historical Archaeology and Ethnohistory*, edited by B. G. McEwan, pp. 242–264. University Press of Florida, Gainesville.

Waselkov, Gregory A., and Marvin T. Smith (editors)

2017   *Forging Southeastern Identities: Social Archaeology, Ethnohistory, and Folklore of the Mississippian to Early Historic South*. The University of Alabama Press, Tuscaloosa.

Waters, Gifford

2006   *Mission San Francisco de Potano's 400th Anniversary: Phase 1, Archaeological Survey and Assessment, Alachua County, Florida*. Miscellaneous Project Reports in Archaeology No. 58. Florida Museum of Natural History, University of Florida, Gainesville.

Weiner, Annette

1992   *Inalienable Possessions: The Paradox of Keeping-While-Giving*. University of California Press, Berkeley.

Weisman, Brent Richards

1992   *Excavations on the Franciscan Frontier: Archaeology at the Fig Springs Mission*. University of Florida Press, Gainesville.

Wernke, Steven A.

2007a   Analogy or Erasure? Dialectics of Religious Transformation in the Early Doctrinas of the Colca Valley, Peru. *International Journal of Historical Archaeology* 11(2):152–182.

2007b   Negotiating Community and Landscape in the Peruvian Andes: A Trans-conquest View. *American Anthropologist* 109(1):130–152.

2013   *Negotiated Settlements: Andean Communities and Landscapes Under Inka and Spanish Colonialism*. University Press of Florida, Gainesville.

Wesson, Cameron B.

2008   *Households and Hegemony: Early Creek Prestige Goods, Symbolic Capital, and Social Power*. University of Nebraska Press, Lincoln.

Westbrooke, Caleb

1685   Calendar of State Papers, Letter of Feb. 21, 1685, British Public Records Office, Vol. 12:5. London.

Wheeler, Ryan J., James J. Miller, Ray M. McGee, and Donna Ruhl

2003   Archaic Period Canoes from Newnans Lake, Florida. *American Antiquity* 68(3):533–551.

White, Richard

1991   *The Middle Ground: Indians, Empires, and Republics in the Great Lakes Region, 1650–1815*. Cambridge University Press, Cambridge, United Kingdom.

White, Sam
2017   *A Cold Welcome*. Harvard University Press, Cambridge, Massachusetts.
Whitehead, Neil L.
1992   Tribes Make States and States Make Tribes: Warfare and the Creation of
            Colonial Tribes and States in Northeastern South America. In *War in the
            Tribal Zones: Expanding States and Indigenous Warfare*, edited by R. B.
            Ferguson and N. L. Whitehead, pp. 127–150. SAR Press, Santa Fe.
Whitley, Thomas G.
2012   *Archaeological Data Recovery at Riverfront Village (38AK933): A Mississip-
            pian/Contact period Occupation in Aiken County, South Carolina*. Report
            submitted to South Carolina Department of Transportation. 2 vols. Brock-
            ington and Associates, Inc., Atlanta.
Widmer, Randolph J.
1988   *Evolution of the Calusa: A Nonagricultural Chiefdom on the Southwest
            Florida Coast*. The University of Alabama Press, Tuscaloosa.
Willey, Gordon R.
1953   *Prehistoric Settlement Patterns in the Viru Valley, Peru*. Bureau of Ameri-
            can Ethnology Bulletin 155. Smithsonian Institution, Washington, DC.
Williams, Mark
1994   The Origins of the Macon Plateau Site. In *Ocmulgee Archaeology, 1936–
            1986*, edited by D. J. Hally, pp. 130–137. University of Georgia Press, Ath-
            ens.
Williams, Marshall W.
2009   *The Estatoe Towns*. LAMAR Institute Publication 142. LAMAR Institute,
            Savannah, Georgia.
Williams, Stephen
1983   Some Ruminations on the Current Strategy of Archaeology in the South-
            east. *Southeastern Archaeological Conference Bulletin* 21:72–81.
1990   The Vacant Quarter and Other Late Events in the Lower Valley. In *Towns
            and Temples Along the Mississippi*, edited by D. H. Dye and C. A. Cox, pp.
            170–180. The University of Alabama Press, Tuscaloosa.
2001   The Vacant Quarter Hypothesis and the Yazoo Delta. In *Societies in Eclipse:
            Archaeology of the Eastern Woodlands Indians, A.D. 1400–1700*, edited by
            D. S. Brose, C. W. Cowan and Robert C. Mainfort Jr., pp. 191–203. Smith-
            sonian Institution Press, Washington, DC.
Wilson, Gregory D.
2010   Community, Identity, and Social Memory at Moundville. *American Antiq-
            uity* 75(1):3–18.
Wilson, Gregory D (editor)
2017   *Mississippian Beginnings*. University of Florida Press, Gainesville.
Wilson, Gregory D., and Lynne P. Sullivan
2017   Mississippian Origins: From Emergence to Beginnings. In *Mississippian
            Beginnings*, edited by G. D. Wilson, pp. 1–28. University of Florida Press,
            Gainesville.

Winters, Howard D.
1969   *The Riverton Culture: A Second Millennium Occupation in the Central Wabash Valley.* Reports of Investigations No. 13. Illinois State Museum, Springfield, Illinois.
1981   Excavating in Museums: Notes on Mississippian Hoes and Middle Woodland Copper Gouges and Celts. In *The Research Potential of Anthropological Museum Collections,* edited by A.-M. Cantwell, N. A. Rothschild and J. B. Griffin, pp. 17–34. Annals of the New York Academy of Sciences 376. New York Academy of Sciences, New York.

Witter, J. B., and S. Self
2007   The Kuwae (Vanuatu) Eruption of AD 1452: Potential Magnitude and Volatile Release. *Bulletin of Volcanology* 68(3):301–318.

Wolf, Eric R.
1982   *Europe and the People Without History.* University of California Press, Berkeley.
1990   Facing Power—Old Insights, New Questions. *American Anthropologist* 92(3):586–596.

Wood, Peter H.
1989   The Changing Population of the Colonial South: An Overview by Race and Region, 1685–1790. In *Powhatan's Mantle: Indians in the Colonial Southeast,* edited by P. H. Wood, G. A. Waselkov, and M. T. Hatley, pp. 35–103. University of Nebraska Press, Lincoln.

Woods, William I.
1987   Maize Agriculture and the Late Prehistoric: A Characteristic of Settlement Locational Strategies. In *Emergent Horticultural Economies of the Eastern Woodlands,* edited by W. F. Keegan, pp. 275–294. Center for Archaeological Investigations Occasional Paper No. 7. Southern Illinois University, Carbondale.

Woodward, Henry
1911   A Faithfull Relation of My Westoe Voyage. In *Narratives of Early Carolina, 1650–1708,* edited by A. S. Salley, pp. 130–134. Charles Scribner's Sons, New York.

Worne, Heather
2017   Temporal Trends in Violence During the Mississippian Period in the Middle Cumberland Region of Tennessee. *Southeastern Archaeology* 36(3):171–182.

Worne, Heather, Charles R. Cobb, Giovanna Vidoli, and Dawnie Steadman
2012   The Space of War: Connecting Geophysical Landscapes with Skeletal Evidence of Warfare-Related Trauma. In *The Bioarchaeology of Violence,* edited by Debra L. Martin, R. P. Harrod and V. R. Perez, pp. 141–159. University of Florida Press, Gainesville.

Worth, John E.
1993a   Prelude to Abandonment: The Interior Provinces of Early 17th-Century Georgia. *Early Georgia* 21(1):24–58.

1993b   (translator) Relation of the Island of Florida by Luys Hernández de Bied-ma. In *The De Soto Chronicles: The Expedition of Hernando de Soto to North American in 1539–1543*, Vol. 1, edited by L. A. Clayton, V. J. Knight Jr., and E. C. Moore, pp. 221–246. The University of Alabama Press, Tuscaloosa.

1995   *The Struggle for the Georgia Coast: An Eighteenth Century Spanish Retrospective on Guale and Mocama.* Anthropological Papers No. 75. American Museum of Natural History, New York.

1998   *The Timucuan Chiefdoms of Spanish Florida,* Vol. 1. University Press of Florida, Gainesville.

2000   The Lower Creeks: Origins and Early History. In *Indians of the Greater Southeast: Historical Archaeology and Ethnohistory,* edited by B. G. McEwan, pp. 265–298. University Press of Florida, Gainesville.

2002   Spanish Missions and the Persistence of Chiefly Power. In *The Transformation of the Southeastern Indians, 1540–1760,* edited by R. Ethridge and C. Hudson, pp. 39–64. University Press of Mississippi, Jackson.

2004   Yamasee. In *Handbook of North American Indians: 14. Southeast,* edited by R. Fogelson and W. C. Sturtevant, pp. 245–253. Smithsonian Institution, Washington, DC.

Wright, Alice P.
2013   Persistent Place, Shifting Practice: The Premound Landscape at the Garden Creek Site, North Carolina. In *Early and Middle Woodland Landscapes of the Southeast,* edited by A. P. Wright and E. R. Henry, pp. 108–121. University Press of Florida, Gainesville.

Wright, Alice P., and Edward R. Henry (editors)
2013   *Early and Middle Woodland Landscapes of the Southeast.* University Press of Florida, Gainesville.

Wright, J. Leitch, Jr.
1981   *The Only Land They Knew: American Indians in the Old South.* University of Nebraska Press, Lincoln.

Yaeger, Patricia
1996   Introduction: Narrating Space. In *The Geography of Identity,* edited by P. Yaeger, pp. 1–38. University of Michigan Press, Ann Arbor.

Index

CHARLES R. COBB is curator and James E. Lockwood Jr. Professor of Historical Archaeology at the Florida Museum of Natural History. He is the author of *From Quarry to Cornfield: The Political Economy of Mississippian Hoe Production* and editor of *Stone Tool Traditions in the Contact Era*.

CPSIA information can be obtained
at www.ICGtesting.com
Printed in the USA
BVHW040218180919

558716BV00006B/13/P